A Kind of Private Magic

A Kind of Private Magic

PATRICK BELSHAW

ANDRE DEUTSCH

First published in Great Britain in 1994 by
André Deutsch Limited
106 Great Russell Street, London WC1B 3LJ

ISBN 0233 988 718

Printed in Great Britain by
St Edmundsbury Press, Bury St Edmunds, Suffolk

In memory of my mother's brother, Charles Lovett,
and his three lifelong friends.
With great affection and respect.

Contents

Contents

Illustrations

Patrick, aged 11, in Trafalgar Square on the day he met E. M. Forster.

Patrick in hotel on the Isle of Wight: Forster 'kept it on his mantelpiece, he did, for ages afterwards. Or so he said . . .'

'Sebastian' Sprott, the image maker.

'Sebastian' Sprott, lecturer in psychology, University of Nottingham, c. 1928.

Ted Shread, aged 16: 'proud as a peacock', in Sprott's Clumber Street flat, 1929.

Charles Lovett at the time he met Jack Sprott.

Charles Lovett (extreme left) at the wedding of Patrick's mother and father, 1931.

Ted Shread, hotel porter, c. 1952.

Ted Shread in his Sneinton flat, two months before he died.

Charles Lovett during his convalescence, 1964.

Bob Buckingham, Jack Sprott, May Buckingham, Morgan Forster, Robin Buckingham.

He achieved physical sex very late and found it easier with people outside his own social class, and it remained a kind of private magic for him – an almost unattainable blessing, for which another person was mainly a pretext. He valued sex for its power to release his own capacities for tenderness and devotion, but he never expected an equal sexual relationship.

P. N. Furbank, from his biography
E. M. Forster: A Life

Acknowledgements

A. Archivists and Librarians

Jacqueline Cox, modern archivist, King's College, Cambridge; Dr Michael Halls, formerly modern archivist, King's College, Cambridge; Suzanne Johnston, archivist, Clare College, Cambridge; Cathy Henderson, research librarian, the Harry Ransom Humanities Research Center, the University of Texas at Austin; Nicholas Hinde, the archivist, Felsted School, Felsted School, Dunmow, Essex; Dr Stephen Fleet, the Registry, University of Cambridge; the principal archivist and staff at the Nottinghamshire Archives; the staff at the Nottinghamshire County Council's Local Studies Library; the archives of the Ministry of Defence.

B. Individuals

P. N. Furbank, Forster's official biographer, for permission to use his words, 'a kind of private magic', as my title, and for permission to reproduce his letter to me, dated 1 December 1991, on the subject of Charles Lovett; Mary Robertson, formerly senior lecturer in social sciences, the University of Nottingham; Gordon Wright, MD, Clare College, Cambridge; the late Velda Sprott; the late Ted Shread; my wife, Kathie, for her patience and tolerance; my youngest son, Christy, for permission to quote from his school project, and for unwittingly rekindling my interest in Charles Lovett; Ted and Daisy Manning of Langham, Holt, Norfolk; Merlin Holland, grandson of Oscar Wilde, for drawing my attention to Wilde's first biographer, Christopher Millard (*nom de plume*, Stuart Mason); Stephen Reiss, for permission to reproduce an extract from his letter to Humphrey Carpenter, concerning Benjamin Britten, dated 5 February 1991; Lady Harrod, for permission to quote from R. F. Harrod's *The Life of John Maynard Keynes* (Macmillan).

C. Permissions Regarding Previously Unpublished Material

The Provost and Scholars of King's College, Cambridge, for permission to reproduce extracts from the Forster Papers; the Master, Fellows and Scholars of Clare College, Cambridge, for permission to reproduce extracts from the Lady Clare Magazine and the Clare College Association Annual; the Harry Ransom Humanities Research Center, the University of Texas at Austin, for permission to reproduce extracts from letters which were the property of J. R. Ackerley; the principal archivist, Nottinghamshire Archives, for permission to reproduce extracts from the Basford Council School Log Book; the Nottinghamshire County Council's Local Studies Library, for permission to reproduce extracts from the Nottingham Medical Register (1928) on the subject of encephalitis lethargica, and from the Nottingham Civic News, March 1971, on the subject of the Nottingham Cosmopolitan Debating Society, and for local accounts of the Nottingham Ragged School.

D. Permissions Regarding Published Works

HarperCollins Publishers Ltd., for permission to quote from *W. H. Auden: A Biography* by Humphrey Carpenter; David Higham Associates Ltd., for permission to quote from *The Letters of J. R. Ackerley*, ed. Neville Braybrooke

(Duckworth), *My Sister and Myself: the Diaries of J. R. Ackerley*, ed. Francis King (Hutchinson) and *My Father and Myself* by J. R. Ackerley (The Bodley Head); The Orion Publishing Group Ltd, for permission to quote from *This Small Cloud* by Harry Daley (Weidenfeld and Nicolson); Hodder and Stoughton Ltd, for permission to quote from *Morgan: A Biography of E. M. Forster* by Nicola Beauman, and from *Aspects of E. M. Forster*, ed. Oliver Stallybrass; Random House UK Ltd., for permission to quote from *The History of the World in 10½ Chapters* by Julian Barnes (Jonathan Cape), *Granite and Rainbow: Essays by Virginia Woolf*, ed. by Leonard Woolf (Chatto and Windus), *The Diary of Virginia Woolf*, ed. Anne Olivier Bell (Hogarth), *The Letters of Virginia Woolf*, ed. Nigel Nicolson (Hogarth), *Virginia Woolf: A Biography* by Quentin Bell (Hogarth), *A Marriage of True Minds* by George Spater and Ian Parsons (Hogarth), and *The Loving Friends* by David Gadd (Hogarth); Reed Book Services Ltd, for permission to quote from *E. M. Forster: A Life* by P. N. Furbank (Martin Secker and Warburg Ltd.), *Christopher and His Kind* and *Lions and Shadows* by Christopher Isherwood (Methuen) and from *Dickens* by Peter Ackroyd (Sinclair-Stevenson); Routledge and Kegan Paul Ltd, for permission to quote from *Woman of Letters: A Life of Virginia Woolf* by Phyllis Rose, and from *Women of Bloomsbury: Virginia, Vanessa and Carrington* by Mary Ann Caws; Constable & Co Ltd, for permission to quote from *Ackerley: A Life of J. R. Ackerley* by Peter Parker; Penguin Books Ltd, for permission to quote from *Human Groups* by W. J. H. Sprott, and from *Phaedrus and Letters VII & VIII*, Plato, translated by Walter Hamilton; Faber and Faber Ltd, for permission to quote from *Benjamin Britten: A Biography* by Humphrey Carpenter; A. D. Peters, for permission to quote from Robert Skidelski's *John Maynard Keynes*, vol. 2, *Economist as Saviour* (Macmillan); A. P. Watt Ltd for permission – on behalf of The Literary Executors of the Estate of David Garnett and the Sophie Partridge Trust – to quote from *Carrington: Letters and Extracts from Her Diaries* ed. David Garnett (Cape); Curtis Brown Ltd for permission to quote from Oliver Stallybrass's Introduction to *The Life To Come and Other Stories* by E. M. Forster and from *Selected Letters of E. M. Forster*, eds. P. N. Furbank & Mary Lago (letters of E. M. Forster © 1983 by the Provost and Scholars of King's College, Cambridge. Selection and editorial matter © 1983 by Mary Lago and P. N. Furbank. Reproduced by permission of Curtis Brown London Ltd on behalf of the author); the Society of Authors, as agents for the Forster Estate, for permission to quote from E. M. Forster's published works, and, as agents of the Strachey Trust, for permission to quote from *Letters of James and Alix Strachey: 1924–25*, eds. Perry Miesel and Walter Kendrick.

Preface

———◆❀◆———

This book was written in memory of four of the many uncles I remember from my boyhood. However, only one member of the quartet – Charles Lovett, my mother's brother – was actually a blood relation. The others, though always addressed affectionately and respectfully as uncle Ted, uncle Jack and uncle Morgan, belonged in fact to an interesting and unusual 'extended family', all male, whose members I encountered from time to time, usually at the house of my uncle Charles.

All characters in the book are real people; their lives have been the subject of many years of research on my part. Only one of the four main players, Ted Shread, was alive at the time I sat down to write in 1991; the others had been dead for twenty years or more. In this respect, Shread was a lone figure in the drama: as usual, he was the odd one out. For this reason I decided to introduce an element of fantasy to the work, enabling him to become 'reunited' with the other three. The device used for this purpose – a locution allowing the dead a voice, and dialogue with the living – demands a degree of imaginative reconstruction and characterisation. Thus, in parts of the text – and these will become obvious to the reader – fact has to be interwoven with strands of speculation. The rest of my book is wholly factual, with all sources duly acknowledged.

Patrick Belshaw

Patrick

———◆———

As a boy I had more than my fair share of uncles, though the vast majority of them were not blood relatives, nor in-laws even; they were simply friends of the family. The reason for this will soon become apparent.

Some of these non-familial uncles, it turned out, were men of considerable standing in the world. Take my uncle Jack. He was a professor at Nottingham University. His house wasn't really posh – though it seemed so to me at the time – but it was full of unusual things. For example, he had a room which was called a study, with a typewriter that stood on a big oak desk, and lots of books and papers and box-files everywhere; and in his kitchen he had interesting gadgets, like coffee grinders, corkscrews, food mincers, nutmeg graters, cheese wires and soda syphons. And on racks there were rows of reclining wine bottles, in greens and browns and ambers, some slim, some full-bellied, with colourful labels and foreign writing on them. Oh yes – and in a large cage, he had a crested cockatoo, handsome and exotic, with a loud squawk, a shifty eye and a treacherous smile . . .

Voices from Elysium

———◆◆◆———

MORGAN: . . . Listen! I think I hear something. Murmurings, and the sound of a rainbow forming.

JACK: Hark! Unless my ears deceive me, there are whispers coming from the mists above Acheron.

CHARLES: I'm sure I can hear faint voices rising from the waters of the Everlasting River. I say, is anybody there?

MORGAN: Yes, I can hear a rainbow. The noise has died into the faintest murmur, beneath which another murmur grows, spreading stealthily, steadily, into a curve that widens but does not vary. And in widening curves it is spreading from the horses' feet into the dissolving mists. What colours! It is more like the rainbows you can tread on. More like dreams. Or more like memories, perhaps? . . .

Patrick

―――◦❈◦―――

. . . A visit to uncle Jack's was always a special treat for me; it held a kind of magic. Uncle Charles used to go to the house to work, often when uncle Jack was away, and he would sometimes take me with him. We would usually be there for most of the day. We made the journey from Welbeck Street to Portland Road on foot, my hand in his as we crossed the two main roads, Huntingdon Street and Mansfield Road, always taking the same route along Peel Street, turning right into Waverley Street, then second left into Portland Road which was almost opposite the high, wrought-iron gates of the Arboretum. There was an aviary just inside those gates, and we would hear the squawk of a parrot or the screech of a peacock above the clamorous cheeping of countless small birds as we turned into uncle Jack's road. Sometimes, if uncle Charles wasn't pushed for time, I would be taken to see the birds. They were really fascinating to observe – especially during the mating season, when you could see their funny courtship displays – and at any other time I would have been grateful for the opportunity, but on 'uncle Jack days' I was always impatient to get to the house.

These visits to Portland Road were something I looked forward to with great excitement for days and days ahead. There were a number of reasons for this. First, in the early days, out walking with uncle Charles, I could pretend that I had a dad. I was told that my real dad would soon be home from the war, and I yearned for that day. I couldn't remember what he looked like, but I was beginning to need him rather badly. Some kids' dads had been home for months already, bringing them presents and taking them out to exciting places; it wasn't fair. So, for the time being, uncle Charles became the unsuspecting surrogate. In this role he would serve as well as the next man. Strangers were not to know that he hadn't even been a soldier, never mind a holder of the Burma Star like my real dad.

3

Secondly, I could have a bath at uncle Jack's. A proper bath, I mean – in a real bathroom, with a heated rail to make your towel warm and cosy, and a wooden bath-rack which contained an assortment of soaps, flannels and brushes, including a long-handled bath-brush whose dark bristles could resemble the conning-tower of a submarine when the brush was allowed to surface from a 'dive'. In our house we didn't have a bathroom; we didn't even have a proper, plumbed-in bath. Ours was a zinc bath that hung from a nail on the wall in the backyard. It was brought in once a week on 'bath night' and placed on the mat in front of the fire, where it was filled by kettles of hot water heated on the gas stove. The water was used by all three of us in turn: Rita first, then me, then Brian – with Brian and me pleading for additional kettles to raise the temperature of the cooling water.

Uncle Jack's bath was a huge, enamelled, Edwardian affair – so deep when filled that I could float in it, sometimes face down, practising holding my breath and opening my eyes under water. It rested on four cast-iron feet that looked like a lion's paws, and it had large, shiny brass taps – powerful faucets which released deluges of water, the hot mixing with the cold to form a roaring Niagara, giving off clouds of vapour that hung about the room for ages, shrouding you in a warm mist which seemed to induce the most delightful daydreams. Half an hour later, when drying in front of the large, framed mirror, you could still write your name in the condensation and then watch it vanish slowly, as if by magic, as you finished dressing.

Thirdly, it was at uncle Jack's that I discovered books. There were no books in our house. Reading was something you did at school. It was a mechanical skill at which, true, from an early age, I found myself proficient. But like most things we did at school, it was left behind in the classroom. It never occurred to me that this might be unusual. After all, I was also quite good at mechanical arithmetic – and nobody expected you to do that at home. No, school, and what you were made to do in the classroom, was one thing: how you chose to occupy yourself in your life outside was quite another.

Then came my first visit to Portland Road. Here, I not only found books – more books than I had ever seen before, even at school – but I began to read them. And not as an exercise, either, but for pleasure. It was here that I realised what a joy it might be to have books of my own – at hand, ready to be taken down at

4

will and opened up for information or sheer delight. Yes, there were books at uncle Jack's, all right. They were in every room; hundreds of them, stacked on shelves from wall to wall and from floor to ceiling, and in some rooms – for example, uncle Jack's study – piled in precarious little cairns about the floor. There were books of all sizes, colours and thicknesses, and on every conceivable subject, it seemed. Some books, I confess, were opened and quickly discarded as incomprehensible; but others, mainly literature, were read hungrily and often with wonderment. For the newly-embarked traveller, each one was a potential adventure; and collectively they represented an Aladdin's Cave to which I had an open sesame each time I visited the house.

The routine of my visits to uncle Jack's house was simple and unvaried. First, I had my bath – always a long, luxurious ritual – after which I would settle down to read. Sometimes I would read for hours, pausing only when food was prepared. I read indiscriminately – untutored; unnoticed, even – sitting or lying in isolation in one room or another, the silence broken only by occasional squawks from uncle Jack's cockatoo and the sounds made by uncle Charles as he went about his chores.

Looking at me – on the face of it, an underprivileged boy from the backstreets of Nottingham; father away soldiering; mother away all hours, barmaiding – who would have guessed that these magical hours were my occasional privilege? And all down to chance. All thanks to my uncle Charles keeping house for a university professor . . .

The Celestial Omnibus

———— ✸ ————

MORGAN: ... Yes, there are memories in the air. Come along, Jack, my dear fellow. And you, Charles, my darling boy. Rouse yourselves! There could be work for us here.

JACK: Ah, it is you, Morgan dear. Thank goodness. But I heard other sounds, I thought. Soft sounds they were, at first, gently penetrating my consciousness. Then suddenly they were amplified to produce such a ringing inside my head. Oh, my poor head! Can Death have left me with a hangover? Are you there, Charles? Attend me, dear boy. Relax me. I need your playful fingers about the muscles of my neck.

CHARLES: I'm here, Jack dear. Ready to serve, as always. There, is that better? But tell me, Morgan, what's this about work to be done?

MORGAN: Well, you heard them yourself, didn't you? The memories, I mean. Coming in on the air? I thought I heard you say so? But wait: let's get Ted settled first. Good evening, Ted. Welcome aboard the Celestial Omnibus.

TED: Hey, what the bleddy hell's going on? One minute I'm waiting to wheel myself across the road to the Wheatsheaf for my evening pint, and the next thing I know this funny old carriage, pulled by two panting horses, draws up. Would you believe, it had ...

MORGAN: ... two great lamps shining through the fog against the alley walls, turning it into tissues of fairyland, you mean?

TED: Yes, and the driver was all huddled up in a cape. Then suddenly my brake was off, my chair was in the carriage and we were away. I know it sounds daft, but we seemed to drive away ...

MORGAN: ... through a blank wall, so neatly and so silently? I know.

TED: Yes, that's right. Then – hey, wait a minute! How do you know all this? And how come you know my name? Turn round, you bogger, and let me get a proper look at you.

MORGAN: I'm sorry, Ted. It's cruel to tease you so. Behold, your driver!

TED: Morgan!

MORGAN: The same. I apologise for behaving so theatrically, but we had to find some way of allowing you to join us here on the Other Side on a temporary basis. We've borrowed the Celestial Omnibus, a little creation of mine, because it offers you the return option.

CHARLES: So be sure you don't lose your ticket, Ted dear.

TED: Charles! You as well! It is you, isn't it? Well, I'll be boggered!

JACK: Not where you are going, you won't, ducky!

TED: And you, Jack! Christ: it's like a bleddy dream, seeing you all again like this! It *is* a dream, isn't it? It must be. Come on, Morgan – what's happening? Am I dreaming? If not, what am I doing in this contraption?

JACK: I would have thought that it was all too obvious. But then – and it must be the Lethe – I had almost forgotten what a stupid little man you can be.

CHARLES: I say, Jack, steady on! You'd be confused yourself, surely? Anyone would. And you're forgetting about Ted's – you know: about his condition.

TED: It's all right, Charles love, I can take it. He never liked me, I know that. I was always a little man in his eyes, and now I'm even smaller. But I'm not stupid, Jack. Uneducated, yes; but not stupid. They haven't taken my brain off, you know: just my legs. And I seem to remember that you knew a fair bit about being legless yourself! Anyway, I may be ignorant, but at least I'm still alive – I am, aren't I, Morgan? – which is more than can be said for you, you bogger!

JACK: Bugger, indeed! I'm flattered, I'm sure. As for Death, you should try it sometime! I don't mind my transcendental state, I assure you. There was precious little to live for towards the end, anyway. All one's friends dying – first Joe; then dear Morgie here, followed with indecent haste by you, Charles dear. It was all too cruel. By that time, even the gin couldn't help. Temporary oblivion was not enough. Life had become tasteless – almost as tasteless as ducky here, whose drab mortality I envy not the slightest.

7

MORGAN: Come, come, Jack, my dear love. And you, Ted. No scratching at one another, please. Let us try to conduct ourselves in a civilised manner. For, as I was about to explain to Charles, there is work to be done. I'm almost sure of it. It is work, moreover, involving the four of us. We heard memories, you see, Ted. Patrick's memories. We heard them in the air. He seems to be gathering thoughts and ideas for some reason. For some sort of book, I shouldn't wonder.

TED: Well, I could have told you that. I've been in touch with him for months over it. How far's he got, then?

CHARLES: Not very far; he's only just started. Just a few boyhood memories, that's all.

TED: Is that all? Christ! With all the stuff he's had from me – and all those trips he's made to your old college, Morgan – I would have thought he'd be nearly finished by now.

JACK: If you knew anything at all about writing, ducky, you would know that these things take time. Research can be slow and frustrating, sometimes impeded by false trails. Patrick's probably having trouble finding information about us.

TED: Well, he knows enough by now, surely? What's he playing about at, for God's sake? And what are we doing in this musty old bus, riding over rainbow bridges and daft things like that, when we could be nagging him to get on with his story? Or, at least, I could. Sorry, you three!

MORGAN: Don't be sorry, Ted. Dead we may be, but we are far from being without influence, you know. And be careful what you say about these rainbows. Remember where you are. Enter into the spirit of the occasion, lest you should fall from our conveyance and plummet to the ground! There is light upon the shores of darkness, I would remind you, but only for those who can see.

JACK: I hate to admit it, Morgan, but it occurs to me that ducky here may have a point. Isn't there something we could be doing? To give the process a little nudge, so to speak? Ted may be in the dark, but at least he knows who he is – which is more than the reader does! If Patrick is having difficulty, perhaps we should help him out . . .

Uncle Jack

———◦❈◦———

... When I first met Charles Lovett in 1926 I was still calling myself Sebastian, a name I began to use somewhat pretentiously during my early days at Cambridge. It was a name which suited my Bloomsbury persona; in that circle of friends it fitted me comfortably. But in my new life in Nottingham – away from the University, particularly – I wore it with increasing self-consciousness and ill-ease, so that within three or four years I had reverted to Jack. However, my Bloomsbury friends continued to the end to call me Sebastian; and despite my intimate relationship with Morgan, it wasn't until September 1932 that he felt comfortable with my change of name and began to address his letters accordingly.

The move from Cambridge to Nottingham marked the beginning of a new phase of my life, and I approached it with a mixture of excitement and trepidation. Cambridge for me had become synonymous with so many satisfying and pleasurable experiences.

It had come to stand for stability, for example. Throughout my six years at the University I had lived at the same address – 7 Brunswick Walk, alongside Midsummer Common – and this modest lodging had become my home and a refuge within which I felt comfortable and safe.

Cambridge had also come to stand for success. I had not been successful at school – or rather, I left Felsted *feeling* that I had not been successful. I was, in fact, a scholar, and a member of the Probationers' Sixth, but I failed to get into the élite top form known as the Headmaster's Sixth. Nor was I successful in the army, from which I had been invalided out in 1917 – not with war wounds acquired heroically, but with a bad back! My early teaching experience – between leaving the army and going up to Cambridge in 1919 – was hardly illustrious, either. At my

9

first school in Edgbaston, Birmingham, I had problems with discipline; and my move to a second preparatory school, this time in Brighton, soon began to persuade me that the problem was perhaps attributable more to the teacher than the class.

After that period of drudgery and failure as a teacher, Cambridge was like a breath of fresh air. I had gone up as a mature student, on a war grant – there were a few of us in this category – and I suddenly received an injection of confidence. I was a man among boys! Oh yes, the young ones were clever all right; and they had the advantage of recent, disciplined study. But I had seen life – in the Great War, no less; and as a private soldier, too, not as a privileged officer. I had also been obliged to earn a living in the workplace, where I had learned to act and think independently. Above all, I was highly motivated: I had been given another chance to prove myself, and I wasn't going to fail this time. I worked hard, and at the end of my second year, to my great delight, I got a First in part one of the Moral Science tripos.

I had not neglected my social life, however. During the Easter vacation in 1921 I toured Algeria and Tunisia with a Cambridge don, Maynard Keynes. Many years my senior, and a brilliant scholar, this man was my hero. Dora Carrington once referred to me as Maynard's 'attendant slave'[1] and it was true: my regard for him was the nearest I ever came, I do believe, to blind devotion. Our visit to North Africa was ostensibly a business arrangement: the curious were informed that I was Maynard's 'companion secretary', charged with the responsibility of indexing his book on probability.[2] In fact, this task consumed very few hours of our time together: the holiday was mainly an opportunity for us to celebrate a loving relationship. Sadly, shortly after that idyllic sojourn in the desert sun, our affair began to peter out. It was Maynard's fault, not mine. He met a ballerina named Lydia Lopokova – 'Loppy', as he called her – and, overnight almost, his friends were asked to believe that he had turned his back on his homosexual past.

The following year I gained another First, in the second part of the tripos, having specialised in psychology – and this time I was able to celebrate by going to Venice with Lytton Strachey. Dear Lytton! He worked so hard, and fussed a great deal, to make that holiday successful. The sleeper train, he said – writing to me from The Mill House, Tidmarsh, on 6 June 1922 – would

10

be equipped 'with beds and all complete', and there would be a gondola at our disposal 'all day and night'. He even managed to make one of the disadvantages, the heat at that time of the year, sound almost attractive:

> The chief drawback will be mosquitoes (to some extent) and fasciste (heavens knows to what extent). It will also be decidedly hot, but I hope you won't dislike that. Bed in the middle of the day circumvents the disagreeable part of it.[3]

Afterwards I travelled into Central Europe, seeking a meeting with Sigmund Freud, but Lytton was kind enough to ensure that a letter, containing his assessment of the holiday, would reach me:

> *July 18th 1922*
> Dearest Sebastian ... I was very glad that you really enjoyed Venice. I did, too, and in my opinion you are a perfect compagnon de voyage ... Freud is away from Vienna. But I fancy you will succeed in running him to earth ... I felt terribly lonely in the train [from Venice]. When shall we swim in a gondola again? And pace the Piazza? I often long for the key, the stairs, the ice-factory, the iron ship, and the vast dark spaces between our rooms, lit by a single fiammifero. Curiously impressed it all is upon one's mind! ... I send you my best love.[4]

Yes, Cambridge had come to stand for success – not simply in terms of scholarship, but socially and sexually as well. I had friends and lovers who, as intellectuals, were held in the highest esteem, and they were to provide my introduction to the Bloomsbury group.

Cambridge had, of course, also come to mean the 'Apostles', the name given to the Cambridge Conversazione Society, whose aim, according to one of the early members, was 'the pursuit of truth with absolute devotion and unreserve by a group of intimate friends'.[5] The 'Society', as it was often called, was a secret fraternity composed entirely of an intellectual élite. To gain entry one had first to be proposed and seconded by existing Apostles, and then gain the majority support of undergraduate members, who were the only Apostles allowed to vote. I was sponsored by Maynard Keynes, who had taken wing from the Society back in 1910 but had remained closely associated with it ever since, and my joy on being accepted knew no bounds. This was the accolade for me. My election represented the fulfilment of an ambition which was, in many respects, perhaps, more important to me than my formal academic successes.

Oh, how I loved those Saturday evenings! Each one, it seemed, a kind of re-enactment of *The Symposium*: civilised proposition and debate, plus refreshments – though, unlike the Greeks, we did not permit alcohol. You will not be surprised to learn that this somewhat puritanical convention put me off rather in later years. But at the time intellectual rigour, based upon unblurred judgement, was all-important; and I have to say that without booze we managed to create an atmosphere of great warmth, intimacy and gaiety. The Apostles opened doors for people, too, rather like the Freemasons: everyone knew that. Through one of those doors I gained access to the Bloomsbury coterie; through another I met a well-known novelist who was about to achieve immortal fame with a novel about India that was almost ready for the publishers. I refer, of course, to Morgan Forster . . .

Patrick

....

... It was thanks to uncle Charles and Ted – and mainly to my uncle Jack, though I didn't know it at the time – that at the age of eleven I first came to meet uncle Morgan. I remember being told his full name. It was spelled out for me – E. M. F O R S T E R – slowly and solemnly. I think I was supposed to be impressed, but the name meant nothing to me. All I knew was that the man in whose London flat we were staying – the man with whom I was going to spend the afternoon, in fact – was supposed to be somebody famous who wrote books. Now that *did* interest me. As you have heard, I had recently discovered books. They were exciting – a bit like adventures, in a way – in that you never knew what you might find inside them, or what might happen next. But I never gave a thought to the people who wrote them. In fact, I don't think I thought of authors as people at all. They were just names. And this was not a name I had come across.

'What shall I call him?' I remember asking uncle Charles and Ted anxiously.

Interestingly, I always referred to these two uncles in this way: under a single avuncular heading, as if they were one. I suppose this was because I was used to seeing them together, as a pair. In fact, uncle Ted was not really an uncle at all. Like uncle Jack, he was one of those friends of the family; and I was about to meet another.

'Just call him uncle Morgan. He'll like that. He's not as lucky as you. He's got no brothers and sisters. So he can't be a real uncle, you see.'

I can't remember who answered me – it was uncle Charles, I think – but the words went something like that, as far as I recall.

We were feeding the pigeons in Trafalgar Square at the time, waiting for him to appear. For a laugh, uncle Ted scrubbed bird seed into my hair – and suddenly my untidied thatch became a temporary nest for two or three squabbling pigeons! I felt their claws scratching against my scalp, and the draught from their wings was cool upon my face. The birds were surprisingly heavy, and their excited flapping was rather disconcerting; but I managed to hold the pose long enough to hear the click of the camera's shutter, which was just audible through shrieks of laughter and encouragement. In all the confusion and good humour, I almost forgot my nervousness.

Then, suddenly, he was there. He seemed to materialise from the fine mist around the fountain. Not that I thought for one second that it was he. This man wore an old raincoat and carried a cloth bag with a bit of shopping in it. He didn't seem very tall – with his stoop, not much taller than uncle Ted – and he had a bristly moustache. There was a squirt of pigeon shit on his left lapel. I stopped laughing and retreated slightly. Then he stepped forward – and I stepped backwards and to the side, sheltering behind the bulk of uncle Charles. But my apprehension quickly turned to surprise. My uncles seemed to know this tramp! In fact, they greeted him – and he them, uncle Charles particularly – most warmly.

After a few minutes uncle Charles and Ted went off somewhere, as arranged, and I was left with my new uncle. My heart was beating twenty to the dozen: even faster than a pigeon's. He offered me a boiled sweet from a crumpled bag. This was a good move. At that time, just after the war, sweets were a rare treat. My fear of this strange, stooped figure began to dissolve slowly, like the warm, sweet stone I had popped into my mouth. He took my hand to cross the busy road; his palm was warm and clammy. Thankfully his grip was loose, and as we walked up the steps of the National Gallery I was able to slip my hand away during a natural break in our stepping rhythm.

Inside the Gallery, he steered me from room to room. I was wide-eyed! I had seen a few pictures in uncle Jack's house – though the only one I could remember was of a weird-looking chap with glasses and a big black beard – but here there were hundreds and hundreds of paintings, with some of them so big that you only got three to a wall! Some of them were rude, too. I was a bit embarrassed in front of the bare women; but fortunately uncle Morgan seemed to stand behind and to the side of me most of the time. I was beginning to like him. He seemed almost as shy of me as I was of him. And the nice thing was that he didn't ask a lot of boring questions about your favourite subject at school, or your hobbies, like most grown-ups did. He seemed content just to be with me, showing me around and observing my reactions to the pictures. On several occasions I turned to find him smiling beneath his moustache – even chuckling, on one occasion: a funny chuckle, more down the nose than in the mouth – at something I had said, or at a face I had pulled. He continued to be generous with the boiled sweets, too – producing, like a magician, the same greyish bag that never seemed to get any emptier.

Afterwards we had a cup of tea in the tea-room, and I remember he got up to fetch me a second jam doughnut. He said very little; but by now I had warmed to him, so that the silences were not embarrassing. His eyes smiled a lot, sometimes twinkling – or was that the light catching his glasses? I think we smiled a lot together. He seemed to derive a simple pleasure from attending to my welfare and happiness. After the tea we had time to browse in the bookshop among the prints and cards and catalogues.

'Just as a matter of interest, if you could have one of these prints which one would you choose?'

He had suddenly materialised again in that strange way of his, and had spoken these words – or words similar – as if out of idle curiosity. Then, seeing my confusion, he had added, 'I mean, only supposing, of course. And there's no hurry. Look at them all again, and let me know before we go. I shall be interested in your choice, that's all.'

My choice amused him visibly. It was Titian's *Bacchus and Ariadne*. He seemed pleased. Perhaps the subject appealed to the classicist in him. Or he may have admired Titian's work – particularly the way the artist presents such a potent mixture of refinement and excess, formal perfection and heavy sensuality. Or perhaps he simply admired the naked male body which figures so prominently in the picture. I don't know. All I felt at the time was a sense of relief that I hadn't disappointed him. Not that he said anything, mind you – other than to suggest that I might visit the lavatory before the tube journey back to the flat.

When I returned he was nowhere to be seen. I waited almost a quarter of an hour, getting more and more anxious as the minutes ticked by. Then there he was, suddenly at my side again, presenting me with a flat, brown-paper parcel and a National Gallery catalogue. I half-guessed what might be in the parcel, of course – though I had not expected the print to be mounted behind glass and set in a wooden frame. I expressed my gratitude enthusiastically, and he responded with little repressed snorts of pleasure that seemed to shake his whole body.

I felt pleasure, too. After a somewhat inauspicious start, I'd had a very happy afternoon – and I was still blissfully ignorant of the fact that my self-effacing companion was not only internationally famous but had worked at the National Gallery during the early part of the First World War, cataloguing many of the paintings I had been viewing. It had been my privilege to be shown around by an important man, who happened also to be something of an expert on the pictures I had seen. Yet somehow he had managed to make me feel that I was the important one, the one whose opinions on the nation's art treasures – communicated non-verbally, largely – were the ones that really mattered.

Looking back, I cannot help thinking how terrified I would have been in anticipation of that meeting – indeed, of the weekend as a whole – had I known then what I know now. Had I known, for example, that my older brother, Brian, had also stayed in uncle Morgan's flat with uncle Charles and Ted a year or so earlier.

Brian was a 'difficult' child – too difficult for my mother to handle once my dad had gone away to the war – and for this reason he had lived with uncle Charles and Ted since early 1943. Preparing for their weekend visit, uncle Morgan had corresponded with uncle Jack, his closest friend, through whom all the arrangements were made; and in his letter of 23 June 1945 he had written:

> Now some questions – a crescendo in their delicacy. What is little Brian's surname (Balham or like that?) Secondly, does he pry so that had I better lock things up in the flat when he comes?[6]

Brian's behaviour during that visit had regrettably run true to form, it seems – or so the following extracts, taken from subsequent letters from uncle Morgan to uncle Jack, appear to confirm:

> N.B. I am not too keen on little Brian having further free hands there. He pinches the matches, nor have we any emotional kick, since he declined to come and meet me.[7]

> ... the china tea service I gave Charles is really valuable –

16

Worcester. Will you pass this on and suggest that it be put away for best, and that little Bryan [*sic*] be anyhow not permitted to gobble off it.[8]

It seems likely, then, that when I met my uncle Morgan for the first time on that Saturday afternoon in 1947 he may not have held the name of Belshaw in the highest esteem. And I would have been even more nervous than I was had I known that the family honour was now in my hands. Moreover, the solicitous reader might have been nervous on my behalf, seeing me walk away hand-in-hand with a man who talked of an 'emotional kick' to be gained from meeting young boys . . .

Uncle Jack

———⟨❂⟩———

... Morgan had become an Apostle during his fourth year at Cambridge – back in 1901, I think it was – but thereafter he attended a number of meetings over the years. Membership of the Society was for life, you see: when you left Cambridge you simply 'took wings' and became an 'angel', with the freedom to fly back to the nest whenever you felt so inclined. And that is how I came to meet the Archangel Morgan! He graced one of our evenings with his presence. I cannot remember the date – or, indeed, the main topic of discussion for that evening: perhaps Morgan can oblige? – but it was some time in the autumn of 1922, I believe. It could not have been 1923, because by the middle of that year I had received several letters from him, including this interesting one, dated 28 June, which seems to indicate a friendship already well established:

> Dear Sebastian ... I am sorry you are unhappy. I have given up expecting for myself happiness of the kind I want for you, but that is only because my friend went and died, it is no argument for general pessimism. – I am a little doubtful perhaps about your application of 'psychology' to your difficulties, though your psychology is of course better than other people's. Science, when applied to personal relationships, is always just wrong ... and when you analyse the obsessions & reactions of D.W. and yourself, I'm not convinced that you have got on to either of the two people concerned. Art is a better guide than Science. Ho! I wish I could expand that remark. Gracefulness is so important – I'll try that. We agreed that it wasn't graceful of me to send Alec & Maurice to a hotel after the British Museum, tho' it would have been 'sound' from their point of view. We agree we want modern beauty ... that's the quality that makes a love-affair successful.[9]

By this time, you see, we must have known one another for several months – for not only had we exchanged confidences over lovers, there had also been time for me to receive and comment on a copy of *Maurice*, which Morgan had shown only to a small number of intimates. How well I remember being amused by that reference to my wrongly applied psychology! Not that I can now recall the identity of D.W. – nor, indeed, any misery he may have caused me. I was frequently in and out of misery caused by such affairs; but I remember no real unhappiness at that time.

Quite the reverse, really – for it was during the early part of this year that I achieved another major ambition: an introduction to Virginia Woolf, whom I regarded as my entrée to the Bloomsbury inner sanctum. By March 1923, after we had met on just two occasions, Virginia was already referring me to the influential patroness, Lady Ottoline Morrell:

> ... his great wish was to meet you. He is a friend of Lytton's ... apparently agreeable and and intelligent. I really think he is very nice, and very young.[10]

When we met for lunch the following week and she told me that she had mentioned my name in a recent letter to Lady Ottoline, well, I could hardly conceal my joy – or my burning ambition, seemingly! Virginia, of course, sharp as a barber's razor, seized upon this immediately. In her diary for March 1923 you will find the following entry:

> Sprot [*sic*] and I lunched at Mary's; then, tipsy with echoing brains, went to tea at Hill's in [Kensington] High Street. Infinitely old and rich I felt, he is very poor. His mother used to attend Barker's linen sales, so that he knew the High Street ... His father is a solicitor at Crowborough. He wished to meet Ottoline. He is hungry as a wolf, & snapping up delicacies in an alarming way. If at his age I had met Ottoline! – still, I wasn't much older.[11]

Yes, she had a way of seeing through you, our Virginia. She didn't have to be told, for example, that when it came my long-awaited meeting with Lady Ottoline was not an outstanding success – and if you read her letter to Lady Ottoline, dated 24 September 1923, you will see also how ready she was to cover herself should future meetings prove equally unsuccessful for me:

> Instinct tells me that Mr Sprott was not a success – partly because of his name. But he is Lytton's Sebastian – not mine. I only handed on his request.[12]

I quickly detected this hard edge to Virginia's character, and my enthusiasm for her began to cool quite early in our relationship. Perhaps I saw in her too much of myself. Certainly, although we kept in touch for many years to come, we never recaptured the warmth and intimacy of that heady afternoon in Kensington.

That letter to Lady Ottoline also contained an intriguing reference to my name, don't you think? My old Cambridge friend, A. T. Bartholomew – Barty, dear boy! – would have been amused. He it was, in my undergraduate days, who went on endlessly about the credibility of plain Jack Sprott. It sounded far too much like 'Jack Spratt', he thought – and with a name like that, the world could never take a fellow seriously! No, if I had to have a surname like Sprott, he teased, the least I could do was change my first name. And that, simply, is how I became Sebastian. One day, when Barty was trying to think of a suitable alternative, somebody came into the room – I don't remember who it was: Furbank suggests Dent,[13] and he's probably right because I must have told him – carrying some music by J. S. Bach, and immediately there was a cry of 'Sebastian'!

I admitted that I thought it had a ring to it – you may remember that it was used by dear old Oscar Wilde, who rejoiced in the pseudonym 'Sebastian Melmoth' during his final years in exile – and I changed to it there and then. Having done that, however, I was soon to discover that the problem really lay with my surname. It was a pity I couldn't have changed that at the same time! I remember Carrington, the dear, sad, Doric thing, once confessing to me that she had described our first meeting in a letter to Gerald Brenan, writing 'Sebastian Sprott. Yes that is really his name!'[14] In fact, initially at least, the whole of Bloomsbury seemed to find the name 'Sprott' faintly ridiculous. Mind you, I am not so sure that at first some of its members did not find my sexual leanings rather comical, too. For all their apparent liberalism, one or two of them seemed to regard our sort as curiosities. Just occasionally one felt like an exhibit in a sideshow. Admittedly, one might have been somewhat hypersensitive on the subject of one's sexuality; but it was more than just a feeling one had. Even someone as liberal and progressive as Virginia Woolf – who once claimed, 'We discussed copulation with the same excitement and openness that we had discussed the nature of Good'[15] – found something unreal in boy-boy love. She could accept some buggers as persons, but she had difficulty coming to terms with the concept of male homosexuality. Extracts from her letters and diaries were to confirm this:

> Lytton, by the way, talked about S....[odom]y; & agreed that the b.....[ugger]s are all namby pambies & sentimentalists. He is himself, he said. To be a b. one must be unvirile, unpossessive, very nice indeed, but tending to be sentimental. And then their tastes become so degraded.[16]

> Have you any views on loving one's own sex? All the young men are so inclined, and I can't help finding it mildly foolish; though I have no particular reason. For one thing, all the young men tend to be pretty and ladylike, for some reason, at the moment. They paint and powder, which wasn't the style in our day at Cambridge ... Then the ladies, either in self-protection, or imitation or genuinely, are given to their own sex too. My aristocrat [Vita Sackville-West] ... is violently Sapphic ... I can't take ... these aberrations seriously.[17]

> I wish I liked buggers – Lytton is giving a party at the Ivy on Monday; and I know they'll all be of that persuasion – Duncan's all right, so's Morgan: but the insipidity of the rest passes belief.[18]

By this time, I dare say, the reader will be bursting to ask an obvious question. Why was it – if Cambridge was so idyllic and had become synonymous with stability, academic success, the Apostles, Morgan Forster, Bloomsbury, sexual conquest, extravagance of style, and other forms of hedonistic self-indulgence – that Sebastian Sprott decided to leave? Well, it was a question that I asked myself many times during my first year in Nottingham, I can tell you; for initially – up to the time I met Charles, in fact – I was wretched and full of misgivings. Within a year I was declaring my misery to Maynard Keynes, and seeking his influence and support for a plan to return to Cambridge:

> *29a Clumber St.*
> *May 1926*
> My dear Maynard, I'm sick of this place and I'm sick of teaching psychology to half-wits. I want to give it up. The Secretaryship of the library at Cambridge is vacant, Peter says, and I have written to him to say I should like it ... Then there's Moore's lectureship, which entails Part 1 Logic which I wouldn't relish, but I'm thinking of applying for that. I wonder whether you have anything to do with the former? I want that badly ... better than this unending vague lecturing ... My love and please help me. Sebastian.[19]

Yes, as things turned out, I had a rather unhappy and uncomfortable first year in Nottingham. But I had no way of foreseeing this. At the time, I was keen to leave Cambridge, and I was fairly clear about my reasons – or, at least, I thought I was.

Virginia Woolf had put her finger on the main one, perhaps. I was poor. No, that is not quite accurate. I was very poor! You see, upon graduating in 1922 my war grant had run out. I had hoped for some form of scholarship award to support my intended postgraduate work; but I was to be disappointed, as the following extract from my college magazine explains:

> We have an increasing number of people who, when asked what they are doing, shelter themselves behind the mystic word 'Research'. Sprott at the Psychology Laboratory, Godwin at the Botany School, West at the Cavendish, Hickson, Green and Walker at the University Library. The College has decided to aid research by splitting a Fellowship in two. The first Lady Clare Research Scholar is Harry Godwin.[20]

So, I had become involved in what my College viewed suspiciously as the mystical world of research! But unlike Harry Godwin – and W. A. Walker, who became the second Research Scholar in 1923 – I was not officially recognised and supported financially. I was expected to conduct my research in what little spare time I could garner from my duties as a demonstrator in the Psychology Laboratory; and the remuneration I received for this work barely allowed me to live above subsistence level. My father helped a little – as, indeed, did my dear Morgan; and Lytton, too, was generous – but for the next three years, yes, I was poor. No poorer, perhaps, than in my undergraduate days; but the difference was that I now *minded* being poor – which probably came from my mixing with the well-off and famous. It wasn't that I begrudged people like Morgan and Lytton their money; but I did begin to resent the fact that, unlike them, I would have to work for my living, and that most probably I would never have the luxury of regarding money as of little consequence. I envied Lytton's attitude to money; it appeared so carefree to me. Thus, he sometimes needed reminding that for others, cash – or the lack of it – could often be a problem. And because, dear man, he gave to his friends so freely and painlessly, he failed to understand how painfully embarrassing it could be for some people to ask

for money. I well remember a letter he wrote to me shortly after
my move to Nottingham:

> Dearest Creature, you are really rather a wretch ... I was told
> ... that you couldn't go away for weekends in the summer for
> lack of money ... why didn't you write and tell me that you
> were short of cash? What am I here for, I should like to know,
> if I'm not to be applied to in such circumstances. I enclose a
> cheque, in rather a rage, and command you to let me know if
> you would like another for the same amount – or any amount
> – little villain![21]

My second reason for contemplating a move from Cambridge
was linked to the first. After six years of undergraduate and
postgraduate work, it was time I got myself a real job – one
that brought with it not only money, but status. My work at
the Laboratory had been interesting in many ways – and it had
certainly rekindled my interest in teaching – but I was little more
than a factotum, running hither and thither at everybody's beck
and call. And from time to time it was galling to see my so-called
superiors take all the credit for successes that owed much to my
careful preparatory work – and were derived, in some cases,
from *my* research. However, there was no doubt that the job
had provided the type of experience and discipline which was to
qualify me for my first post. This appointment you will find
announced in the 'Clare College Association Annual':

> W.J.H. Sprott, B.A., appointed a Lecturer in Psychology at
> University College Nottingham.[22]

I was soon to be on the move, then – a fact which prompted
an enquiry, followed by a quirky observation, from Morgan:

> When do you leave Cambridge, and when do you go to Notting-
> ham? ... As for Nottingham ... the apex of a pyramid whose
> basis is Blackpool and Wigan.[23]

Meanwhile, once I had accepted the reality of the move, I
was able without difficulty to persuade myself that there were
other good reasons for leaving Cambridge. Maynard was one.
We remained good friends, he and I – as late as 1924 we still
went riding together on Saturday afternoons[24] – but it irked me
to see him with Lopokova. And when he came to tell me he was

engaged, and that he and Loppy planned to marry in the summer of 1925 – well, you can imagine my feelings! I think I still loved him, you see.

Apart from this, though, at twenty-eight years of age I was at last beginning to outgrow the life of a student. Was there not a danger, I was beginning to ask myself, that seductive Cambridge could hold me in its enchanting, suffocating embrace for ever? If I remained for much longer in this rarefied atmosphere, did I not risk being unable to breathe normally again outside? And was I not wearying of this incessant regard for one's image? Was there not a danger that affectations of dress, accent and mannerism could transform me permanently, so that even I might have difficulty identifying the 'real me'?

Yes, once I had made up my mind to do it, there were reasons aplenty to support my decision to leave Cambridge. There was a subconscious element at work, too. And at this point I have to confess that Cambridge was not quite the unalloyed success I have described. Maynard's desertion had hurt my pride, for one thing. But there was another conspicuous embarrassment; one which caused me even more anguish.

Early in 1923 I had been given the privilege, as we have heard, of reading Morgan's daring, unpublishable novel, *Maurice*. In an accompanying letter he had written:

> I send MS to 7 Brunswick Walk . . . better pretend that no one has ever heard of it. The history of its fame would be a curious one, and perhaps could not be entirely written by me. Lytton has read it, also Maynard and G.L.D. [Goldsworthy Lowes Dickinson].[25]

The book excited me, and before long I had begun work on a novel of my own. Not surprisingly, perhaps, it had a homosexual love theme. By the beginning of 1925 I had completed the final draft of the work in half-respectable manuscript form. Morgan, the only person in whom I had confided up to that point, showed great impatience to read it. From his newly-acquired West Hackhurst, he wrote:

> We moved in yesterday. It has been a rotten time and among other things I have no news of you. Are things fairly right? When can I read your novel? I want to read it so much.[26]

Well, I sent it to him immediately – and whether or not

24

you were simply being polite, dear Morgan, I don't know, but you said you thought it had sufficient merit to risk showing it to Virginia, with a view to possible publication by the Woolfs in their flourishing Hogarth Press. This response made me deliriously happy, and I wrote off to Virginia immediately. Her reply was not unencouraging. In a letter from Tavistock Square, dated 18 February 1925, she wrote as follows:

> Dear Sebastian, I look forward to reading your novel, but it has not yet come. I'm afraid that it may be some little time before I am able to read it, as I have been having a relapse from influenza and have to be very quiet for a bit. This also makes it rather doubtful whether we can come to Cambridge as you suggest – much though we should both like to.[27]

I remember being irritated with Morgan for causing a delay by not returning my manuscript promptly. However, after a reminder, it arrived within a few days; and by the end of the month I had posted it to Virginia.

The next three weeks or so found me in a state of exquisite agony. Morgan's kind words had possibly blinded me to any stylistic defects in my writing; and my friendship with Virginia, who was well-known for her avant-garde views, had perhaps persuaded me that the somewhat delicate subject matter would present few difficulties to a sympathetic and courageous publisher. I saw myself in print already: a brilliant new talent being groomed for a promising literary career by the astute patronage of Virginia and Leonard Woolf. And an end to all my money problems! There were moments of doubt, of course; naturally there were. Supposing I had no real talent, and Morgan had not had the heart or the stomach to tell me? Supposing artistic worth had to yield to commercial considerations, or to an out-moded morality? Yes, there were doubts. But I was a romantic, a dreamer – a believer in fairy tales coming true! And Cambridge had not prepared me and my kind for failure. We were intellectual gods on whose lives the sun never set. We were Olympians who dwelt in the company of the Muses. Our vanity had grown big on the ambrosia and nectar of privilege and scholarship. We could do anything we cared to put our minds and lofty spirits to. We were the golden boys, the chosen ones. Was it not the case that, Midas-like, everything we touched would turn to gold?

Imagine my dismay, then, when I received Virginia's verdict.

Perhaps the reader should see the whole letter, dated 25 March 1925:

> Dear Sebastian, Your book has interested me very much, but on the whole we don't think we can publish it; though we are extremely sorry not to. My feeling is that you don't get going till rather late – it seems as if your theme interested you, and not the people; so that in spite of the fact that the end gets an emotion which is quite genuine, it is too late to tell; and as a whole the book is not pulled off. I only give you these criticisms as you asked me; honestly, I don't trust myself on other people's novels, simply because, as I write them myself, I get my eye out. I feel that you ought to stand more on your own feet, and that at present you accept too brilliantly what other people tell you and are afraid of your own observations. But this may well be nonsense. The other point is that the public won't like the theme or understand it, which of course makes it risky from the publishing point of view. But it will be very interesting to see what you write next, though after this plain speaking we have no right to ask you to let us see it. Would you send Angus [Davidson] a card to say where you would like the MS sent? I suppose you are no longer at Cambridge? Yours, Virginia Woolf.[28]

I was devastated. It was not simply the rejection – though that was bad enough: the news of Sprott's failed novel would soon be winging its way through Bloomsbury! – it was the fact that I seemed to be incapable of isolating one clear reason why the Woolfs had found my work unacceptable. Ironically, in her desire to be helpful and honest, Virginia had been too conscientious in her critical analysis, offering too many points for my consideration. Was it my style, or my technique? Was it true that I was more interested in my theme than my characters? And did I really mistrust my own observations? In my arrogance, I was inclined to dismiss what had been written on the lines and look for the real reason between the lines. Perhaps it was something personal? Yes, that was a distinct possibility – for was it not true that my relationship with Virginia had cooled somewhat of late? Or was the real reason my 'risky' theme? – or rather the Woolfs' cautiousness and lack of courage? Whatever it was – and I was able to get no more out of Virginia, apart from a somewhat patronising plea for me to go on trying – I entered a period of catatonic depression. As I began to emerge from this, I had but one healing thought: I would soon be off the scene. In the end, it was almost a flight from Cambridge. I couldn't get away quickly enough. That damned novel had soured a whole glorious bowl of cream! I remember throwing the manuscript into one of the tea-chests brought in by the removal men, so it must have travelled to Nottingham with me. But I do not recall ever seeing it again . . .

The Celestial Omnibus

———◆———

MORGAN: ... This is fascinating, Jack dear. I interrupt only because I sense that the lads would like to say something. Ted seems particularly keen to make a comment.

TED: You bet your life I am! First of all, I'm surprised that Jack had the nerve to mention that bleddy fancy name he used to impress his la-di-da Bloomsbury friends with. Christ, no wonder it became an embarrassment to him later on!

MORGAN: Oh, but you should have seen him in his Cambridge days, Ted. Sebastian suited him then. It went with the Bloomsbury accents, and with the clothes he wore with such éclat – his oriental dressing-gown, and the large black hat and cloak he used to wear about town. Yes, he cut quite a dash, I can tell you. I think it was Lytton Strachey who described him at that time as 'debonair, dashing, and an acknowledged leader'.[29] It is true that he was too exquisite for some; but most people loved his flamboyance. And plain 'Jack Sprott', you must own, hardly had a ring to it. It simply did not match his image. We must permit the young, Ted, to indulge in a little harmless affectation. We have all been guilty, I am sure?

CHARLES: Yes, Ted, what about your first suit of plus-fours? Do you remember that? You strutted about like a peacock in that outfit!

TED: Well, perhaps I did. But that was different. It was my first decent suit. Before that, all I had was an old jacket and two pairs of ragged trousers – one with the arse worn out, the other with the knees worn through. For 'best' – and to hide my shame, really – I used to wear both pairs of trousers, the one hiding the bare bits of the other! Yes, I did fancy myself in that suit; but no wonder. And even then, it wasn't a new suit was it? It was one of yours, Charles, wasn't it, that Miss Jephson had altered for me?

JACK: You were still indulging yourself, though, ducky. And

in other ways, too. We notice, for example, that your speech has improved vastly since last we met. There are fewer vulgarisms, and we are no longer deafened by the sound of dropped aitches.

TED: Again, that's different. I'm not putting on airs. I'm just trying to do something about the way I talk, that's all. I'm not swanking, and bleddy name-dropping, like you.

JACK: Oh dear, ducky, you really are too tiresome. I wasn't name-dropping. I didn't have to. Those 'names', as you call them, were my intimate friends. It was only natural that I should mention Maynard and Lytton, and people like that, because they were an important part of my life. We had such gay times together in my student days. And they did everything, some of those people – Lytton, in particular – with such style, such panache. And with frequent displays of charming eccentricity too. I remember Lytton once writing to me – it was in November 1923, as I recall – and addressing the envelope as follows:

> Kind *Cambridge* postman, please do not forget, through loitering, love or talk, to leave this letter with the SPROTT who lives at 7 Brunswick Walk.[30]

Yes, he had quite a line in dry humour, had Lytton. It was too wicked for some, I fear, but it was never directed against me. He amused me greatly. For example, commenting on my latest affair shortly after my move from Cambridge to Nottingham, he once wrote:

> Your clerk appals me. But I gather, via Philip, via Philip's brother, that virginity is, now at any rate, not one of his drawbacks.[31]

MORGAN: Oh, delightful, Jack dear! Yes, Lytton could be very amusing, I grant you – when he wasn't being bitingly critical, that is: for you must admit that some of his gossip had a cruel edge to it? He nicknamed me 'the Taupe', you know. Not that there was any great malice in that, I'm sure. It derived in part, I believe, from the way I had of slipping, silently and unobtrusively, in and out of company and conversations – though I suppose it could also have been an observation on my physical appearance. Hardly flattering, perhaps, to be compared to a mole; but I took no offence.

TED: If we can move on, I also want to ask Jack what he thinks it means to be 'very poor'? Because when he got to that bit – well, if I'd had any feet, I would've laughed my bleddy socks off! What does he know about real poverty? Does he know what it's like to go all day with only a slice of bread and margarine in your belly? No, he doesn't – but I do! Does he know what it's like to go to school without shoes on your feet? No, he doesn't – but I went to school with kids who did. And my own shoes, perhaps third or even fourth-hand from Jacky Pownall's, were so worn that if I stepped on a ha'penny I could tell you whether it was heads or tails. Does he know what it's like to have bugs in your beds, or to shit in a tub across the yard, or to take your dad's only suit, the one he got married in, to the pawnshop every week – or to have brothers and sisters who died of disease and malnutrition? Of course he bleddy doesn't! But I do. So talk to us about your posh friends and your university degrees, Jack, and we might listen. But don't talk to us – or to me, at any rate – about being poor, because you've got absolutely no bleddy idea what it means.

MORGAN: Yes, Ted, we take your point. Don't overexcite yourself. I'm sure that Jack understands more than most that being poor, like being rich, is relative. And so is hardship. Of course Jack has never known the degree of poverty that you had to endure; he simply meant that he experienced relative hardship at that stage in his life.

TED: Well, he shouldn't have talked about being poor then, should he?

JACK: I'm sure that I wasn't poor in your terms, Ted; and, believe me, I'm sorry for anyone who was. But to pursue Morgan's point, compared with most of my friends at that time I was very poor – and compared with my parents' standard of living, even, I was experiencing hardship. Anyway, let's change the subject. Did you want to make an observation, Charles dear?

CHARLES: Yes, but first I must say that I agree with Ted about poverty. Mind you, I don't think I was quite as poor as he was, although I certainly went to school with kids who were. You couldn't help being born above such things, Jack; we all understand that. But sometimes it made us mad, you know, listening to the middle classes going on about being poor – when we knew that what they really meant was two trips abroad instead of three, eating in slightly less expensive restaurants and ordering a case or two less of wine that year. But let's not dwell on these things. I was more interested in your reference to – what did you call it? – the Apostles? I'm sure it's nothing like it, really, but it reminded me of the Cosmo. Did it you, Ted? That bit about the aim of your Society, for example, struck me as being rather similar to the object of the Cosmo. Am I right?

JACK: Well, yes, I suppose there is a similarity in a sense; in their quite different ways, you might argue, both were concerned with the pursuit of truth.

MORGAN: What exactly was this Cosmo, Charles dear? Jack mentioned it once or twice in his letters, I remember, but I was never really sure of its aims – or if I was, I have forgotten.

CHARLES: Oh, it was a marvellous institution, wasn't it, Ted? It was sometimes referred to as 'the working man's university', but it was the name by which the Nottingham Cosmopolitan Debating Society was always known. Bits of its aims were always appearing in its annual syllabuses. One year, I remember, there was printed across the top of the syllabus, 'A thinking man is the worst enemy the Prince of Darkness can have' – a quotation from Thomas Carlyle, it said – and across the bottom were the words, 'Our object is the furtherance of knowledge and truth by means of free discussion. All truth seekers have here an open door and a kindly welcome'.[32] In other syllabuses – and Patrick has copies of these; they take me back with a mixture of pleasure and sadness – you can find other quotations, like:

> Truth is a frail spirit that must be sought with patience and calm investigation. Its pursuit should be conducted with dignity and especially with scrupulous honesty.[33]

> The Cosmo is formed for the free and open discussion of all subjects, tabooed or otherwise, and any Lady or Gentleman, Member or Non-Member, desiring to ventilate his or her own opinion, can have a free platform and courteous treatment by applying to the Hon. Sec., F.H. Groocock.[34]

> The Cosmo . . . is unattached to any political or religious organisation, its endeavour being to give a fair and impartial hearing to all speakers on all subjects . . . the Society appeals to all lovers of Truth and Justice, and to those interested in the cause of Progress and Reform, to assist by becoming members and making the Society known to their friends.[35]

MORGAN: Most interesting, Charles dear; thank you. And when was the Cosmo founded?

CHARLES: Aah, now Patrick made some notes on that; perhaps we should take a look at them:

The Nottingham Cosmopolitan Debating Society
Notes made by P. Belshaw from the *Nottingham Civic News*, March 1971

In 1898 a Labour Church was in existence and the local secretary, Frank Keeling, commented to the President, William Robinson, 'I think if we had a debating society as an adjunct to our Church it would help to improve our speaking'. The idea obviously commended itself to Robinson because in 1916 writing of the Society he said, 'It has had my best thoughts, it has preceded my business, it is interwoven with my very life'. The Debating Society, as it was then known, thus began as an adjunct to the Nottingham Labour Church in 1898.

The first meetings were held in Cobden Hall, Peachey St., and in these early days a very motley crew from the Labour Church attended. No outside speakers were invited at that time, and every meeting was opened with a prayer given by the Chairman. Later meetings were open to the general public and outside speakers, many of them eminent, were invited. 'The cranks came in. We became alive and firmly established', wrote William Robinson. When Keir Hardie MP was guest-speaker the Chairman's prayer was, 'May they, Lord, be so impressed as not to suffer to be further bamboozled in the future'.

Meetings were held each Sunday afternoon; an experiment to attract a larger audience by meeting in the evening failed. A change of name to 'The Nottingham Cosmopolitan Debating Society' was suggested by Fred Groocock, an early enthusiast of the Society, about the time of the Great War. By 1916 a friend of William Robinson, F.W. Dexter, was writing that the Cosmo could 'boast of a type of lecturer and able debater second to none in any debating assembly in the world'.

The leaders in the first decade claimed that the Cosmo was a local parliament to which everyone was welcome and in which there was no discrimination of race, colour or creed. During its seventy years the place of meetings of the Society has been changed several times to accommodate larger assemblies. From Cobden Hall the Society moved to Clarion Fellowship Room and later it hired the Nottingham Orchestral Society's rooms in Parliament St. (now Hopewell's Furniture Showrooms). One Sunday audience grew so large that when they dispersed the police were called by an alarmed citizen who thought there was a riot. The Local Authority condemned the rooms because the means of exit did not conform to fire regulations. The King's Theatre in Market St. (later the Scala and now the Classic cinema) was then hired. There when George Watts and H. T. Newman debated 'Is Socialism possible nationally?' an audience of 1200 attended. The largest ever audience recorded at the King's Theatre was 1600, but when the rent increased to five guineas a new home was sought. The Society transferred to the Mechanics Institute – where members were not allowed to smoke: one of the main reasons why this venue was changed – and then later to the 'Picture Palace' in Upper Parliament St. where a special portable platform was installed to enable the speaker to be seen from the balcony. The 'Picture Palace' became the 'News House' cinema and has since been demolished. The Cosmo's best years occurred between the two World Wars when the Society met in the large lecture theatre of the University College in Shakespeare St. Eminent speakers of international and national reputation appeared and the theatre was packed every Sunday afternoon. In November 1934, when Professor J. Lavrin's subject was 'Russia and the Crisis of Civilisation', an attendance of 529 was recorded. Officers of the committee were told, 'This day the Hall was so crowded that a number of people forced the door, breaking the woodwork. The caretaker telephoned the police and the registrar'. The meetings continued to be held in the Hall, however, with the support of Alderman Huntsman . . .

. . . The Rules of Debate have scarcely changed over the years; they are as follows: 'Chairman's Opening Remarks – 5 minutes; Lecturer's Address – 40 minutes; Questions from the Audience – 10 minutes; Criticisms from the Audience – 50 minutes (anyone catching the Chairman's eye during this period could speak for up to five minutes); Lecturer's Reply to Opposition – 15 minutes.'

Footnote: In its early days the Cosmo was once described by the *Daily Express* as 'a hot-bed of cranks'.

TED: Well, it would say that, wouldn't it, the bleddy *Express*! As Charles said, this was the nearest we got to a university; it made us think – and it made us realise just how much injustice there was in the world. No wonder the *Express* saw us as a threat! Most of us were rather left wing, naturally. In fact, it was thanks to the Cosmo, I believe, that Charles and I eventually joined the Communist Party in the mid 1930s.

MORGAN: Yes, I remember Charles telling me about that, Ted. Well, this has been most instructive – and I hope, Jack dear, well worth the interruption to your narrative? . . .

Uncle Jack

———※———

... To continue, it was hoped that my life in Nottingham would provide a new beginning. In fact, I was about to lead three different and separate lives. I tried to keep each one insulated from the others, quite deliberately – though, inevitably, some seepage occurred across the boundaries. First, despite the shame I suffered with regard to my failed novel, I continued my contact with Bloomsbury. Once or twice a month I would travel down to London or Cambridge to maintain old friendships or cultivate new ones. Such intercourse provided my main stimulus intellectually; it also allowed me to remain within a magic circle of influence and delicious gossip.

Secondly, I had my professional life at the University. Here I earned my living, and learned the tricks of my trade, working hard to improve my lecturing techniques and to earn some respect in my specialised field of social psychology. I met people, of course; and once I had come through the misery of the first year, I found the work interesting, even enjoyable at times. But this was my work place; and I tried to keep all relationships here – with my colleagues on the staff, and with students – on a strictly formal footing. For a man with my sexual proclivities this was crucial in those days. To drop one's guard for a single moment was potentially an act of professional suicide.

The detail and style of my third life, my private life in Nottingham, would have shocked and alarmed the people who belonged to my other two lives – with notable exceptions, of course, including dear Morgan and Joe Ackerley. At one end of the spectrum, a few would have viewed my life style as curiously eccentric; at the other end, a great many more would have regarded certain aspects of it as a loathsome perversion, and in general would have found my behaviour abhorrent. Between these two extremes the majority would privately have registered distaste;

34

but publicly, anxious to appear tolerant and liberal-minded, they would have used coded words and phrases to describe me and my behaviour – words like unconventional, free spirit, iconoclast, libertarian, and so on.

Thankfully, for all these people, prejudices were to remain undeclared. Very few friends crossed the borders between my three lives. As far as I was concerned, of course, there was nothing remarkable about my private life. Indeed, had it 'got out' what would all the fuss have been about? It was simply that I associated almost exclusively with members of the lower classes, all of whom were men and some of whom gave me sexual satisfaction.

My face became familiar in all the well-known haunts of homosexuals at that time – for example, in pubs like the Dog and Bear and the Peach Tree – where I was soon referred to as 'the Professor', a somewhat prophetic sobriquet as things were to turn out. I hasten to add that presumably the nickname derived from my accent and studious mien: I was always careful to tell no one what I did for a living, or where I worked. When I first heard it used I was unnerved, I can tell you. I thought they were on to me. But I soon came to realise that to most of these men anyone who wore glasses and used words of more than two syllables was almost automatically a 'Brains', or an 'Egghead', or a 'Professor'. Selected pick-ups – the more interesting, the more hygienic! – were invited to my Clumber Street flat, where sometimes a number would gather for coffee and sandwiches, and a chat. Some of these men were 'down-and-outs'; one or two had been in prison, and most seemed to live on the fringes of the law. A few took advantage of me – for I soon gained the reputation of being a bit of a soft touch – but most were quite loyal and scrupulous in their way. I enjoyed their company.

The inquisitive reader may care to speculate why I encouraged this apparently unlikely circle of friends. It wasn't simply a question of lust. Over the years I took very few of these men home to bed: I tended to conduct my sexual exploits away from the flat. Perhaps it was egalitarianism? – a late and rather dramatic reaction to the privilege and power I had inherited? Or was it altruism? Did I genuinely hope to improve the lot of those less fortunate than myself? It might possibly have been simply a form of relaxation – a relief from the affectations and intellectual demands of Bloomsbury, or an entertaining diversion from the solemn routine of work? Or was it that these hapless souls provided 'good copy' for the stories I used to recount in epistolary form for the amusement and titillation of Morgan? (For example, I remember telling him about taking Norman, my window-cleaner, for a drive into the Peak District. We had come back through Chesterfield, and upon seeing the famous crooked spire he had remarked that it looked 'just like an old man's prick'![36] Morgan told me that he found such snippets most entertaining.)

A final possibility which may have crossed the reader's mind is that far from behaving benignly I was cynically using my friends as guinea pigs – constantly analysing their behaviour, and keeping records which one day, in my lectures, articles and books, would prove useful. To be truthful, there may have been something in each of these explanations from time to time and in varying proportions. But perhaps, as I say, I simply enjoyed the company of these men.

This was the background to my first meeting with Charles Lovett in the late summer of 1926. I met him – or rather, picked him up – in the men's public lavatory near St Peter's churchyard in the centre of Nottingham, a well-known rendezvous for homosexuals. If this *sounds* sordid, the reality for a man of sensibilities – driven under-ground, literally, because of his sexuality – was even more distasteful. We were engaged in what was known as 'cottaging' – and if you had to wait an hour or so before you got that spark of recognition, that thrill of mutual attraction, you could develop what was known in the trade as 'cottage feet' from standing about too long, welt-deep, in piss! The law and public opinion being what it was in those days, many a tender and long-standing relationship had to spring from such squalid beginnings.

With his round face, clear complexion and blue eyes, Charles was very attractive. He seemed quite intelligent, too, with a good sense of humour; and he wasn't badly spoken, either. We went for a drink and a chat. The name of the pub escapes me, I'm afraid; but I was so impressed that I arranged to spend the following night with him in a discreet hotel I knew. Within a week, after one more night in the hotel, I had broken my general rule and Charles was introduced to my flat. Our relationship quickly became warm and intimate. I was very happy; and I lost little time conveying my felicity to Morgan in my usual, confidential fashion. He immediately showed an interest – as was his wont regarding all of my 'finds' – and his simple enquiry into the nature of Charles' job is contained in a long letter which reveals, quite clearly, the level of intimacy that had by now developed between us; it also offers another delightful example of Morgan's playful humour:

> Dear Mr Sprott ... Mr Forster is as flabbergasted as myself though in a different way, as on opening 'Reading' it turns out to be dedicated to him. I think there is nothing like a writer for giving another one a nice surprise, and one so on the spot too. You would love to see Mr Forster's face. It is in a series called 'These Diversions' – 'Talking' by J.B. Priestley, 'Dreaming' by De La Mare (Dreaming – odd again) 'Idling' by Robert Lynd, 'Wandering' by Hilaire Belloc, and 'Playgoing' by James Agate, and 'Fucking' by Sir William Marchant [this name crossed out by EMF and replaced by 'Lady Gregory'] ... Please write again. I want to hear about Stan very much. I am awfully sorry. What was it, and how long did he get? I went to Weybridge – dully with Mother yesterday to see a play, and secretly and amusingly about six weeks ago. My life is literary and idealistic since then. I hope the calm will not continue. I don't know of a job for Bert – easily found doubtless. Very sad he's going. What arrangements are you making in his place? What's Charles' job? And is Billy Peck cropped everywhere, or don't you know? You must write again – your letter's all title pages. Love from Morgan.[37]

During the following months Charles and I saw a great deal of one another: too much, really, for his future happiness. I quickly came to realise that he was infatuated with me; and although I loved him I was not able to reciprocate his intensity of feeling and, more significantly, his desire for an exclusive relationship. Throughout my life, for some reason, I was never able to love with that degree of commitment – even with Maynard. Sensing this, Charles felt insecure. He suffered agonies of jealousy when he saw me in the company of other friends; in particular he mistrusted the relationship I had with Blackamore, the man I employed part time to clean and cook for me. Charles wanted me to get rid of Blackamore, whose position he sought for himself; that way he hoped to make me more dependent on him. Eventually he got his way; but for the moment Mr Blackamore was the cause of much tension between us.

Apart from his jealousy, I was delighted with Charles; he was proving to be a very sensitive lover. I sang his praises frequently in my letters to Morgan, who began to show more than a passing interest in our affair. He seemed very keen to meet Charles, so I invited him to join a little gathering of some of my newer friends in Nottingham. This was in the summer of 1927. His reply to my invitation included the teasing suggestion, 'Will you not invite two Blackamoors to tea – and better still to dine and sleep?'[38] Behind this playful pun on Mr Blackamore's name was there a hint, I wondered?

My little party was a great success. Charles, in particular, had made quite an impression. Morgan thanked me in a letter dated 1 July, concluding:

> Remember me in varying ways to 'ubert, to Harold, to Charles.
> I like Charles best. Tell him so if you think it will cause him to like me better. But I liked them all.[39]

Within a week he was writing again, apparently unable to keep Charles out of his thoughts: 'Glad that Charles goes on all right – how nice he is.'[40] I sensed that Morgan was angling for an opportunity to meet Charles alone, and after some consideration I thought it would be rather amusing to arrange this. It would make Morgan happy – not to mention indebted to me – and it might be fun afterwards to compare notes! I was quite confident that I couldn't lose Charles, and my apparently casual attitude might deter him from doting on me more than was good for him. Yes, the more I thought about it the more excited I became. This could create a fascinating diversion. . .

Uncle Morgan

———❈———

... When I wrote to say how nice Charles was, I was employing a deliberate understatement for Sebastian's benefit. In fact, with his soft skin and youthful chubbiness, I thought he was just the ticket. His facial features, it is true, were of the type that, in repose, could not combine to make a handsome sculpture; but when he smiled, with that trick of his of inclining the head slightly, his face lit up and was transformed. I believe you will find a reference to this in a letter I wrote to Sebastian thanking him for arranging Charles' first visit to London:

> Dear Sebastian, ... Charles missed the 7.00 which was half an hour late and arrived by the 8.10 which was punctual ... There was time to get him to St Pancras and feed him. He was reluctant to go and I should have asked him to stop if I could have put him up, but it didn't seem worth sending him to a hotel. He has been in an aeroplane and has scandalised the fuck-hole aunts by saying he knew someone who knew Edgar Sackville West ... I asked him if he knew my name. Yes he said – Gordon ... What an ugly glazed, crooked face Charles has – then he smiles and is enchanting. He smiled most of the hour. I was greatly pleased with him. He told me how much you thought of me, altogether a very happy hour, and we have arranged that he is to work an early invitation for me to Nottingham. Tell him when you write that I have the remains of a ... biscuit in my pocket which I meant to fling into his mouth before I left ... Love from Morgan.[41]

Oh, how well I remember that evening! After he had gone, I felt mean about fetching him all that way from Nottingham for an hour or so in a railway station restaurant. But I had to be cautious. Charles was indeed charming; he had a sort of boyish innocence which I found captivating. And despite his naivety, I was sure he was capable of discretion. However, these were first impressions. I had to learn a lesson from the past and avoid committing myself

39

too soon. The situation was complicated because I already had a lover, a man named Harry Daley; and it was complicated further by my concern about constructing yet another triangle, this time involving Sebastian, my friend and confidant, whose respect I was anxious to maintain. Yet I could not get Charles out of my mind. I desperately wanted to see him again. Yes, I knew he belonged to Sebastian; and the more rational half of me doubted the wisdom of allowing a relationship to develop. Nevertheless, I accepted the invitation to Nottingham when it arrived. 'Tell me which train to arrive by', I found myself replying excitedly, 'and Charles to meet it.'[42] It couldn't do any harm just to see him again, I persuaded myself.

During this visit I saw Sebastian and Charles, and no one else. Sebastian was in gay mood throughout; his insouciance was infectious, and there was much tempting and teasing, helped along by liberal draughts of wine. I got the impression that Sebastian was offering Charles to me; he seemed keen, certainly, for Charles to come and stay with me in London. Oh, how I was tempted! And how strong I had to be to include in my next letter the following rejection of Charles:

> I have decided to do a renunciation stunt over Charles. When close to him I didn't want to, but closeness is too narrow a basis on which to construct a triangle. Some triangles there must be, there shall be; but as few of them as possible in my position. So I shall let the London invitation slide ... Give best remembrance to Charles and 'ubert, and to black Harold.[43]

The fact was that I was already involved in a painful triangle. And, moreover, I had but lately escaped from an earlier one. I have never been able to get away from triangles, it seems. Throughout my life this geometrical figure has gone on reproducing and insinuating itself. The age, size, shape and background of my lovers may have varied from time to time, but almost all of them led me into three-sided affairs. And not a right angle in sight! On the contrary, they have always been acute in terms of the pain inflicted, and obtuse regarding my determination to persist well beyond the stage of construction at which a third side begins to push the other two sides apart. The entire history of my emotional life might well be represented by a mosaic of tessellated triangles. I have no regrets; but to the observer, what a sad tale this picture would appear to tell. For as Jack was to write in one of his books, derived from painful personal experience, I'm sure:

> It is in the pair relationship that the sharing of specific experience reaches its height, and a certain weight of responsibility is placed upon each of the participants to keep the group intact – there is, in fact, no group 'outside' the individual members to blame for anything that goes wrong. The presence of a third is notoriously interruptive. Each member of the original pair is likely to have a different relationship to the third, and so the triad tends to shift into three pairs: AB, BC, AC, with one left out. A fourth and a fifth make less difference to a triad than a third added to a pair.[44]

I first began to play triangles – or rather triangles first began to plague me – during my relationship with Hugh Meredith. He and I were undergraduates together, and fellow Apostles. When we left Cambridge we both went on to lecture at the Working Men's College. As classicists we understood, and were drawn to, the Greek ideal of love; indeed, we may have been as much in love with that ideal as we were with one another – or rather, as I was with Hugh, for I was much keener than he. To understand something of our relationship – or of my idealised, romantic notion of it, at least – the reader might try my novel, *Maurice*:

> Clive had expanded in this direction ever since he had understood Greek. The love that Socrates bore Phaedo now lay within his reach, love passionate but temperate, such as only finer natures can understand . . . He led the beloved up a narrow and beautiful path, high above either abyss. It went on until the final darkness – he could see no other terror – and when that descended they would at all events have lived more fully than either saint or sensualist, and would have extracted to their utmost the nobility and sweetness of the world . . . Love . . . in order that two imperfect souls might touch perfection.[45]

Elsewhere in the novel I had Clive say that with Maurice he sought 'a particular harmony of body and soul' which he doubted 'women have even guessed' – then, within three years, I had him marrying Lady Anne Woods! Although in Maurice, as I explained later, I had tried 'to create a character who was completely unlike myself',[46] I was here creating a deliberate echo of the progress of my affair with Hugh Meredith. I had dreamt of Hugh and myself achieving that harmony of body and soul, only to discover that he had become engaged – first to Caroline Graveson, and then to Christabel Iles whom he married in 1906. Masochistically I kept my side in the triangle; and as the third side got longer, my misery grew proportionately. Mercifully, however, I was soon to be diverted from this anguish and disappointment.

The year Hugh was married I took a job as tutor to Syed Ross Masood, the grandson of Sir Syed Ahmed Khan. Over the next few years we developed an intimate friendship which, on my part at least, became love – despite Masood's openly declared relationships with a number of girlfriends. My masochistic streak again! Our relationship was never consummated; but we holidayed together in France and Italy, and in 1913 he joined me during my first visit to India. Then in 1915 he suddenly announced his intention to marry – and my second triangle was under construction.

A third began to form the following year, during my service as a 'searcher' with the Red Cross in Alexandria. I became friendly with a young Muslim tram conductor, Mohammed el Adl, who had learned English at the American Mission School. Our growing intimacy hiccuped a little at first; I became overexcited at our first physical contact, and it was some time before Mohammed consented to go to bed with me. But after that – oh, what bliss! Not only was I fulfilled by this, my first full physical relationship, but in a single, bold expedition I had crossed successfully the frontiers of race, religion and class. I could hardly contain my happiness; indeed, it spilled into my correspondence with Florence Barger, the wife of an old Cambridge friend, who had for some time been my confidante. 'Wish I was writing the latter half of *Maurice*', I wrote to her in 1917, 'I now know so much more. It is awful to think of the thousands who go through youth without ever knowing. I have known in a way before, but never like this. My luck has been amazing.'[47]

Sadly, after a year or so, things began to go badly for Mohammed and me. He took a new job, working for the army in the Canal Zone, and this meant that we saw one another much less frequently. Then, in 1918, his father died. He inherited the family house – and suddenly, out of the blue, he decided that as a man of property he needed a wife. He married in July 1918. Fortunately, with the war at an end, my work with the Red Cross was terminated; and less painfully than perhaps I deserved, I was able, in January 1919, to break out of this triangle by returning to England – although I corresponded with Mohammed for several years thereafter, and I was much saddened by the news of his death in May 1922.

To explain the construction of the fourth triangle, one may as well begin with my letters to Joe Ackerley between 1924 and 1926 and allow extracts from these to tell their own story:

My dear Joe. Excuse two letters in a single day, but the man I told you about has just asked me to go and see him. My alleged superiority in the French language was the pretext. He fired, out out of the gloom, a parlez vous Francais suddenly, and was amazed when I understood the words, and later in the day he as abruptly invited me. You, of course, would have said, 'Yes', but I said 'Yes', too . . . Lives with wife and child in a large derelict house in the field behind. Perfectly simple and ordinary, I think . . . But I am amused and excited, of course. I go tomorrow evening. The worst of it is I can't find my easy French books, and I said I had heaps. With love. Morgan.[48]

My mother . . . says he has mistaken my class, thinks it is a little higher than his own (instead of infinitely higher) and will see his blunder when he comes to the house. I am afraid this may be so, still I shall go ahead until rocks are visible – it is quite a good substitute for courage. If we pull through the interview, perhaps you might come down and inspect.[49]

Dear Joe. I liked your sympathy. I didn't mean that when I had a feeling it was returned (that alas! would be a grotesque claim for me to make); only that I must be a pretty good judge of character, for I have seldom ventured and drawn a dud. I don't care much for what are usually called 'good looks', and this does assist one towards a correct estimate.[50]

Tom has just called to say he can't come in this evening – relatives. He was gentle and friendly and surveyed the well-carpeted hall without visible emotion. 'Any day next week', were his words. I shall wait till my mother has gone off again. Perhaps Joe is right, and I don't look like a gentleman or the house like property, but it seems too good to be true.[51]

My dear Joe. I've just discovered the trouble over Tom. Bess won't let him come. I'm pretty well resigned to the inevitable sadness of life and shall probably settle down . . . He served me the same last week – he and she, both on the bus and very pleasant, said he should turn up but he didn't. Then today – I left Cambridge early for the purpose – I asked if I might come and see him; when I got round Bess was in the dark and a temper. I asked Tom (according to my plot) to come off with me to my house for a few minutes, and until he did I didn't like to come into his. He said, 'She's a bit nervous – she doesn't like to be left' – no doubt true; and she said crossly, 'I see nothing of you all the day'. So I retired, defeated I suppose, but on the way to internal relief. I think he would have liked to come. He is weak . . . with nothing to him beyond friendliness and charm (a great deal, those qualities, but they provide no handle to get hold of). I could not forget him in Cambridge . . . I did not mention my trouble to anyone but you. You have helped me a great deal by allowing me to write and talk. I don't anticipate you will hear much more in the future, for it is not my policy, even if it were within my power, to break up homes.[52]

Haven't heard from Tom. Wish I could get him alone, with plenty of soap, on a desert island, though perhaps with his physique it might end badly.[53]

Dear Joe. The enclosed [photograph] has at last been to see me. Let me have him back, with something comforting. It is not like his face, and Bess tilted the camera. The visit was sticky, but friendly and physically superb. At the end of an hour a ring at the door – Bess and baby unable to walk alone across the field. The name is not Tom but Dudley . . . I have not much hope of a meeting in town, since he never has an opportunity to get off. I feel a bit upset, but nothing to the pain of 3 months ago. I feel sure he likes me, and I think he would have pity on me if he understood, but there is no approaching him through the intellect. In spite of all, what a privilege it is to be brought close to anyone outside one's own run. A queer ending to my 20 years sojourn in the suburbs.[54]

When I said it had been a pleasant evening he replied, 'It was all right, but it ought to have been an hour longer'. Mother – 'How like the lower classes to give you his photograph at a first call. They always think we're in love with them after the slightest civility'.[55]

The worst of it is I see no future. When and where are we to meet except in his house, which I dislike? . . . I cannot stir body or soul for furniture here.[56]

My mother would not stand much of Tom. He came twice to the house to get his stuff and to help me shift some heavy things. He wanted to go to tea which affronted her . . . I don't think Tom has more than charm and heart.[57]

. . . and when I made some remark about plans [he] said, 'Oo, celebrated author again' and touched me lightly and gaily with his hand. I think this is pretty good . . . I wish it could have an intellectual basis.[58]

My mother says she doesn't like him, doesn't trust his face by the way . . . West Hackhurst you see is impossible. I long to leave it and shall do so on Sat.[59]

I feel gloomy and useless – masturbation perhaps, but why masturbate?[60]

I was not as happy yesterday as I hoped – I suspect a general caution before starting from Bess, for the trustfulness has almost evaporated, and those foolish lies! On the other hand why write such letters, why come at all, and why certain moments of charm – turning back again and again to wave goodbye. I felt yesterday that I was being foolish, but today that I am a wise man trying to do a difficult thing.[61]

All was gay and lovely again. London must have intimidated.[62]

Am nearly off my head with happiness . . . 9 hours. He would have stopped longer, but Bess is expecting a child any moment. We saw a lot of interesting things at Wembley, also talked and ragged no end – 'It's been another vernon bruiser all day' – 'Look at them 'owards Ends being lifted in packages for export'.[63]

Tom is on the bus again, but I fear only temporary. I had a drink with him in the pub down Thames St. 'Hullo, old sport' – all very fresh and friendly. The child is a boy. He wants to come to town again, but I don't see how to arrange it yet.[64]

I ran down to see Tom who was very gay and nice though looking like Owen Nare owing to a coiffeur [sic]. I may have him up next Sat – the 18th.[65]

My mother, I notice, features in a number of these extracts, and rightly so, perhaps; she was a powerful influence in my life. Anyone I brought to the house had to get past her; without her approval, any openly declared friendship had little hope of flowering. I mention this because, since we are talking triangles, I suppose it can be said that she formed the third side in the largest of them all – the unspoken, unacknowledged triangle that cast its shadow each time I took a lover. This hidden triangle involving my mother was the one into which each of the others had to fit. Not that I was any more than partially aware of this at the time. My consciousness rarely extended beyond feelings of frustration and irritation at her interference in my affairs. It was these feelings that drove me – shortly after the move from Harnham to West Hackhurst, during the episode with Tom – to take a flat in town, in Brunswick Square. I did not leave home. I could not have done that; mother needed me. But I now had a *pied-à-terre* in which I could conduct a private life, and a life in private. I thought a great deal of my mother; but as I grew older I developed what the moderns would call a love-hate relationship, I suppose. My ambivalent view of her is perhaps best conveyed in the following extract from a letter I sent to Joe Ackerley from

West Hackhurst; the letter is undated, but I must have written it some time in 1937/38:

> Although my mother has been intermittently tiresome for the last 30 years, cramped and warped my genius, hindered my career, blocked and buggered up my house, and boycotted my beloved, I have to admit that she has provided a sort of rich sub-soil where I have been able to rest and grow. That, rather than sex and wifiness, seems to be women's splendid gift to men.[66]

You will have noticed that the references to my Weybridge bus driver – whose real name was Arthur Barnet,[67] by the way, not Tom, Dudley, or any of the others he tried on me: he told such lies! – began to decline during the later part of 1925 and the early part of 1926. The reason for this was that Fate had taken up the compasses again, and a fifth triangle was in the making.

I was introduced to Harry Daley by Joe Ackerley towards the end of 1925; he was a policeman stationed at a Section House in Hammersmith. He and Joe had met earlier in the year, and although they had soon become intimate friends they were never, each of them swore, lovers. It would have been naive to take Harry's word for this, but I was inclined to believe that Joe was telling the truth: he could never resist telling the whole world about his conquests! No, Joe was not a rival; I was certain of that. Quite the reverse, almost. For if this was a triangle at all, in the same sense as the others, it was probably one that I came to welcome. Harry was wildly indiscreet and not at all to be trusted; I needed Joe as a mediator, a middleman, through whom certain aspects of our affair could be arranged. Harry came to resent this. 'Ours isn't a friendship', he once asserted during one of our many arguments, 'it's a conspiracy!'[68] He was right; but without that conspiratorial dimension our brief, two-year affair would have ended much sooner.

We were not really suited, Harry and I. Afterwards, I could admit that. But at the time, I was blind to our differences. He excited me, and I was flattered by his attentions. 'I found myself too excited to do anything but walk about', I wrote to him on 18 July 1926, after we had gone to bed together for the first time, '– it is the happiest day I have spent for a very long time.'[69] Our days were always numbered, however. For one thing, I began to realise, Harry's preference was really for younger, heterosexual men; he was like Joe in that respect. But mainly it was because I was too often made to suffer through his brashness, his bouts of ill-temper and his many indiscretions; towards the end it became unbearable. Writing of one of my liaisons, I once confessed to myself in my diary, 'I have suffered no end, don't know what to do: it's an illness not an affair'.[70] This description could well have been applied to my affair with Harry. But if it was an illness – and I suppose it was a sickness, of sorts: it certainly affected me bodily – a remedy was already presenting itself in the form of Charles Lovett and triangle number six.

My so-called 'renunciation' of Charles lasted about three weeks! By the first day of December 1927 I was writing to Sebastian:

> It is short notice, but I am asking Charles if he can come up to town for the weekend, Dec. 10th. I don't expect he can . . . After Xmas – which may be more possible for him – may not be for me. Lovett is Charles' name is it not . . . His visit would be a pleasure . . . Give him my love.[71]

Well, Sebastian – my angel, my arch-organiser – made sure that it was possible. Just a few days later I was writing to thank him for arranging my first weekend alone with Charles, expressing my excitement as follows:

> Wonderful news – I am so astonished and pleased. The only thing I want to know is how to feed him when he arrives. I thought of a gentlemen's tea in my rooms, followed by meat meal with beer before the theatre . . . I expect we shall enjoy ourselves.[72]

Most certainly we did. 'One can't thank enough', I wrote to my organiser on 12 December 1927, adding:

> Visit to remain undeclared to the 'Cat Circus' [a reference to Joe Ackerley's Hammersmith circle] . . . When seeing him off he said he shouldn't like to live in London – Nottingham preferable . . . don't you think he is getting a good wage for what appears to be unskilled work? . . . Tell him I thought about him even more than I expected – because he'd taken off with the matches and I had to go off for an automatic machine.[73]

And we kept the pot simmering over the Christmas period, too:

> My dearest Sebastian . . . Charles has sent me a Xmas card – crossing a h'kerchief which I sent him.[74]

47

I ended the year feeling less troubled than I had done for a long time. Indeed, my customary diary entry for the last day of the year made me sound very contented and middle-aged at that time – filtering out, it seems, the alternating agony and ecstasy of my rum affair with Harry Daley:

> Moreover Charles, whose goodness and Sebastian's encircles me as I write (Seb. so unhappy himself is in London now) Charles, dear Charles – it's an elderly man's love. Tom was the last of my lusts – whenever I think of you I am soothed.[75]

Yes, Charles was precisely the remedy I needed; he was a safe haven from the emotional turmoil of the past few years. I was so grateful to Sebastian. Incredibly he didn't seem to mind lending me this gentle, accommodating lover – and the loan was always offered so graciously, so civilly, and without the slightest hint of jealousy afterwards. I have never been able to understand, let alone match, that degree of trust and generosity. Thankfully, he took care of all the arrangements, too. It was so much safer that way, I thought. Charles was an unknown quantity, after all, with qualities yet to be revealed or confirmed, whereas Sebastian's discretion was proven. It also meant that I was spared the embarrassment of making the more delicate advances and presenting the more awkward, inconveniencing plans. At the beginning, certainly, Sebastian's role of a 'go-between' was invaluable to me. He was my aide-de-camp, and a perfect secretary; he smoothed out all the difficult creases – some of which, no doubt, never even reached my attention – leaving me free to pursue my writing, my lecturing and my new lover unimpeded.

The progress of my developing affair with Charles Lovett can be plotted through the following extracts from letters to my organiser, some written from West Hackhurst, others from Brunswick Square – and almost all of them revealing how much I owed to Sebastian's tireless work as my go-between:

> *1 January 1928*
> What will Charles feel if I come up [to Nottingham] to tea Sunday?[76]

> *15 January 1928*
> Don't let anyone 'spoil' Charles ... though he seems perfectly sensible and resistant. I wish I hadn't mentioned 'Paris' to him – got excited. Think it had better lapse. And he shouldn't, for

his comfort and others, talk more than he needs about my being a prominent writer. If he needs a hint you'll give it.[77]

24 February 1928

Tell Charles to say what time he arrives, also how long he can stop, also give the names of 2 or 3 things he would like to see Sat evening and I'll try to get tickets. I'd like to pay his fare please. Tell him so, so that he shall not be put to the expense.[78]

28 February 1928

Tell Charles to arrive at 4.30 as planned and if I am not there to meet him [I had been called to a Fellowship Electors' meeting at King's College] to go to 27 Brunswick Square where he will find a note from me awaiting him on the mantelpiece. I enclose key so that he can let himself in without interviews and he will remember the room – second floor . . . I shall certainly be there for dinner and the theatre, but of course I wanted to be there to greet him. Give him my love and tell him I am sorry.[79]

8 March 1928

I was so very happy. I lived for those 29 hours in a world of good health and good temper that is almost closed to me elsewhere. I knew he was happy too and didn't stop to think whether he was equally happy – that sort of comparison doesn't exist. Well, it is over now – but not the sense of security it brought with it . . . Got seats in theatre behind Christopher Wood who saw the whole thing at a glance . . . but Charles didn't appear to worry at all . . . Am I a famous author? I think Charles had better not tell people I am when he can avoid it . . . Those who saw us saw 'a well matched pair'. An unhelpful tendency.[80]

25 March 1928

We will talk about Charles. I haven't unfortunately staged him here [at West Hackhurst] very well for a possible appearance in the flesh. Have conveyed indeed a false impression of Mr Lovett, and of course a slight one.[81]

18 May 1928

Still, fancy if Charles *was* free and willing to run up Sat (still more Friday) to town! How nice for Morgan.[82]

30 May 1928

What a happy time. All I find to fuss over is that I believe Charles to be a little fussed by a sore place in his mouth – his father's illness may be in his mind, though for no reason. He said it's nothing . . . I noticed his breath; was odd, just occasionally so probably is everyone's[83] . . .

The Celestial Omnibus

JACK: ... Charles, dear boy, you are looking a little discomfited. Is there anything wrong?

CHARLES: No, Jack, there's nothing the matter, except – well, there is something, actually. Oh, what's the point in trying to conceal things when you're dead! It's a silly thing, really – and goodness knows, I'm aware of the beam in my own eye – but I never realised that Morgan had had so many affairs. And all those sad triangles. If I were alive now, dear Morgan, I wouldn't know whether to weep for your disappointments or to rage against the number of men who seemed to be special in your life before I came along.

MORGAN: Oh, come now, Charles, dear, I was twice your age when we met. You must have known I was no beginner?

CHARLES: It's interesting you should say that, because that was exactly what I thought right up to the time you told me about Harry Daley. I really did think you were a beginner. You were so nervous in those early days and weeks: not at all the sophisticated, confident celebrity I was expecting.

MORGAN: I was always nervous at the start of any relationship; it sprang, I think, from anxieties about possible failure. I worried about physical performance, you see. It happens as you advance in years. The older you get, indeed, the more aware you become that life in general holds fewer and fewer certainties. But to return to the number of men in my life, I would hate you to think that because you were not the first – or, indeed, the last – you were not very precious to me. There is a sense in which each one of us is special, of course – you know the place of people and personal relationships in my credo – but some people are more special to us than others; and some, a cherished few, are

50

deserving of a highly treasured place in our hearts. Rest assured, my dear Charles, that you number among that few.

CHARLES: Thank you, Morgan; that makes me feel better. But you say I was not the last? Are you referring just to Bob Buckingham – because I knew all about him, of course – or are you telling me there were others?

MORGAN: Yes, there were others, I have to confess. But don't look so gloomy, Charles. They were just casual affairs – excitements, diversions, passing fancies: call them what you will – that developed, sometimes quite spontaneously, from my fondness for people. You know how it is. I am sorry to admit that I had one of these affairs in 1929. Oh dear, I see by the look on your face that my honesty shocks you – for, yes, you are quite right, it was during that same year that you and I had some of our most memorable moments together. But I was away from England – had been for several weeks, on a tour of South Africa with George and Florence Barger initially – and I suppose I was feeling lonely. Achille was his name. He was a French sailor, and I met him by chance in Toulon when I stopped off in France. We had a gay, if very brief, time together. We might have seen more of one another – for I had intended to spend several days in France, visiting the Maurons – but news of the death of Joe Ackerley's father took me hurrying back to London.

JACK: But afterwards Achille wrote to you, didn't he?

MORGAN: Oh, yes, he did; quite a few times – and very entertaining letters they were, too. And I have to say, since we are being honest, that the affair didn't end there, either. I spent two very diverting days with him in November 1934, when again I was on my way to see Charles Mauron and his wife. But you have no need to upset yourself over this, honestly, Charles. They were gay interludes, that's all. And I would say the same to Bob Buckingham if he were here. In fact, to anyone I may have upset by offering warmth and comfort to others I can only say, please forgive me. It was never my intention to hurt anyone. So pardon if you can, my very dear Charles, your gently philandering Morgie.

CHARLES: Well, I can forgive you if you can forgive me – for you never know, I may have a few confessions of my own . . .

Patrick

. . . I was very fond of my uncle Charles. Everyone was. It was hard to dislike him. For many years – during the war, particularly – he was the next best thing I had to a father. He was good to my mother, too; to the whole family, in fact. He and my uncle Ted both. They were the first people my mother turned to in a crisis. And she ran to them very frequently – indeed, sometimes almost literally, traipsing us kids across the city in the blackout, to arrive at Welbeck Street breathless with her latest problem. 'Consulting the Oracle', I came to call it. She was always assured of my uncles' protection – and of tea and sympathy, at least – and she acted unquestioningly upon the advice she was given, displaying a childlike faith in the infallibility of her brother's counsel.

Uncle Charles was a burly chap – or so he seemed to me as a child – but he had a genial and gentle nature. He had big, warm hands, I remember, and eyes that were easily moved to tears. He was very sentimental. But for me he usually had a smile. He had a nice smile, had uncle Charles. His round, chubby cheeks were always in high colour anyway – due to a combination of high blood pressure, shaving rash and fondness for a tipple – but when he smiled his whole face seemed to light up.

He rarely said much to me, my uncle Charles; but I warmed to his physical presence and his easygoing nature. Most of the time, he was phlegmatic and conciliatory; but if he did lose his temper, his face would flare up alarmingly, and foam would appear at the corners of his mouth. I saw him in such a rage on two occasions only, both in confrontation with my aunt Gwen, a wild-eyed, intimidating harridan who, as my mother put it, was enough to provoke a saint – which was what uncle Charles was, as far as my mother was concerned.

Yes, I liked my uncle Charles. But he had some curious habits. Periodically, for example, he would suddenly clear his throat in protracted and raucous fashion, as if he were trying to rid his passage of a serious obstruction. An embedded fish bone, perhaps? Or stubborn mucus, at least? Yet he never brought anything up. And I never saw him spit. Why, therefore, did he resort to this laryngeal extravagance? It puzzled me. Even more puzzling, and alarming, was his habit of drinking cough medicine – or any kind of medicine: he wasn't fussy! – straight from the bottle in huge draughts, rashly ignoring the prescription on the label. And not just his own medicine, either. He would help himself to other people's, applying the same profligate and dangerous technique with complete abandon, as if he were swigging lemonade. Give him his due, though: he never failed to offer his surprised donor an opinion, delivering a brief verdict on the pharmaceutical vintage with the gravity of a wine taster. Come to think of it, perhaps these two habits were not unconnected: years of medicinal abuse had probably done irreparable damage to the lining of his throat. Another habit uncle Charles had was something my dad used to tell me off for. He nearly always had his hands in his pockets – his trouser pockets, that is. 'Playing "pocket billiards", perhaps?', I came to speculate, when I was old enough to understand such things.

After I left home and got married I rather lost touch with my uncle Charles. I lived away from Nottingham, for one thing. Also, I became preoccupied with my own family. Sadly, I was away at the time of his death. And no one thought to invite me to his funeral! An odd thing, that, don't you think?

I rediscovered an interest in my uncle Charles years later when my youngest son, Christy, was working on a school project entitled 'My Family History: 1870–1970'. In a section devoted to my mother's side of the family, I read:

> Bede Ben-oni Lovett and Ada Elizabeth Daft were married at Nottingham Register Office on the 9th of April 1901. Bede was thirty six and his wife was twenty five – a difference of eleven years. Ada left her job at Griffin's fashion department to marry Bede who was working as a coal agent. The couple rented rooms from a Mr William Thomson M.B., a consultant surgeon, at 66 Carlton Road. Here the couple's first child, Charles Athelstan, was born on the 2nd of August 1901.

The information in this project, researched mainly from register offices and census returns, made interesting reading. I remember discussing the findings with my son – for example, the startling fact that so many people of that generation, and the one that followed, were conceived out of wedlock – and I was able to provide him with a lot of personal information about the Lovett family. Much of it was too detailed to be included in Christy's project, of course, but he was fascinated to hear his great-uncle's name linked with people like Morgan Forster, Joe Ackerley and Professor Sprott. At the time, the project engendered enormous interest throughout the family, on both sides. Unwittingly, my son may have been responsible for the genesis of my own research; at the very least, he may have sensitised me to my subject. For later in that same year, I opened my own file on Charles Lovett.

For me, the Lovett affair – as I came to call it – began with a chance encounter. I was browsing in a public library one day when I came upon Furbank's biography *E. M. Forster: A Life*. Having met Forster when I was a small boy – and knowing that uncle Jack Sprott had been one of his closest friends – I was immediately drawn to the volume. I turned to 'Sprott' in the index and began to work my way through the many references. Towards the end of the book I read about Forster's seventieth birthday treat:

> For his seventieth birthday Plomer and Ackerley organised a party in a Soho restaurant, inviting various of his closest friends.

At this point on the page the reader was referred to the following footnote: 'The guests were Anwar Masood and his wife, the Buckinghams, the Wilkinsons, Rose Macaulay, Elizabeth Poston, Hugh Meredith, E. K. Bennett, Sebastian Sprott and his friend Charles Lovett, and John Simpson.'[84]

The mention of my uncle's name took me completely by surprise. I became excited. And small wonder, perhaps. A famous writer has a private birthday party – for a select group of 'closest friends' – and my uncle Charles is invited to attend! But, wait a moment. I had to be careful not to jump to conclusions. Was he there merely as Sprott's appendage, I wondered? I was unable, it seems, to take in the possibility that uncle Charles might have been important in his own right . . .

Uncle Charles

————◦❂◦————

... Morgan's reference to my father is an appropriate point for me to pick up the story, partly because I did have good reason to feel upset about his illness – as you will hear in a moment – and partly because we have stumbled across something quite rare, namely, some evidence about my early life. You now know for a fact that my father was still alive in May 1928; you also know that, sadly, he was very poorly at this time. I can add to that information. His 'do's' – as my mother used to call them – were getting worse each time, and this latest period of illness was causing more than usual concern. My father's life was drawing to a close. These are facts that Patrick will be grateful to have come across, because the sad truth is that although I am his uncle, his mother's brother, the only blood relative he's got in this quartet, he probably knows less about me in some respects – certainly, up to the time I met Ted in 1929 – than about the other three members.

Ted is still alive; he can speak for himself and answer specific questions about his past. And Patrick is in touch with him. Morgan isn't a problem, either. He is famous; he has been officially biographered – if that's the word: if it isn't, you know what I mean – and dozens of other books have been written about him and his novels. You can even get to know a bit about him through reading his books. And not just those like *The Hill of Devi*, in which he describes his experiences in India, but his novels as well, if you know where to look. He once told me that. He said a writer puts a lot of himself into his work, and that in his case, particularly, he could only write from his own experiences. After our love-making, when he was more relaxed, he used to talk quite a lot about writing. Not that I was expected to understand much of it, mind you; most of the time I think he was just rehearsing what he was going to write, or say in a lecture

55

somewhere. I was simply his captive and captivated audience. This comes out quite neatly in one of his letters to Jack:

> Yes, I had five happy hours with Charles, sometimes lecturing him on Ibsen but not always ... How comfortable and safe one feels with him – so gentle and so definite.[85]

'But not always' – oh Morgan, how you loved your little jokes! I can see you now, smiling – even chuckling, in that funny way of yours – as you wrote that. Looking back, it couldn't have been very good for Morgan, mind you – except for boosting his ego, that is – because I was too adoring, and almost entirely uncritical. I was content just to sit at his feet, with my head against his knee, his fingers in my hair, and listen to him talk. Yes, what with his talks, his articles, his books, and all that has been written about him, Morgan should be quite well known to Patrick. And of course, Patrick met him on one or two occasions, as we have heard, so there are personal memories as well.

Patrick will know less about Jack, perhaps – simply because there aren't any books written about him. But he has plenty of memories of him, I'm sure. When he was a boy he used to go with me quite often to Jack's house on Portland Road; and Jack took a great interest in his educational progress, particularly after he passed to go to High Pavement Grammar School. He won't know as much detail about Jack's life, of course – compared with Morgan's, that is. But at least Jack went to the sort of school and college where records would be kept; and there will be details, I'm sure, of his career at Nottingham University. There are his books, too, though I never tried to understand those; they were too technical. And anyway they wouldn't tell you much about Jack as a person. There would have been obituaries, though. Oh yes, and his sister might have talked a bit about him. I know that Patrick managed to visit Velda on at least one occasion before she died. There may even be one or two people still alive, who might be able to help with information. Ted and Daisy Manning, for example, who did domestic work for the Sprott family in Blakeney, and who remained loyal friends to the end. And there may even be former university colleagues of Jack's who are still alive and willing to volunteer information or personal memories. I'm thinking of one in particular. I knew her well; met her many time. Mary, she was called – but her surname escapes me. Oh, how annoying! This is one of the problems with death: it dulls the memory. Anyway, Jack took this Mary Doings under his wing when she joined his department just after the war. He thought a great deal of her, I know; she was one of the few women he could stomach. So yes, come to think of it, one way and another perhaps, Patrick might know quite a bit about Jack.

But what does he know about me? And more to the point, perhaps, why does he – why does anybody? – *want* to know anything about me? I'm not exactly a figure to be proud of, am I? I'm a nobody, really. As you've heard, just a footnote in a famous biography. Yes, a footnote: that just about sums me up. Not much to show for my three score years and nine, is it? I have often wished that I could have been famous in my own right: a celebrated writer, like Morgan, or a learned professor, like Jack, or a well-known editor, perhaps, like Joe Ackerley. If I had been, Patrick could have looked into my life with some pride. But what pride can he take in an uncle whose only claim to fame is that he was a nancy boy – yes, that's what they called us, among other things, in those days – who had the good fortune to be fancied by a famous novelist? 'My uncle was E. M. Forster's bit of rough!' Hardly much to crow about, is it? Things might have been different, of course, if I had started out with Morgan's or Jack's advantages. But then again, would they? I was always easy-going, you see. I liked the quiet, easy life; one without strain and effort. One without sweat on its brow. Morgan had me on about it quite often, sometimes lecturing me gently on the subject. On several occasions – in letters to Jack, of course – he complained about my slackness. Jack read me bits from one or two of those letters. In one of them, for example, he wrote:

> Charles said he would write to me when he ordered his suit and he must. Indicate to him ... that idleness and diffidence were twin sisters ever.[86]

Joe Ackerley, too, thought I was rather casual about things. In fact, he thought I was a bit of a loafer. Jack told me that. He said that Morgan had received some such comment in a letter from Joe:

> I spent two nights in Jack's house last week, and glad I went, painful though much of it was. The 4½ hour coach journey, half of it down the M1, was wretchedly tedious and dull, the landscape

mostly hideous. I took a Christmas present of whisky to Charles and gave him lunch at the Black Boy also; he didn't deserve either, he is an idle fellow.[87]

Jack and I both thought that was a bit strong – especially since I was recovering from a heart attack at the time – and I went off Joe a bit after that. Mind you, there were other things by then that were sending people off Joe – like his preference for animals rather than people, for example. That didn't go down too well with his friends, as you can imagine. He once lectured me about the way I looked after my cat; and on another occasion, in a letter to Morgan, he said that I was 'an animal lover without a clue to the animal mind'.[88] Well, look where his understanding of the animal mind got him – treating his Alsatian bitch like a lover! He was crazy about Queenie, was Joe. He thought the world of her. She came as close as anyone to being the special friend he was always searching for. And when she died, he nearly went off his head with grief.

However, I have to say, looking back, that Joe was right about me; and so was Morgan. I did prefer to take life easy if I could; in this respect, I took after my father – though with him it was understandable, I suppose – and my mother, for that matter. So, even with better opportunities, I might not have made more of myself, perhaps. It took quite a lot of hard work, making yourself famous; I could see that with Morgan and Jack.

Oh, Patrick, I'm sorry you can't be more proud of your uncle Charles. I was always proud of you, you know – though perhaps you didn't know, come to think of it. You were always such a good boy – and nice-looking, too. Do you remember that photograph Ted and I took of you? The one taken on the bed in the hotel when we took you to the Isle of Wight? Perhaps I should explain quickly to the reader that you were fully clothed and everything; there was nothing improper in it. But we liked that photo, Ted and I. We sent a print of it to Morgan. He liked it, too. Kept it on his mantelpiece, he did, for ages afterwards. Or so he said . . .

Patrick

—◦❀◦—

... I longed to know more about the Forster–Sprott–Lovett connection. The relevant passages in Furbank's book had whetted my appetite regarding Sprott, but there was no further mention of Lovett. I was very disappointed. Then, in Furbank's notes and acknowledgements, I read about the Forster Papers which are kept by the modern archivist in King's College, Cambridge. Within a few weeks, permission to inspect these papers had been sought and granted. At last I was on the trail, nose sniffing like a truffle hound; and it wasn't long before I made a number of exciting discoveries.

First, that early doubt in my mind – regarding whether or not uncle Charles was really a friend of Forster's – was soon to be settled. Indeed, it was confirmed by Forster himself. In a letter to the publishers, André Deutsch, in which he turned down an invitation from them to contribute to a proposed T. S. Eliot seventieth birthday celebration anthology, he wrote:

> I am amused at the contrast between the preparations for his seventieth birthday and the actualities of mine. Mine consisted of a meal with fifteen beloved and uneminent friends. I hope he will have that type of celebration too, for the memory of it certainly helps.[89]

So, my uncle Charles had numbered among E. M. Forster's 'beloved and uneminent friends'. There was a thought to conjure with ...

Uncle Charles

———❖———

. . . Yes, I wish I could have been more famous for you, Patrick; then you wouldn't be scratching around the way you are for information about me, would you? Oh, I know that you managed to talk to your mother about me just before she died; but she wasn't much help, was she? About my *early* life, I mean? One or two childhood memories, that was all. For example, one of me looking after her during a 'flu epidemic. And a much more vivid one of me doing the housework and looking after my sisters during my mother's last confinement. That was a memory I always found very painful to recall. My father was ill in hospital; my mother was in bed giving birth to her fifth child; my youngest sister, Gwen, was barely two years old and still needed a lot of attention; we had no money, and there was little food in the house. Things were pretty grim, I can tell you. But as if that weren't enough, our new brother was born a 'blue baby' and died a few days later. For me, there was even worse to come. Dorothy, who must have been about seven at the time, would presumably remember only the outline of the hideous task which now fell to the eldest in the family. I had to wrap the cold, blue-black body of that creature who should have been my brother in an old shirt of father's, put it in a cardboard box – and I was eleven at the time, remember, trying not to cry, trying not to be sick, trying to be a man – and take it to Basford Cemetery for burial. I felt I ought to walk slowly, out of what I thought to be respect for the dead – but all the time I wanted to run like hell, so that I could deliver that grim parcel as soon as possible. It was the longest mile I ever walked, and I had nightmares about the whole episode for months afterwards.

Apart from these memories, Dorothy had little recollection of my early life. But that's hardly surprising, perhaps? I was four years older than her, so we didn't play together much; and we didn't have to share a bedroom. After the family moved from Whitemoor Road to Westgate, I had my own little room in the attic. The three girls slept in the back bedroom, with Dorothy and Gwen sharing a double bed, and Win, privileged as the eldest girl, in a single. My mother and father slept in the front bedroom. It was a very small house. And although Dorothy and I went to the same school at one stage – Percy Street (where we all went after we moved to Old Basford) – the girls and boys were taught in separate departments, and in any case we were in different standards. I was rather a private child, too. Being the only boy made me feel separate, of course, but I rather enjoyed my own company anyway. And as I grew older and the truth about my sexuality began to dawn on me, I became even more private. I now had a special secret to keep. When I left home we saw very little of one another; and then when Dorothy got married a few years later there was even less contact between us. We each led our own separate lives. It wasn't until the war that circumstances threw us together a bit more. I guess it's the same in many families: what do you really know about your brother or your sister? My sisters are all dead now, anyway – first Gwen, then Dorothy, then Win – so there's no one to help Patrick out, even if there were memories.

This is why Patrick will have seized on that letter of Morgan's, the one that mentioned my father. It will have given him some factual information about me. In that respect, it was a very unusual letter. Yes, it is true that in the correspondence between Morgan Forster, Jack Sprott and Joe Ackerley you will find hundreds of references to me – and that's not bad, you may think, for someone who was a mere footnote – but one of the reasons why I remained a footnote, perhaps, was that the letters offered very little hard fact about me and the life I was leading when I wasn't travelling backwards and forwards between Jack and Morgan. I was like a parcel being passed around without anyone really knowing, or revealing, what was inside it. Or to put it another way – because I sometimes felt that I was merely an item in the Sprott–Forster library service – I was like a book that was kindly on loan between friends but rarely opened and read properly.

If we dip into a few extracts from the letters Patrick has read in the King's College archives, you may begin to see what I mean. First of all, you will see that the letters are addressed to Jack. Morgan very rarely wrote to me. Almost everything was arranged through Jack; I was merely the third person. Secondly, most of the references – and we'll just take the ones from letters leading up to the time Morgan met Bob Buckingham and I met Ted – seem to show me as a kind of object, a love object, to be organised and talked about as if I had no real identity, no real life of my own. Anyway, see for yourself. It won't take long: most of them are just snippets, but you'll soon get the picture:

Don't you think Charles would take it well if I paid for your ticket as well as his . . . It was a fat year for Morgan![90]

Have had a very charming and attractive letter from Charles. Give him my love.[91]

He seems to be in greater and more constant need of you than he was a year back, and this isn't for the happiness of either of you.[92]

Give my dear little Charles my love – for in a sense he is mine.[93]

Since you won't be back till the Sunday afternoon I won't come. I can't trust myself to entertain Charles for so long.[94]

I shan't put Charles off, am too fond of him, but I shall want a bit of looking after I'm afraid and it's very unlikely I shall be able to meet him at the sta . . . Two days later (Thurs) ankle still painful. Charles will have to ring and walk up Sat. We shall dine out and go to 'Lucky Girl' in the evening and lunch out Sunday – afraid that's the extent to which I can gallivant, but he'll understand. I didn't want to put him off for so many reasons.[95]

Some day I must speak to C. upon his weeping; we have already furtively agreed that it is no good my hanging around when Jack's about; and the subjects almost coincide. I think about him very often. There are few people who give me so much happiness.[96]

I arrive from Putney at Waterloo on Sunday at 5.25, so could 'you' who is really the solitary Charles be in the refreshment room at that hour and get picked up there . . . If I don't turn up . . . he must go to 27 Brunswick Square, W1, tele. 5596 . . . I suppose it's that ceaseless 9.55 for Charles on Sunday and no chance of him staying the night? . . . Looking forward to coming again to Nottingham before I sail.[97]

Is there any possibility of C. coming to stop with me in London on May 25–26. I fear it may be too soon after Whitsun for him to get away . . . However, I hope to be up in June to see you both . . . Joe [Ackerley]'s father is very ill. He is much worried.[98] [To which Sprott had replied: 'How sweet of you to write your last letter – yes I think Charles can come for May 25th. I don't see that is to say any reason why not, but like a bloody fool I forgot to ask. I shall leave this letter open and add something when I see him at 6 this evening . . . Charles is here and says 'Yes' (or rather 'Ah') about the 25th.']⁹⁹

Let me know how C. is. I didn't like him going off with a bad thumb and having to wake up at 3.00. I had a clean bandage, but no lint. It was a deep cut. I think he should go to a doctor. Remind him he promised to visit a dentist too, and fix him up at a good one – I would see to the bill. I am happier and happier with him every time . . . send me a silkish handkerchief, the gift of Joe, which I gave to C. to bind up his finger with. Love to you. Love to him.¹⁰⁰

Shall meet C. at just before 4 tomorrow unless I hear to the contrary. He had better have the address of Joe's flat if you can get it to him: 6 Hammersmith Terrace.¹⁰¹

Do see that C. goes on and through with his teeth. He had pain in the one that was stopped and said there was more to be done elsewhere . . . We had such a lovely time.¹⁰²

I am annoyed at the news about teeth. I guess C. is pretty smart to himself about the upper classes, how one feels all right until they interfere for the best and regardless of expense. I see nothing for it, however, but to pursue the path of decadence further.¹⁰³

. . . but now I am tired and only my memories of Nottingham are bright. I should rather like to give C. a watch for Xmas – the present one drains his salary most dreadfully. Could you take him to choose one for £2–£3?¹⁰⁴

I have had the sweetest line from him, also a handkerchief – helps me through this dreary season.¹⁰⁵

Charles was so wonderful. My only blot is that I have lost his handkerchief in China Town together with a commercially desirable scarf – at least they are not at the hotel or at the pictures.¹⁰⁶

I think I have spoilt Frank V[icary], that part is sensible, and I am worried today how to unspoil him, and also how to avoid spoiling Charles – C. has no sign of it yet, but both you and I must be careful not to let him get soft. (Alas that I should live to write that adjective!)¹⁰⁷

I think C. had better come. Will you say I will expect him on the usual train Sat., and should be very grateful if he could help me with staining the surround of the sitting room – 'chocolate' or 'treacly' . . . I shall get tickets for some play I want to see on Sat. evening so that it shall be all my treat and not Charles' at all.¹⁰⁸

Shall Charles' great coat be chosen now or in the autumn? I should think now, and if you agree will you get it in motion. I think he has grasped the importance of proper innards. Tell him I shall be writing to him.¹⁰⁹

Now this great coat. Yes, very nice indeed, I have no doubt, and here is the cheque, but what about a line from the mannequin itself, rain or no rain.[110]

I hope the reader hasn't found these extracts too boring. To me they're not, naturally. They're commonplace, perhaps – but revealing, none the less. They show, for example, how genuinely fond of me Morgan was. I am touched and much flattered by some of his comments. They indicate, too, how generous he was, and how concerned he was for my welfare in his motherly, rather fussy fashion. In one or two of them he reveals – with a sad note, perhaps: another of those eternal, or infernal, triangles! – that he understood the depth of my feelings for Jack. He knew, too, that it pained me to see Jack with other men; he was aware that ours was not the only triangle. And of course the letters reveal quite clearly – as did the ones that Morgan referred to when he was doing his piece – the extent to which Jack and Morgan had taken over my life.

But however you view the references to me in these letters, I think you can see my point that they offer little information about me as a person – about the way I was living and thinking and feeling – and in this respect Patrick must have found them frustrating. On the few occasions when Morgan wrote to me instead of using his pet carrier pigeon, there was a bit more detail. But not much; and sadly, only one of those letters from the early days has survived anyway. That was me being casual again, perhaps? – though at the time I just didn't appreciate the importance of saving the letters of someone like Morgan. But that's by the by.

The fact is that Morgan showed very little curiosity about my life outside our relationship. Unlike Joe and Jack, I don't think he was really interested in getting too involved in the lives of what he called the 'lower orders'. Affairs with them, yes, but that's another story; attempts to improve them, yes, that was all right, too, at a distance. But real involvement – committed involvement of the sleeves-rolled-up type – no, I don't think Morgan wanted that. As I say, he didn't even show very much curiosity – which, now I come to think of it, was unusual for a writer, surely? I think Patrick will find that Jack, too, was a little puzzled by Morgan's lack of curiosity in this direction; and there's evidence to that effect, as well. For example, Patrick will discover, I'm sure, that when Jack was invited to contribute to a book written in honour of Morgan's ninetieth birthday in 1969, he decided to do a piece about Forster as a humanist. I wouldn't know about the other parts of his essay, but when he came to the subject of Morgan's curiosity about people I reckon he was really struggling to make a case. A short extract should make my point, but the reader might care to study the whole section before deciding whether or not to agree with me:

> Forster himself has characterised humanism in writing about Gide (*Two Cheers for Democracy*, p. 233). 'The humanist', he says, 'has four leading characteristics – curiosity, a free mind, belief in good taste, and belief in the human race.' How does Forster make out on these criteria?
>
> Curiosity? I have to admit that before reading these words I had not thought of Forster as particularly curious, but on reflection I realise I was wrong. His range of literary criticism displays an inquiring mind. He ranges with ease from William Barnes to d'Annunzio. He is curious about music. He is curious about places, in the sense that wherever he goes he is sensitive to their distinctive features and to any oddities which present themselves. When it comes to people, his curiosity is, I think, a little hampered by his standards. He dislikes anything that smells of grandeur, he shrinks from it and may miss something of interest as a result.[111]

I think you could add that he didn't like ugliness, or bad taste, or rough manners; these things upset him deep down, I could tell. And he was very much afraid of poverty, you know, which was strange in one who was never short of a bob or two. Perhaps he thought, too, that the lower orders, largely uneducated and unrefined, would be bound to lead dreary lives. He hated dreariness more than anything. But he was lucky, wasn't he? He had the luxury of being able to choose to fill his life with exciting people who had lively ideas, so he could always avoid dreary people and dreary situations if he wanted to. Anyway, perhaps it was for reasons like these that he didn't want to get too involved in the lives of my sort, my class? I don't know. But I think that this lack of involvement shows in his books. I'm no expert, of course, and my opinion probably isn't worth very much; but it seems to me that he does seem to shy away from writing about working-class people. And when he does occasionally attempt it, my honest opinion is that he doesn't do it very well. We're back to writing about what you know and what you've experienced yourself, I suppose. Not that Morgan lacked opportunities to find out about the working classes. But for some reason he never took full advantage of them. He was always kindly, mind you; and he fussed a great deal about your health, which was nice. He liked to see you happy, too; other people's sadness made *him* feel sad, he said. But I never felt that he was interested – really interested – in what was going on inside my head.

If he had really taken an interest in me, he would have realised that my father's illness was likely to be very much on my mind. And the reason for that could have been expressed in one word: guilt. Even after three years, I still felt guilty about leaving home. Not that it was a decision I had come to without a great deal of consideration. Nor, indeed, that my reasons were not valid. It was true that I had my own little attic room at Westgate; but with six of us in that small house, we were always on top of one another. Once Gwen had started work it was difficult in the mornings, particularly, with four of us trying to get out on time. All washing had to be done at the kitchen sink, and there was only one WC, situated outside the yard. If one of the girls got in there first – and Gwen was the worst: she always took ages – it could be agony! With me out of the way, I argued, Win would be able to have my room – which in turn would mean that Dorothy and Gwen could sleep in separate beds. And Win wouldn't be disturbed when the other two came in late from dances.

Dorothy and Gwen were mad on dancing. Dancing, and chaps. Or rather, the pleasure of stringing along the chaps they met at dances, and taking them for every penny, every port and lemon, they could. I felt sorry for all those poor devils: they were no match for the wiles of women. Particularly women like my sisters. Real heart-breakers, they were, my sisters. And prick-teasers, too, I shouldn't wonder. Oh yes, and they were mad on clothes as well, those two. There were clothes everywhere, all over the house. I was sick of ducking under stockings drying on the line in the kitchen, or of finding someone's knickers soaking in the sink when I went for a shave. They were so untidy, and generally thoughtless, my sisters – and to my alarm they were beginning to tease me about never bringing home any girlfriends. For a while, in a silly attempt to throw them off the scent, I encouraged the attentions of a girl who lived next door. I knew she'd been keen on me for a long time. Once she got to know me better, of course, she too began to sense that there was something wrong. It became obvious to me that my secret would not be safe for much longer.

I just had to get away. It would be so much more convenient for work, too – now that I was working for Goodacres on Canal Street – if I could find somewhere nearer the city centre.

Getting away wasn't easy, mind. It was my mother who raised most of the objections. How was she going to manage without my money coming in? Especially now that my father was almost a permanent invalid and unable to work? Did I want to see her starve? And what was it going to be like for her without a man in the house? My father didn't seem to count. To pacify her, I had to promise to allow her two-and-sixpence a week out of my wages – oh yes, and I also had to promise faithfully to visit every weekend, to see everyone, and to tackle any odd jobs that might need doing. Years later, when I was living with Ted, we were still observing this ritual of the Sunday late-afternoon visit. My mother invariably greeted us with a list of jobs to be done; and upon our arrival I was still handing over my two-and-sixpence, now intended to cover the cost of the special tea of tinned salmon and tinned fruit, never varying, that she had prepared!

After all her objections had been met, my mother played her trump card: my father's illness. How I had the heart to leave my father in his condition, she just did not know. As if I wasn't feeling guilty enough already! For I had to admit to myself that beneath all the sound, well-rehearsed arguments, my basic motive for leaving home was a selfish one: I wanted to lead my own independent life. In the end it was my father who saved the day; he found enough breath to argue on my behalf, saying, 'Let the boy go: we all have our own lives to lead'.

And so I went to live with aunt Harriet, my mother's sister, in Muskham Street, a district not too far from the city centre, between the railway station and the Trent, known as The Meadows – or 'The Medders', as most of the locals pronounced it. I took with me two carrier bags containing most of my clothes and my private possessions, the blessings of my family – most of them genuine – and very few regrets. I was free at last! I had passed the first really important milestone in my life. I was now able to do as I liked. But I was not, and for years would never be, free from very strong feelings of guilt. Had you asked, Mr Forster, why my father's illness was preying on my mind – had you shown just a little curiosity about this member of the lower orders – I would readily have unburdened myself. And then you would have seen some weeping!

The second major milestone in my life was my meeting, and subsequent affair, with Jack Sprott. And Jack was right: from the beginning, I was besotted with him. He was not my first lover, however. From the freedom of my Muskham Street base I had made one or two conquests before I met Jack; and as a trial, to test my aunt's reactions, I had even taken one of them home to tea. To my great relief, it had all passed off quite smoothly; aunt Harriet had been charming, and above all she had shown no tendency to pry. But these early affairs were brief and rather shallow. Although they excited my flesh, I can now admit to myself that they scarcely touched my heart. Jack was my first real love – and I fell hook, line and sinker! Apart from the excitement of being physically close to him, I used to love to listen to him talk in his learned and gently lecturing fashion; and while he was at work at the University there was nothing I liked better than sit in his Clumber Street flat, among his books and his papers, pretending to be him preparing scholarly lectures to be delivered with wit and charm to rows of adoring male students.

This was an exciting time of my life. I now belonged to a widening circle of homosexual friends, most of whom, like me, were enjoying their new-found freedom. Except for Jack – he was different, special, a cut above the rest of us in all sorts of ways – we were all so relieved to have unburdened ourselves of a secret which had hung around our necks like a millstone, weighing us down since adolescence, that it now felt as if we were walking on air. I was dizzy with happiness. It wasn't just the sex – though I must say I enjoyed that! – but a shared excitement, and a strong sense of belonging, of having found one's place at long last. I talked to Jack about this one day. He understood. He said he had felt the same when he left home. How did he put, now? Oh, yes – that we were all a bit like butterflies just out of the chrysalis: liberated, new-fangled with the freedom, and flying a bit crazy! Something like that. I thought it was very clever. But he always did have a way with words, did Jack. So did Harry Daley, actually, for all he had no formal education to speak of; and I'm sure Patrick will have come across the way Harry phrased it in that personal memoir of his:

> So far as I knew there was no other person like me in the whole world . . . Many people, young and old, carried a burden of guilt which would have floated away like a balloon had they been able

to 'air' the subject and discover how commonplace was the secret 'thing' that weighed so heavily upon them.[112]

Like butterflies, or like balloons: same difference. A weight had been lifted from us.

Apart from Jack, four friends stand out from this period of my life. One was a chap called Charlie Pownall. His family ran a rag-and-bone business in Nottingham. He was never short of a bob or two, was Charlie, and we had some good times together. I shall always remember our trips to Blackpool. Another was a chap called Harry Dawes, who was mad about bikes – push-bikes, I should say, not to confuse him with an even closer friend of mine, Boyd Jephson, who used to ride a motor-bike. The fourth friend's name was Norman Edwards. Patrick has discovered a couple of letters from Jack to Morgan, the first of which contains a reference to Charlie Pownall, though not by name, and the second a marvellous description of Harry Dawes and his family, plus a mention of Norman Edwards:

> Charles is much better, came to dinner yesterday, and comes tonight to the Empire. His rag-and-bone friend is being run after by a lad from Heanor.[113]

> . . . on Sunday I went to Somercotes to spend the day with Harry Dawes – the young lad from the Summer School. It was moving. He lives in a small house with mother (pretty – almost beautiful) father (feeble, with his head on one side) brother (most of this time at an Exeter College, and considering himself the gentleman of the family) and sister aged 5 (but lively, intelligent). I was left with mother and brother in the kitchen and put my foot in it, 'Do you work at the same place as Harry?' 'No, I work at – I am at Exeter – at a college there.' 'He doesn't do anything, other people have to support him. He doesn't have to work.' There was pride, bitterness, shame – all three in her voice . . . saw his cycling photographs. He is a champion cyclist . . . Charles is well, but has had a cold. He stayed last night (Thursday). We went to the 'Student Prince' – a dreadful musical affair. His new boyfriend Norman Edwards wrote to him and complained of neglect. Charles was wildly excited and entertained, rushed around, 'Look, kid, a letter from our Nooooorman'.[114]

I remember that I was all for dropping dear Norman at this point, but Jack wouldn't hear of it, suggesting later in the same letter that I might arrange to spend time with each of them:

Wednesday with Norman, Thursday with me . . . Norman sounded
charming from his letter. Charles then wanted to do me a good turn.
I don't think it wise, but am infinitely curious. It is essential that
he has another interest when I'm not here, and I think he agrees.
I feel so sure of him, so I believe I would be secure enough to dis
– rather than en - courage.

Harry is mentioned again in two other letters from Jack to
Morgan, the second of which is very humorous and includes a
mention of Boyd Jephson:

Harry Dawes and Hugh Gaitskell (whom I think you met –
economics) are here for tonight . . . C. will come at 3 and we
shall buy a green shirt for him to wear with a marvellous jumper
H.D.'s mother has knitted for him.[115]

And Charles? He can come to London if you like on Saturday
next. The week after he goes to Mansfield and after that he is
again free . . . Of course I have flown off in the face of your
advice: you knew I should? Yes, I have a new boy friend, he lives
with us, he is great friends with Charles who has introduced him
to his mother and to Boyd, and when I am away he will live with
Charles. He is very affectionate, a little noisy, inclined to peck at
you, kisses delightfully and as Charles says, 'lets you do anything
with him, kid'. In short, my dear fellow (as I should have written
in 1860) I have bought a Cock-atoo. It was a white one when I
got it . . . Then Charles and I went to the fair [the Goose Fair]. I
didn't do anything because I felt my stomach wouldn't stand that
on top of the mixture I had earlier. When they offer you a drink
you must have a cheap one. I was exhausted when I got home &
flopped into bed and went to sleep. Charles, who stayed the night,
complained I was hasty tempered and awkward which is true, so
we have decided not to go to fairs again . . . On Monday Harry
Dawes came and brought us a cycle, so I go about now with my
arse in the air and my head in the front wheels, 'Game', as Charles
says, ' to the bloody last'.[116]

Perhaps I should point out that although Harry Dawes was
a member of our group, and he and I were quite close, he was
really Jack's special friend, not mine. In fact, for a time Jack
seemed to think more of Harry than he did of me. He was always
going on about him – being deliberately cruel, I thought: I was
madly jealous! – to people like Morgan and Joe, and to Lytton
Strachey and Dora Carrington. I remember reading one of Dora
Carrington's letters which Jack had carelessly left lying around.
'And how are your Nottingham intrigues?' she had asked. 'I hope

you are enjoying yourself and your . . .' – and here she had done a funny little drawing of a chap on a bike, who could only have been Harry – '. . . friend is king.'[117] No mention of me! I was put out. I was also puzzled by the signing-off: 'My very fondest love your fond Carrington', with three kisses. Kisses – from a woman! That seemed odd. It was only when Dora killed herself shortly after Lytton's death in 1932 that Jack felt able to tell me how close they had been. She had been corresponding with him for years, apparently – though it was only a platonic relationship, I was told. So was the one each of them had with Lytton. It broke her heart, it did, Lytton's death; and she wrote a lot of letters to Jack afterwards. Cries for help, I suppose they were. I remember him receiving from her some of Lytton's ties, and a belt, as a keepsake.[118] He was very touched. And when she committed suicide like that – well, poor dear, Jack was beside himself. It was one of the few occasions on which he was unable to hide his feelings. But, sorry, I'm drifting away from the point.

It was Jack who introduced me to Boyd Jephson. And we had something in common right from the start, he and I. We were both under Jack's spell. We were drawn together at a time when each of us felt neglected, excluded, by Jack's latest 'excitement' – I forget who it was at the time – and for a while we became very close friends. In those days, before his tragic illness, Boyd was a popular member of our circle. Although he was well-educated and, like Jack, talked with a posh accent, he got on well with everybody because there was no side to him. I used to love riding pillion with him – particularly in the summer time when we weren't bandaged in layers of clothing and I could feel the warmth of his body pulled close to mine as I clung tightly to his waist.

Then in 1927, suddenly and dramatically, the man we all knew and loved was stricken by a disease for which there was no known cure. Within a matter of a few weeks, this bundle of energy, this gifted musician with the promising future ahead of him – and such a sense of humour, too: oh, how he enjoyed those jokes about his talent for the organ! – was reduced to a helpless, dribbling cripple who was unable to speak or move a muscle. The transformation was swift, cruel and terrifying to observe. It left our little community stunned. Boyd had contracted 'sleeping sickness'. It was a rare but dreaded disease at that time, and it had a long, medical name which I can't remember. A look at Patrick's notes should tell us more about it:

71

A Kind of Private Magic

Encephalitis Lethargica
Notes taken by Pat Belshaw
from the Nottingham Medical Register for the year 1928

Encephalitis Lethargica, otherwise known as 'sleeping sickness'. A viral disease, first separately described in modern times by von Economo, of Vienna. The recent epidemic had its beginnings, it is speculated, when the disease was brought into Britain by returning soldiers who had served in the Middle East during the First World War. The first recorded death from the disease in Nottingham in recent times was in 1916; between then and the end of 1919 [the first year that cases were compulsorily notifiable] there were six more deaths. Thereafter, for the next nine years, the number of deaths and reputed and notified cases, respectively, were as follows: 1920 – 5 and 6; 1921 – 3 and 2; 1922 – 1 and 4; 1923 – 1 and 4; 1924, the year of maximum recent prevalence in Nottingham and Sheffield [the 'storm-centre' of the disease] – 10 deaths and 25 new cases; 1927 – 7 deaths and 8 new cases, including one male in the 15 to 25 age range [this was Boyd Jephson, surely? He was 24 years old in 1927]; and 1928 – 2 deaths and 3 new cases. The number of cases treated at home were very few because the victims needed constant and devoted attention, including feeding and toileting: 1922– 1; 1923 – none; 1924 – 2; 1925 – 2; 1926 – 10; 1927 – 1 [who must have been Boyd Jephson]; 1928 – 1 [the same patient as in 1927: Boyd Jephson].

It was Boyd's sister, Emily Hickman Jephson – always known to family and friends as Dickie (taken from her second name) but commanding a respectful 'Miss Jephson' to everyone else – who took on the heroic task of looking after him. In fact, she sacrificed her own life to the work, nursing him at home with great courage and love for almost thirty years. I think he survived longer than almost any other victim, and the doctors were amazed. But it was due entirely to Dickie's devoted care and attention. Towards the end, by which time Dickie herself looked old and worn out, they had become for one another a reason for living; and deprived of what had provided such purpose to her life, Dickie survived Boyd by a few years only.

In the first year or so Dickie had nursed Boyd in the family home, but she was soon looking for somewhere else to live – somewhere away from pitying friends and an over-emotional mother who hadn't been able to come to terms with her son's condition. Unexpectedly, out of the blue, there was an opportunity for me to help. Aunt Harriet had just inherited a little house in Lenton, and she announced her intention to move in as soon as possible.

Her eyesight was failing and she didn't want to be a burden to me, she said, so why didn't I stay on at Muskham Street, with Dickie and Boyd as co-tenants? Why not, indeed! Boyd had visited Muskham Street on several occasions before his illness, so he was familiar with the house. He seemed pleased with the idea. And that was enough for Dickie. It was an arrangement which suited everybody. I was glad to be of service to a good friend; Boyd and his sister would have some company; and Dickie would be relieved of her duties for a couple of hours each time I took Boyd out in his wheelchair. We were still living together in Muskham Street when I met Ted in 1929. In fact, Ted became a popular visitor to the house. He had endless patience with Boyd, and came to spend more time with him than I did; for this reason, mainly – though I think she also felt sorry for him and liked to mother him a little – Dickie seemed to take an instant liking to Ted. In 1934 the four of us were to move to 19 Wiverton Road, Sherwood Rise, where Ted and I lived in the rooms above Dickie and Boyd. Patrick will find a number of brief references to the Jephsons, and one to Muskham Street, in Morgan's letters to Jack:

> Miss Jephson wrote a nice letter about Boyd's cap. Will you ask C. to thank her for it.[119]

> I wrote to Charles at Muskham St. yesterday and mis-spelt it.[120]

> Also – *very kind* – could you take to Notts a pair of polished leather evening shoes for Boyd Jephson. They are in the big cupboard where the empty bottles go.[121]

> Charles' foot is rather disgusting from what he and Miss Jephson write.[122]

> What news about Charles? Much too risky for Miss J. to move. I shall say. It might so easily end in unpleasantness and financial loss.[123]

> Miss J. was right [about a recent BBC broadcast] – I had a cold, also they put me too near the mike. I heard my record – hollow, slow, deep – helpful, such an experience.[124]

But forgive me, I am running well ahead of myself. We should return to 1927 and to the third milestone in my life, my meeting with Morgan Forster – and, through him, my chance to meet other celebrated figures, too . . .

Patrick

———◆———

... My series of visits to King's College archives revealed several hundred references to Charles Lovett in the correspondence between Morgan Forster, Jack Sprott and Joe Ackerley; and these references confirmed a remarkable fact. It was one that took me completely by surprise. My uncle Charles had been one of E. M. Forster's lovers!

I could hardly contain myself. What a revelation! I sensed immediately that I might be in possession of sensitive, if not sensational, information. Indeed, I regret to say that the thought did cross my mind that the story might be of interest to one or two of the Sunday newspapers. From the outset, however, nobler instincts came into play: my excitement was tempered by strong feelings of obligation and guardianship. If this account were to be written at all – and from the beginning such a notion began to germinate – it had to be done caringly and responsibly. I had fond memories of uncle Charles – and, from my boyhood, of uncle Jack and uncle Morgan – and it was to be hoped that, whatever the outcome, there would be no betrayal of the affection and respect I felt for these men.

Plans for crafting the material into some sort of book soon began to develop, though I was unsure what literary form the book might take. An idiosyncratic history, perhaps? One dwelling on minutiae in the domestic lives of my main characters, rather than on larger, outside issues? That would keep faith with the spirit of Forster's own biographies, come to think of it. A pleasing thought – though in the case of Goldsworthy Lowes Dickinson's life Forster had no choice, he said, but to focus on internal matters because there were no big outside events:

It is difficult to think of a life where so little happened outwardly. He was never shipwrecked or in peril, he was seldom in bodily pain,

74

never starved or penniless, he never confronted an angry mob nor
went to prison for his opinions, nor sat on the bench as a magistrate,
nor held any important administrative post, he was never married,
never faced with the problems of parenthood, had no trouble with
housekeeping or servants.[125]

Presumably, that was how he came to linger over small,
quirky items. Like Goldie's ineptitude with the typewriter, for
example:

> He is said to be the only man who could make a Corona type upside
> down. He struck the keys rapidly and violently, thinking of what he
> thought and not of what he did, with the result that he doubled lines,
> halved them, threw capitals in the air, buried numerals in the earth,
> broke out into orgies of ?????? or %%%%%%, and hammered his
> ribbons to shreds.[126]

Such descriptions give this biography its great charm. Forster
had time to dwell on things which, in fuller, more momentous
lives, are so often omitted. For example, he wrote:

> . . . nonsense is too seldom recorded. Wit and humour get put
> into a biography, foolery is missed out. It is too evanescent, it
> needs a gesture or a smile to fix it, and these cannot be transcribed.
> Dickinson could be ever so gay and ridiculous, laughing and talking
> at once, making everyone laugh, shooting out little glints of non-
> sense like flying fish. If one could convey the little glints, the sea
> and the sky would take care of themselves.[127]

Forster could, and did, create some marvellous 'flying fish',
and I found myself yearning for a fraction of his talent, that I too
might attempt to convey one or two 'little glints'. But given the
exciting material I was collecting, I told myself that even I ought
to be able to write something half-readable at least; and the idea
soon became real and alive and growing inside me. It was rather
like a pregnancy, one imagined: a weight to be carried around,
yet an excitement, never a burden; a part of me, yet separate;
an object of wonder and hope, yet on occasions overwhelming
me with apprehension. Fed by my initial exhilaration, it quickly
grew large and importunate, gaining an identity, making demands,
making itself felt. It was my child – and goodness only knew how
it would turn out.

As I became able to view things rather more objectively, however, the initial euphoria gradually began to wear off. I started to

have doubts. Was I really unearthing startling revelations which it was my duty to make public? Or was I merely grubbing up sordid banalities which should, out of kindness if nothing else, remain private? Was I involving myself in genuine, worthwhile research, or merely satisfying a vulgar taste for voyeurism? And at the end of the day, there was another crucial question to be answered. Would this story really be of interest to anyone other than a few members of my family, a handful of curious friends and a small number of literati? Sadly, I had to admit that probably it would not. My excitement began to evaporate slowly; and accordingly, the living weight I was carrying inside me began to shrivel.

Then came what appeared to be an extraordinary discovery, and with it a sudden and dramatic resuscitation. I can date it quite precisely: the time of my second visit to King's. I had returned in a state of delirium almost, clutching a batch of pencilled notes which included the following extract from a letter from Forster to Sprott:

> I had on the whole a good time in France. Charles is the most civilised friend I've got, I think, and it's very helpful being with him.[128]

It seemed inconceivable. Uncle Charles had always been kindly, of course: a natural gentleman, you might say. And I had even discovered that he had been abroad with Forster. But the novelist's 'most civilised friend'? No, surely there was some mistake. It would not have been out of character, it was true, for Forster to confer such an honour on an uncelebrated friend. But did Charles have the necessary credentials? It seemed unlikely, and yet here apparently was clear, documentary evidence leaping up at me from the page. Oh, how I wanted to believe it! Oh, how ready I was, my spring coiled tightly by the discovery, to jump to this conclusion.

But my bubble of excitement was soon to be pricked. A short time later, checking facts, I re-read parts of Furbank and came across references to the scholar and philosopher, Charles Mauron, who had translated *A Passage to India* into French. I discovered with sadness that the date of the letter matched Forster's stay with the Maurons during the spring of 1937. I had followed a false trail which had led me to the wrong Charles!

My literary foetus now went into a rapid decline; and it

was some time before it flourished again. Fortunately, I managed to revive it by enlivening its diet with fresh, nourishing titbits brought back from subsequent visits to King's, and from other sources. This new material revealed that although Charles Lovett's affair with Forster may have been very special – and for a time, at least, of this there was no doubt – it was certainly not exclusive. It also showed, interestingly, that Lovett and Forster represented two sides of a complex triangle whose third side was Sprott. In fact, I unearthed a complicated tangle of relationships – usually developed into anguished triangles, some of them interlocking – involving these three men, and others, which would require handling with some delicacy. So much so that I was left in something of a quandary. In my desire to research and write an account which would demonstrate that my uncle Charles was worth more than a footnote in any biography of Forster, I ran the risk, if I were not careful, of damaging the memory, if not the reputation, of a group of people who had always commanded my respect and regard . . .

Uncle Charles

———◦✦◦———

... As you might imagine, I now walked with a spring in my step. I, Charles Lovett, knew people who were famous throughout the land. I, Charles Lovett, was having an affair – even if I was on loan from someone else! – with a famous novelist. Not a sordid or meaningless affair, either, but one involving caring and gentleness. He was generous with me, too, my novelist. He bought me clothes and paid for me to go on holiday; he bought me presents; and he took me to hotels and theatres in London and abroad. Why, he was even good, as you have seen, to my teeth! Thanks to him, I lived well above my means. Yes, there were times when I resented the way Jack and Morgan organised my life, particularly when they took me for granted. For it was always assumed that I was waiting at their beck and call, ready to run to one or the other at a moment's notice. But I knew which side my bread was buttered on. The life they organised for me was in most respects of far greater quality than any I could have organised for myself, or that I could have hoped for, coming from my sort of background.

Take education, for example. Patrick was right, in one way, to describe me as 'uneducated'. His research shows correctly that I attended Basford Council (Elementary) School on Percy Street, Old Basford, and that even in this modest institution I was unexceptional. I cannot deny it. The School Log Book for that period includes the names of many boys who were awarded prizes – usually Holy Bibles or Old Testaments – for good work or regular attendance, or who were given extraordinary promotions from one standard to another; but you will find no mention of Charles Lovett. How frustrating for the researcher! I can only apologise, Patrick. But that Log Book gave you some flavour, at least, of life in an Elementary School during the period leading

78

Uncle Charles

up to the start of the First World War – at which point, aged thirteen, I left school:

Notes taken by Pat Belshaw
from the Basford Council School Log Book

16.02.1909 Standard 3 paid a visit to the Arboretum for Nature Study.

17.02.1909 A reference to the 'Children's Exhibition of Drawings' at the Castle; on 1.03.09 24 pupils from standards 1 and 2 visited this exhibition.

07.04.1909 The Headmaster makes a heartfelt observation: 'Some of the boys are very dull and most energetic. . .'

24.05.1909 The School was closed for Empire Day.

07.07.1909 Standard 4 visit Vernon Park.

09.08.1909 Some boys were taken to the Northern Baths to take swimming tests; they were allowed to leave 20 mins early at 4.10 pm.

08.11.1909 Bulwell Wakes [the 'fair' which followed the Goose Fair] had 'an injurious effect on attendance'.

11.05.1910 Empire Day celebrations were deferred until 3 June due to the 'lamented death of our late King Edward VII'.

02.06.1910 Standard 3 were allowed to leave 30 mins early, at 4.00 pm, for good attendance (99%).

07.07.1910 The School was closed all day for the City of Nottingham School Sports.

01.06.1911 The Headmaster was notified that the School would be closed all week to celebrate the Coronation of King George V.

20.11.1911 8 shillings was collected 'for the benefit of the Children's Hospital'.

21.12.1911 'Each boy was given an orange on leaving school, the gift of Councillor Gibbon.' Also the Old Basford Men's Sunday Morning Institute gave 'Treat Tickets' . . . 'for distribution amongst the poor boys'.

10.06.1912 Record of the annual Scripture Report, given this year by a visiting Baptist minister.

07.12.1913 A reference to the football team's last league match on the Forest [one of many references in the Log Book to boys being given time off to play and practise football – in place of 'Drill'].

23.05.1913 'Patriotic songs were sung and lessons on the duties of an Englishman were given to the boys in commemoration of Empire Day' – but, added the Headmaster, it was not easy 'to light a spark of life or enthusiasm'.

02.10.1913 The School was closed for Goose Fair.

17.11.1913 A reference to the annual Drawing Report, which revealed that pupils had to attempt a 'plant form', an 'object drawing' and some 'memory work' in their Art lessons.

24.06.1914 Due to a visit of King George V to Nottingham the School was closed.

18.09.1914 'Mr Ridge left to join the South Notts. Hussars.'
29.09.1914 The Headmaster reported that he 'gave a lesson
on "The Cause of the War" in place of the usual History lesson'.

So yes, Patrick was right: my formal education probably
didn't amount to much. But think how I must have furthered
my education through my association with Sprott and Forster,
and the sort of company they usually kept. Even someone like
me – and it's true, I was no high-flier at school; though I might
have done better if I hadn't been kept off so often to help out at
home – couldn't help but profit from the sort of discussions and
conversations I sometimes sat in on. I don't remember making
any great conscious effort to improve myself, but I suppose
that my knowledge and vocabulary must have widened almost
without my realising it. Speech was a different matter; I did try
to do something about that. I don't mean that I tried to copy
people's accents; I would have felt a bit of a fraud doing that.
But I did try to speak correctly, partly because I didn't want to
sound common, and partly because I didn't want to let Jack or
Morgan down in public. I sometimes used the language of the
streets I was brought up in, just to amuse – Jack, in particular,
seemed to enjoy what he called this bit of 'local colour' – but I
despised it, really; or was it that I feared it, as you often do with
something you have recently managed to distance yourself from?
Travel had helped to broaden my mind and increase my
confidence, too. Patrick has a copy of a letter from Jack to
Morgan which gives an account of one of my trips abroad
with Jack. It shows, incidentally, that old habits die hard, even
in foreign countries:

> Charles and I started on about the 28th July for Brussels ...
> reached there on Saturday morning, found a hotel, and went
> to inspect the town. We found it odder than, but not as nice
> as, Paris. The people were contemptible, though Charles got off
> with a flaxen-haired Queenie – 'Oo kid, good thing you weren't
> there' – in a public lavatory ... on Wednesday we went to Bruges
> which I liked – so did Charles. We liked it best of all. It was full –
> rather littered – with English proletariat holiday parties ... Went
> on to Zeebrugge, returning in pouring rain. I was ill-tempered and
> 'mardy' and Charles said he wished we had never gone.[129]

Then, of course, there was the Cosmo. Inevitably it was
Jack who took me to my first meeting. In fact, in those days

80

the Cosmo used to be held where Jack worked, at the University College building on Shakespeare Street, in the large lecture theatre. You have already heard what an important influence it had on the lives of people like Ted and me. We may not have had the knowledge and the confidence to stand up and speak, like some did; but we could follow the arguments, and sometimes we read up on the topics afterwards. Above all, I suppose, the Cosmo taught us that any subject should be debated fairly, with respect shown for all points of view. Yes, at those meetings we learned an important lesson: namely, to tolerate opinions we did not necessarily share. Throughout the 'twenties and 'thirties the Cosmo became as much a part of my weekend routine as did the football match for other men. For me it was an indispensable element of the ritual of Sunday, just as the church might have been for others. Unless I was away for the weekend, Sundays never varied: a lie-in with the Sunday papers in the morning; Sunday lunch, sometimes with Jack, in which case it would be special; the Cosmo in the afternoon; and finally, the Sunday tea with my family at 21 Westgate, followed by an evening in with the Sunday tipple – beer in a jug, and lemonade, fetched from the local off-licence. Jack mentioned a part of this ritual in one of his letters to Morgan:

> Sunday lunch Charles came; I went to meet him while V got the food ready, and they left at 2.15 for the Cosmo.[130]

I very rarely missed a session at the Cosmo. I loved the atmosphere there. But mainly I liked the way it got you thinking. As Tom Mosely, the President of the Society from 1928 to 1958, once said, the Cosmo was 'the working man's university. Every Sunday afternoon we were transported to the world of Poetry, Politics, Religion, Economics, Philosophy' – even though on Monday morning, sadly, it was 'back again to the same industrial jungle'.

All in all then, Patrick, in reality I was far from uneducated. But I owed it all, as I owed so much, to Jack Sprott and Morgan Forster. Not that our relationship, this strange triangle, was without its disadvantages, mind you. I was really in love with Jack, so you might imagine how shocked and bewildered I was at first to discover that he was prepared to loan me out so readily to someone else. Fortunately, I soon came to like Morgan. I really mean that.

He quickly became, and remained for the rest of our lives, a very dear friend. And although he was almost twice my age, there was none of the revulsion I was afraid I might feel when we became physically close. I think this was because he was always clean, always gentle, and never guilty of gross conduct. He would have found a lack of these qualities in others distasteful, I am sure, so in his usual sensitive way he would have been anxious to ensure that his own conduct should not be found wanting. I think that you will find something to this effect in one of his early diary entries – in 1910, I believe it was:

> However gross my desires, I find I shall never satisfy them for fear of annoying others. I am glad to come across this much good in me. It serves instead of purity.[131]

In fact, his sexual demands of me were usually quite modest. As we have heard, his was an 'elderly man's love' for me.[132] Occasionally, we indulged in mutual masturbation – not always completely satisfying if he couldn't get a stand on, though he got great excitement and pleasure from handling me – but he was often content with kissing, or simple touching, stroking and caressing. For this reason, I very rarely felt that I was betraying the love I had for Jack. Most of the time I was merely giving simple relief and pleasure to a rather sad, middle-aged man who often became overexcited, yes, but who loved nothing more than to be able to return that pleasure. Indeed, if anyone felt guilty I guess it was Morgan most of the time. As you have seen from one or two of his letters, he was well aware of the depth of my feelings for Jack.

Another disadvantage – chafing more sorely sometimes than others – was the thought that through the eyes of other people I might be seen as a kept man. And I think it *was* largely a concern for what others might be thinking, because I never saw myself as some kind of slave whose services had been bought. Morgan may have bought me presents, but he hadn't bought *me*. In fact, I was much more of a slave to Jack – or, at least, to my love for him – and *he* certainly never showered me with presents. What money I received from him was for the hire of my labour. I was a housekeeper in love with the boss – a not uncommon case, I would have thought – and I neither received nor sought anything extra for sleeping with my employer. I had *some* self-respect; and although you wouldn't think it from reading the letters, perhaps,

I did try to keep my dignity by making little protests from time to time. There was the business with the dentist, for example; you've seen that mentioned in the correspondence. Then sometimes I would be awkward over the arrangements being made on my behalf, pretending that certain dates were inconvenient when they weren't; or I would be deliberately casual about thanking Morgan for a gift in order not to appear too grateful. Yet I didn't want to appear ungrateful. They were difficult games to play, these. If I wasn't careful, I ran the risk of killing the goose that laid the golden eggs – and also of hurting Morgan, and I didn't want to do that. But nor did I want him to feel that he owned me, that he was buying the right to control my life.

I suppose that my decision to allow the affair with Ted to develop was a form of protest, too. If Jack didn't mind lending me to Morgan, or mind hurting my feelings with his various affairs, then he oughtn't to mind if I took another lover. What was sauce for the goose was sauce for the gander! Morgan knew that Jack sometimes upset me by making other triangles. In fact, he once mentioned one of these triangles in a letter to Jack:

> I was happier even than ever with C. this weekend ... and I know he liked being with me. I have thought much about the triangle but to no purpose ... to leave V. established at Clumber St. would be too great a strain on C.[133]

I can't tell you very much about V., by the way – other than his name, which was Verney. Not because I don't know any more than his name – I remember him only too well! – but simply because Patrick doesn't know much more about him. Apparently, the rules allow me to tell you only what Patrick knows for a fact, or what he can reasonably deduce from the evidence he has gathered. What I can reveal is that this particular triangle was very painful because it was formed under my nose. In a way, it was the last straw. I had managed to control my jealousy over Jack's affairs with people like Harry Dawes. And I had been very patient, I thought, over his reluctance to get rid of old Blackamore, even though I was again madly jealous, with my imagination running riot at the thought of what they might be getting up to together. For over two years I put up with that! And with what others were thinking, as well – because I knew that Morgan used to make jokes about it. Dora Carrington, too. I remember going through Jack's drawers and coming across a letter in which she referred to him being 'completely engulfed in his boot blacks and blackamoors', adding later, 'I hope you keep well, and enjoy your low life with the blacks'.[134] Oh yes, I had put up with a lot from Jack, I can tell you. But this was something else, it seemed to me. This was Jack openly shitting on his own doorstep, if you'll pardon my French, and then rubbing my nose in it. As you have just seen, at one stage he was actually thinking of inviting Verney to stay in the Clumber Street flat – with me continuing to cook, clean and stay overnight every Tuesday and Thursday as usual, as if nothing had changed. He had to be joking!

I was angry, as you can imagine; but more than anything, I was hurt. And the business was the more painful because it went on for so long. Thankfully, Verney gradually tired of Jack – only to make matters really complicated by showing an interest in me! Hoping to come between them, I encouraged him a little, I'm afraid – and another damned triangle was in the making! For a while, our lives were terribly confused. Verney and I even went away together, staying on one occasion in Morgan's flat. Morgan referred to the visit quite openly in a letter to Jack:

> I expect arch-fiend Charles to come up alone on the 4th. to you and not to see him. I expect him and assistant demon, Verney, to come together on the 11th. and to see them.[135]

Jack described quite well the tangled mess we were in when he confided in Morgan:

> C. is in love with me. I am in love with V. V. is not so much in love as either of us, with both of us in different ways. I don't like seeing C. with him and C. doesn't like seeing him with me. We have things to plan and arrange. V. is bewildered. We talk to him, C. in a confused, half-hearted, ashamed kind of way, and I in highfalutin terms of 'personal relationships'. If he comes to Nottingham & calls on C. on his way to West Bridgford I am distracted . . . Fortunately, I don't mind their being together when I am not there and cannot see them . . . C. says he wishes the whole triangle had never been built and so now do I . . . It makes no difference to my feeling for Charles which seems in-grown to such an extent that he is part of myself. That's a blessing anyway. The odious thing is my obsession which I have about V. He, of course, is gay, insouciant, 'out for a good time' and quite un-understanding.[136]

So yes, I had no right to feel too hurt by Jack's behaviour.

In fact, from the very start, before I got involved with Verney myself, I had no real cause for complaint, you might think, in that by this time I had already met Ted and had been out with him a few times. There was nothing serious in our relationship at this point, but I was feeling guilty about it, and I was afraid that Jack might get wind of it. Poor Morgan! He must have been really confused by now, knowing as he did all about the Verney triangle. 'Is Charles any longer Jack's property?' he must have asked himself. 'And if he isn't, why should I feel guilty about borrowing him?' No wonder he and I were very close at this time.

Ted, then, became an important part of my protest. Two could play the triangle, I thought – little realising at that stage how complicated it was to become. It all seemed so simple at the beginning. Jack had hurt me, so I intended to hurt him. And Morgan? Well, there was no reason why he should even know about it – and in any case, he could hardly play the injured third party when he himself had formed a little triangle recently with a man called Charlie Day. I not only knew about this little fling of his, I was even expected to soothe him, to help him forget, when things went wrong! He mentioned the affair to Jack, confiding that no one 'except Charles could help me and he has helped me tremendously'.[137]

This was how I came to allow my affair with Ted Shread to blossom. At first he was no more than a bit of excitement; and although I was flattered to receive the attentions of a fresh-faced boy of sixteen, his very youthfulness was a problem. To tell the truth, to begin with I was rather embarrassed to be seen out with him. Wasn't he much too young for me? Wouldn't people think I was cradle snatching, corrupting the innocent? Also, he was so – well, so rough and ready. Yes, I think that's about the right description. His manners were rough, his speech was rough and his clothes were even rougher; but he had a ready charm – cheeky, but nice with it – and he was ready to do anything for me. He didn't seem to be my type at all, surely? Yet he had a certain something. And, what was really good, I found I could relax with him, be myself, without caring too much what I said and how I said it.

There was something else, too – something I shouldn't be proud to admit, yet it excited me. For the first time in my life I had power – power over someone else, the way in which Jack and Morgan had power over me. Just as Jack commanded me, so I was now able to command Ted. I was enjoying, for the first time in a relationship, that feeling of being in control.

So I kept Ted on. Partly to spite Jack, partly as a protest against my threesome with Jack and Morgan, and partly because – well, to hell with what people thought! – I was rather enjoying myself. But by the time the Verney affair had died down, and Jack could laugh and talk about it without pain, I was discovering that it was going to be very difficult – ultimately impossible, as it proved – to give Ted up. I had become a victim of my own scheming . . .

The Celestial Omnibus

———⟐———

MORGAN: Your account was excellent, Charles dear, but it has left me feeling rather ashamed of myself for my part in what you referred to as the 'Sprott–Forster library service'.

JACK: I was just about to say the same thing, Morgan. In fact, the whole piece has made me realise the extent to which, throughout our lives, we may have underestimated the sensibilities not only of Charles but of the lower orders in general.

TED: If you really meant that, you bleddy hypocrite, you would stop referring to us as the 'lower orders'. Don't you realise how offensive it is to people like Charles and me? It makes us sound like second-class citizens – or worse: something unpleasant on the sole of your shoe. You really do think you're better than us, don't you? Well, I've got news for you, you stuck-up bogger. We're as good as you, any day. I may not have been able to write books and talk clever like you, but I could mend a car, decorate a house, do my own electrical repairs, fix the plumbing, and do a hundred and one other practical things that you and Morgan were so bleddy useless at. And who's to say that they aren't as important as clever words? Christ, Charles, how long is it since that revolution in France when all them lords had their bleddy heads chopped off – about two hundred years? – and these boggers are still talking about the 'lower orders'! It's no wonder we joined the Communist Party, is it? Not that joining the Commies got us much closer to equality, mind you. Where did it get us, eh, all that talking and dreaming? Abso-bleddy-lutely nowhere, that's where!

MORGAN: Come now, Ted, don't take on so. It was only a figure of speech, you understand. If Jack and I did tend to equate a lack of education with a lack of intelligence and sensibility – and I concede now that perhaps we did – then you should regard it as ignorance on the part of our class. I can assure you that we never regarded you as inferior in other respects. In fact, secretly,

87

I always rather envied your practical abilities, and I was about to rebuke Charles – gently, of course – for regarding himself as a nobody.

CHARLES: But I was a nobody. You can't dispute it. This whole story, in fact, is essentially about a Nobody who happened to know a Somebody, isn't it? Without my connection with you, Morgan, who on earth would be interested in the life story of Charles Lovett?

MORGAN: I know what you mean, Charles dear; and sadly, you may be right as far as strangers see you. But to those of us who knew you and loved you, you were most certainly a somebody; and a very special somebody, too.

CHARLES: Yes, in your hearts, maybe. But out there in the real world we can't all be a Somebody, can we?

JACK: Oh, come now, Charles dear. You're thinking of that line from *The Gondoliers* – 'When everyone is somebodee, then no one's anybody' – aren't you? Oh, tra-la-la! Do you remember those nights at the Empire, dear boy? The lights, the buzz of the audience, the pit orchestra tuning up, the costumes, your face shining with pleasure – and always that mad dash from our 'bar seats' to get drinks at the interval! Oh, how you used to laugh at those Gilbert and Sullivan lines. I can see the tears rolling down your cheeks now. Remember the one from *The Mikado* about playing billiards with elliptical balls? That gave rise to ribald jokes for weeks afterwards – not to mention some light-hearted anatomical investigation! They were meant to be laughed at, those lines, not taken seriously. So laugh again, Charles dear, and be assured that in our eyes you were a somebody.

CHARLES: Thank you, both of you; but I wasn't fishing for compliments. And it remains a fact, doesn't it, that despite all the references to me in your letters, I was still a mere footnote in Furbank's book? I obviously wasn't a Somebody – or even a very interesting Anybody – as far as he was concerned.

TED: Ah, yes, but that could've been because he didn't know anything about you. You may like to know that Patrick has been in touch with that bloke Furbank. He told me when he came to see me just before Christmas. And he's asked him why he said so little about you, Charles, in his book. He got a reply, too; he showed it to me.

JACK: And? Oh, come on, ducky, what did Nick Furbank say?

TED: He said a lot of things. How can I be expected to

remember them all, for God's sake! It was a long letter. Perhaps we could read it?

1 December 1991

Dear Pat Belshaw, The reason why I did not say anything much about Charles Lovett in my biography was that, in the long perspective of EMF's life, I got the impression that Charles was not very important: also, there didn't seem very much that I *could* say, there being very little about him in EMF's diaries, etc. There are one or two others who played a vaguely similar part in his life, in the middle 1920s, and though here I knew somewhat more, I decided to leave them out of the narrative, too. Evidently Charles was important to him at the time – maybe more than I realised, judging from the words you quote – but never what you might call an influence, which is what chiefly interests a biographer . . . There is a passage in one of Sprott's letters to EMF (which I am sure you will have read, as well as EMF's to Sprott?) which made me laugh – a disrespectful description of Charles's inability to remember names and to refer to people as 'Doings', which tended to make his conversation obscure. In September 1968 Sprott wrote to me referring to Charles . . . as 'my greatest friend in Nottingham', which is quite a tribute. All best regards. Nick Furbank.[138]

CHARLES: Thank you for that, Jack dear. Here is proof, if ever I needed it – which I didn't, really: I always knew – of your love and friendship. But I must say I found that bit about me calling people 'Doings' very interesting. I did that to make Jack laugh, actually. It amused him the first time I said it, so I kept it up for effect – which just goes to show, doesn't it, how what may be seen as evidence can be open to interpretation? I said, and did, lots of things mainly to amuse Jack, and Jack wrote lots of things mainly to amuse Morgan; but a biographer wouldn't necessarily know that, would he? Unless he knew us both well, he would have to take things at face value. Fascinating, isn't it, how you can be wrong when the evidence points to you being right? But I was correct, wasn't I, about Furbank not regarding me as important?

JACK: Yes, but he as good as admitted that this was mainly because he knew so little about you. And he came as close as dammit to admitting that he might have been mistaken – that you might have been far more important than he realised at the time.

MORGAN: That is true. Not that we should blame Nick Furbank in any way. Biography, even the most responsible

and respected, is always dependent upon the writer's judgement; indeed, upon his privilege to exercise that judgement.
The biographer must try not to abuse that privilege. However,
the responsibility placed upon him is really quite awesome. To
borrow Jack's line from *The Mikado*, it is just as difficult to
write the real truth about real lives as it is to play billiards 'on a
cloth untrue, with a twisted cue, and elliptical . . . balls'. Which
is why, with hindsight, Nick may wish that he had followed up
the lead on Charles. It might have taken a crease or two out of
the cloth, so to speak.

TED: Good job he didn't, though, isn't it? Otherwise we
wouldn't have a story! . . .

Patrick

. . . My uncle Ted was quite a bit shorter than my uncle Charles. Thinner, too, and more wiry. And much more restless. He was rarely still. And even if his limbs weren't moving, ten to one his lips were. He always had a lot to say for himself, did uncle Ted. And he liked it best when he had an audience. He loved to amuse people, make them laugh, shock them – anything to buck them up, as he put it – and no one worked harder in his attempts to be the life and soul of the party. His conversation was peppered with jokes and little anecdotes, most of which were *risqué* or in dubious taste. He also had a weakness for exaggeration, and that made people laugh as well.

He often went too far, it is true – crossing the boundaries of propriety, taste and credulity in outrageous fashion sometimes – so that people learned to make allowances. You had to take him as he was – and, on occasions, with a generous pinch of salt! I don't think anyone took him too seriously. Least of all, to be fair, uncle Ted himself. You couldn't deny him that: he could always laugh at his own absurdities – which was just as well, really, in view of the number of gaffes he made. I suppose he was what you might call something of a 'show-off'. He liked the attention at the centre of the stage. But most people forgave his little faults. How could they do any other when uncle Ted himself was so good-natured, so tolerant of other people's foibles and weaknesses? Yes, he could be indelicate and tactless at times; but he was compassionate, big-hearted, generous with his time and his money, irrepressibly optimistic and chronically cheerful.

Uncle Ted was about twelve years younger than uncle Charles. He was born on 1 June 1913 in Washington Street, Sneinton, a district of Nottingham known as 'the Bottoms' because – as he liked to put it – you couldn't come from anywhere lower! His name seemed to cause as much amusement as Jack Sprott's – and a great deal more confusion, for it was usually assumed that Ted was short for Edward. In fact, he was registered and christened Ted, in memory of his father's best mate. 'If plain Ted was good enough for my pal, Ted Robinson', Mr Shread senior was fond of explaining, 'then it has got to be good enough for anybody else.'

Mr Shread senior was a bricklayer's labourer – and uncle Ted used to joke that, since he was the youngest of thirteen children, his dad must have done more than his share of labouring in the bedroom! Sadly, not all of those children survived to reach adulthood. Nevertheless, a gathering of the Shread family, I remember, brought together a vast army of sisters and brothers, aunts and uncles, nieces and nephews, cousins and in-laws. Trying to put a name to every face, never mind a relationship to every name, was impossible. And just to add to the confusion, uncle Ted had two sisters with the same name! He used to explain it like this. His big sister had been christened Georgina Anne, but right from being a baby she had always been called Annie. For some reason his dad appeared to forget this when he went to register the birth of his latest daughter – probably, thought Ted, because he was a bit kalied at the time! – and he named her Anne Elizabeth. The new arrival immediately became known, somewhat predictably, as Little Annie, to distinguish her from her elder sister, who was thereafter called – less fortunately – Big Annie.

Uncle Ted was educated – if that's what you could call it, he would joke! – at Colwick Street Ragged School and Bath Street Elementary School. The Ragged School was run by a 'charitable Church-based organisation dedicated to promoting scriptural education and general schooling for the poorest classes in the town'.[139] Such schooling of what were known as the 'ragged children' was seen 'as a way of lessening crime, saving souls and providing the rudiments of educational and social training'[140] . . .

Uncle Morgan

―――――◦✲◦―――――

... It is strange, is it not, how particular elements from one life can be picked up as echoes from another, quite different life?

For example, my father – himself named Edward, though usually known as Eddie – once had an intimate relationship with a man called 'Ted'. In fact, so special had been their relationship that this fellow, Ted Streatfeild, had actually accompanied my parents on a holiday in Paris. Nothing extraordinary in that, you may think; but it was at a time, I one day came to learn, when my mother was carrying me – which perhaps placed a different complexion on things? Certainly, aunt Monie had thought it a queer business, commenting in acerbic tone, 'and no Lady companion except Streatfeild who is very nearly one I own, but not quite'.[141]

Like Ted Shread's, my father also got himself into a muddle over naming his child. In his case, however, it was achieved without the excuse of drink. As agreed within the family, my father registered me correctly as 'Henry Morgan' Forster; but later at my christening, when asked what his son's name was to be, the poor man became confused for some unaccountable reason and offered his own name, Edward Morgan, instead.[142] Like little Anne Elizabeth, then, I was named by mistake!

A third echo was sounded with Patrick's reference to Ted and the Ragged School. When I embarked upon the research for the biography of my great-aunt, Marianne Thornton – aunt Monie, as she was known – I discovered that at one stage she was very interested in the education of the poor. In the days well before compulsory education she set up a school for 'Tradesmen's Daughters'; she also had an interest in a number of other schools – one or two of which she may have partially financed – including a school for 'Raggeds'.[143] When, upon

93

reading her papers, I first came across that reference to 'a school for Raggeds', I remember thinking what a curious designation it was. I had no real idea what kind of institution it described, but the phrase captured my imagination for some reason and I have never forgotten it. It is interesting now to learn that such schools survived well into the twentieth century, decades after universal elementary education was introduced by my namesake – who was no relation, incidentally – through the Education Act of 1870 . . .

Patrick

—————◦❀◦—————

... 'Only connect!' ran Forster's sermon, ascribed to Margaret Schlegel in *Howards End*:

> Only connect the prose and the passion, and both will be exalted, and human love will be seen at its highest. Live in fragments no longer. Only connect, and the beast and the monk, robbed of the isolation that is life to either, will die.[144]

Forster believed that life can be enriched by connections between pairs of apparent opposites. He also thought that the finest connections – his 'rainbow bridges' – could only be built with the mortar of love: ' "Love" at the beginning, in the middle and at the end', as he once instructed a friend.[145]

There was to be no love between Forster and Shread – but 'only connect', and the paths of the Ragged One and the Important One[146] could at least cross ...

Uncle Ted

———————❈———————

. . . Thank Christ! I thought my turn would never come. Last in line, as usual, of course. Still, I'm used to that. It's the story of my life. So I'm not going to waste time moaning. Instead, let's get straight down to business. Let's spill a few beans, shall we? Let's let a cat or two out of the bag.

Take Charlie Lovett, for example. I reckon he comes over – or rather, Patrick lets him come over – as far more refined than he really was. If you like, he seems to speak with a far more educated voice than the real Charles had, using words in a way that I would never have given him credit for. Perhaps Patrick likes to think of his uncle – his only *real* uncle in the story, when all's said and done – in this way? Or perhaps he simply made too much – or rather, made his uncle make too much – of the chances Charles had of improving himself? I mean, Patrick himself might have made the most of those chances – the way he made the most of his own – but the Charles Lovett I knew (and I think I knew him better than anybody) wouldn't have done. In fact he couldn't have done, I'm almost sure. Not to the same extent, at any rate.

To make my point, you take that bit about the Cosmo. Yes, we did find out later that it was sometimes referred to as the 'poor man's university'. And there were some – perhaps the majority, I don't know – who went to the Cosmo on those Sunday afternoons to improve their minds. But I can tell you that some blokes went just to get out of the cold in the winter, or to sleep off a heavy lunch-time drinking session, or to pick up boyfriends in what was a mainly male audience – or just for somewhere to go. You've got to remember that this was before the days of the video, or the telly; in fact, early on, it was even before the heyday of the cinema.

But once you got inside – whatever your reasons for going – it was always entertaining, the Cosmo. We had some bleddy good laughs there, me and Charles. It was better than the pictures, really, most Sundays – and they let you in for nothing, too. Every man had the right to have his say, you see, no matter how daft his ideas were. And there were some right cranks, I can tell you. I swear they were bleddy crackers, some of them! Mind you, there were some really clever boggers as well – and often very witty with it, too, they were. The point I'm making is that we were a funny mixture in that audience. We went to the Cosmo for mixed reasons, so it follows that we must've been just as mixed in terms of what we got out of it. Who knows what Charles might have gained from those afternoons? Or how much they helped to educate him? All I can say is that he loved going – especially for the politics.

He was mad about politics, was Charles: always was, from the day I first met him. Whenever we went to London, for example, we always had to go to Speakers' Corner in Hyde Park to listen to – and sometimes argue with – whoever happened to be on the soapboxes that day. Sometimes we were there for ages, especially if there were people spouting politics – or if there were blokes in the crowd who wanted to turn anything and everything round to politics. That happened a lot. And it was the same with the Cosmo, only more so.

It didn't matter what the subject for the day was supposed to be – whether it was books, or religion, or history, or philosophy – we always seemed to get round to politics in the end. It was amazing. We always saw the funny side of it afterwards. So yes, for the politics if for no other reason, Charles loved the Cosmo – though once he'd left Goodacres and was poncing about as Jack's manservant, that idea of having to return to the 'industrial jungle' the next morning was a bit of a bleddy joke in his case!

For all he was interested, mind you, I don't remember Charles reading books about politics – or about anything else, for that matter. Newspapers, yes – but not books. For example, that book of Morgan's, *The Hill of Devi*, which Charles mentioned earlier, remember? Well, Morgan gave us a copy when it first came out. It was on our shelf for years. I *looked* at it – and we both had a laugh at Morgan in his fancy dress: Christ, he didn't half look a prat in that bleddy silly hat! – but I never actually read it; and I never caught Charles reading it, either. Yet he does give the impression, doesn't he? – or is it just me? – that he was a bit of a reader. On the other hand, you could argue that he wouldn't have been likely to read books when I was around. Certainly not in the early days, anyway. We had better things to do with our time! It's more likely, I suppose, that he could have done some reading at Jack Sprott's. There were plenty of books for him to go at there, after all. And I could imagine Jack encouraging him.

I think it's difficult, though, this business of how much Charles might have picked up from the various opportunities he describes. He certainly spent a lot of time, one way and another, at Jack Sprott's – far too much for my liking. It was the cause – practically the only cause – of many arguments between us. But he never let on how much he and Jack talked, or what they talked about. And the same was true when he came back from his weekends with Morgan. I think they must have done some talking, though, because when we were alone he'd suddenly come out with things that sounded quite clever or witty, and you could tell he was using words he'd picked up from somewhere. Charles never said that much, mind you, when we were all together in a group – particularly when Jack and Morgan, or Joe Ackerley, or anybody like that, was there. He liked to listen. I used to say more than he did – sometimes too much, perhaps, putting my foot in it with subjects I knew very little about! Perhaps that's where Charles was smart: listening, appearing to take it all in – but keeping quiet, and therefore never making a fool of himself. Clever enough not to show himself up, if you like – or clever enough to appear cleverer than he really was! I don't know, really. None of us does. We don't know what goes on in one another's minds, do we? That must be the main problem, I should think, when you're writing about other people's lives. But although I don't have much evidence, as you've seen, I've got a very strong feeling that Charles is coming over as too refined, too educated. In all, you could say, a bit too intellectual. A bit too much like Jack Sprott, maybe? Or at least, a bit too much like Patrick himself?

Also – and this isn't easy to put your finger on, either – Charles in general seems to be coming over as a bit too good to be true, perhaps. All that gentleness and politeness and even-temperedness, if there is such a word. Christ, at times we almost get a picture of some kind of saint! And Charlie Lovett certainly wasn't that. Not that he couldn't be gentle and all those other things, mind you. In fact, I would go as far as saying that most of the time he was.

But he could also be stubborn, and moody – some of his moods lasted for days! – and when he did lose his temper (which wasn't often, to be fair) he could look quite alarming. When I talked to Patrick about this, he told me that in one of Forster's letters to Jack Sprott Morgan had confessed, 'When I cannot "get what I want" I have tempers like collar-burning Charles'.[147] This is a very good description of Charles, because when he got angry his neck and the sides of his face used to burn bright red like a turkey cock.

There's something else, though, that bothers me about this picture we're getting of Charles. Something more important, and more worrying, in a way. It's this business of the way he's seen as some sort of victim who was for ever being used by people. At one point we almost feel sorry for him, don't we, for the way Jack Sprott and Morgan Forster were using him, passing him from one to the other like a bit of baggage, organising his life for him, choosing his clothes and his dentist, discussing him behind his back, as if he was some kind of pet poodle instead of a person, and so on? Then Charles himself goes and spoils this view by telling us that he knew full well he was being used – and that far from pitying him we should understand that he did quite nicely out of the deal, thank you very much, and that if this was what was meant by being used, well, on balance, he was quite prepared to settle for it. This then gives us a new picture of Charles – as a man who was a victim, yes, but a willing victim. And that's the one we're left with.

But it isn't the true picture. This book of Patrick's has taken me back over a lot of old ground – and I've had plenty of time to think in this bleddy wheelchair, as you can imagine – so, slowly, I've been able to come to my own conclusions about Mr Charles Lovett. And they don't paint such a pretty portrait as the one you've been given so far. Charles will have to forgive me – and if he came back now I would still love him, still want to live with him, in spite of everything, in spite of what I'm now going to say – but I don't think he was a victim at all. In fact – and I've talked this over with Patrick, who helped me to find a word here and there – I don't even think that he was manipulated by Sprott and Morgan Forster. Or at least, he might have been at the beginning; but he allowed it to happen so that eventually – and it didn't take long, I reckon – he could be the one doing the manipulating. Yes, he was gentle and peace-loving, and all those other things we've said about him; but underneath that layer I now think there was a cool, calculating brain at work. He may have appeared to be easy-going – lazy, even – but I begin to believe that a part of his brain was always busy, for ever working out what was going to be best for Charles Lovett.

This may surprise some of you. It may even shock some members of his family. But let the facts speak for themselves. This was a man who didn't have to go out to work for most of his adult life. For most of his life he was a kept man. First of all he was kept by his aunt Harriet. He knew he was her favourite, and he was always careful to keep in her good books. And it paid dividends for him. When she died she left him her little house in Lenton, and he got rent from that for the rest of his life. Then he was kept, as you've heard, by Sprott and Morgan Forster. Think of that cushy job he had working for Jack, and the clothes and the gifts he was bought, not to mention the holidays. It all mounts up, you know. And finally he was kept by me. Yes, by me – because once we started living together it was me who brought in most of the money from the various jobs I had over the years. It was me who bought the car just after the war – the first one to stand outside in the road, to the envy of the neighbours, when we lived on Welbeck Street – yet Charles always referred to it as 'our little jaloppy'. And I didn't mind. It was me who found almost all of the money when we bought 74 Dryden Street in 1951 – yet Charles always talked about 'our house'. And I didn't mind. In fact, how could I object when legally it was his house as much as mine – because, foolishly, I'd had it made out in joint names! I say 'foolishly' because I've since come to realise what a perfect idiot I must have been. For what happened when Charles died? Well, I'll tell you. He only went and left his 'half' of Dryden Street to Ken Ball. Ken Ball, I ask you! I've nothing against Ken. He was what he was, a gentle giant; a bit thick, perhaps, though nobody can help that; and there's no denying that at the end he was very good to Charles. But Christ, to leave him what was mostly mine anyway: I couldn't believe it! And what happened to the house that his aunt Harriet left him? A similar story. He left it to Jack Sprott, didn't he! Not to me, of course – and not to his sister, Dorothy, Patrick's mother, who he was supposed to think so much of – but to Professor Sprott. Yes, to Sprott! To the very last person who needed the money it would fetch. That was how much he thought of me at the end. He left me nothing.

Nothing but memories, that is – and this brings me on to another thing that's left me feeling a bit bitter.

Charles always claimed to love me. And I think he did, in a way. I mean, you don't live with someone for thirty years or so, do you, without there being something there, some feeling? So, yes, when we were together – and this is the thing: *when we were together* – I'm sure he did love me. But we weren't always together, were we? This was the point that caused all the trouble. Throughout our lives – every week, regular as clockwork, come rain, come shine – Charles spent Tuesday and Thursday evenings at Jack Sprott's. He only missed when Jack was away somewhere, or if he himself was badly – and he had to feel really bad for it to stop him going, I can tell you. If Charles said he was too ill to go to Sprott's, believe you me I knew he really was ill! Wild horses couldn't drag him away from Sprott's on those nights. And it didn't matter how much I pleaded with him – or how often I tried to explain how much it hurt me to see him go – it made no difference: off he would trot. It was almost as if he couldn't help himself – as if Jack had some kind of hold over him. And to make matters worse, he never would tell me what they did on those nights – those hundreds of lousy nights when he left me for Jack – so that my imagination worked overtime. It didn't matter how many times Charles protested that nothing happened, I always tortured myself with pictures of sexual orgies! I knew only too well, you see, how loving Charles could be.

So you see, Jack Sprott always came first with Charles – and so did anything organised by Jack, like the weekends spent with Morgan. It was Jack Sprott first, make no mistake. Then, for many years early on, it was Morgan Forster second – because in those days if Morgan clicked his fingers and Jack commanded, Charles thought nothing of leaving me to spend weekends in London and Dover with his 'famous author'. And I've only just found out, with the writing of this book, how deeply Charles was involved. Sometimes he must have been alone with Morgan, for example, when I thought he was at Portland Road, or somewhere else, with Jack. Not that it would ever have occurred to me that anything sexual was going on, mind you. I was jealous of Jack, yes; but I never saw Morgan as a threat. To me he was just an old man, and just a good friend to Jack and Charles. I should have realised, shouldn't I? I should have wondered what they did with all those hours they spent together. And I don't think they were spent discussing books and that chap – what's his name? – Ibsen, whoever he was when he was at home!

Jack first, then, and Morgan second, with me third most of the time – and a poor third at that, because somewhere in that order of Charlie Lovett's loves comes money. Yes, money. That surprises you, does it? Well, it's only lately that I've started to think about this; and it's just beginning to dawn on me that when it came to money, Charles was little better than the rest of the Lovetts. They were all much quicker to take than to give. It was in the blood, I reckon; though which side it came from – the Lovetts or the Dafts – I've no idea. Charles was no exception, really; but he was much cleverer than the rest of the family at disguising it. He got a lot out of Jack, and Morgan, and me – but he was clever enough not to get greedy. He made a comfortable living out of us all. It was modest, you have to admit. It didn't make him rich – or even greatly comfortable, for that matter: not by Jack's or Morgan's standards, anyway – but he was clever enough to settle for what he had. And because of that – because he was careful not to make demands; careful not to ask, usually; and always careful to receive gratefully, without show or fuss – people were slow to see through him. I was very slow – though they do say that love blinds, don't they? It certainly blinded me to a lot of things regarding Charles Lovett.

Ah, you must be thinking, now we know about the hold that Jack Sprott seemed to have over Charles. Obviously, he owned Charles. He had bought him. Simple as that. And it is tempting to go for that explanation. Patrick once quoted to me something very interesting, written by some author or other, which went: 'homosexual sex is always bought sex, sooner or later'.[148] Well, I'm not sure about that – or, at least, if it is true, why just *homosexual* sex: why not all sex? – but I think it was true of all the relationships involving Charles. In fact, to some extent it might have been true for all of us. It doesn't completely explain, though, why Charles always went running to Jack, and why he always jumped when Jack called. I mean, at one time – when I was making plenty of money from tips and fiddles as a hotel porter – I could have given Charles far more things than Jack Sprott ever could. In fact, I did. But it didn't keep Charles at home on Tuesday and Thursday nights, did it?

No, although Charles knew he was on to a good thing, there was more to it than money and introductions to famous people, and all those other things that Jack stood for. The plain fact is that although I lived with Charles all those years he never really loved me the way he loved Jack. I can bring myself to admit that now. Just as I was infatuated with the first real love of my life, so it was with Charles. Charles was first and last with me. Jack was first and last with Charles. And sadly – I see it all now, reading about the way Jack treated Charles – it seems that neither of us had our love returned by the same amount.

I'm sorry it's all coming out like this, Charles, but it's got to be said. The trouble is, though, you'll probably think that I'm just trying to get my own back for the way I felt cheated by your love for Jack. I know the others will. They'll probably put it down to spite, because they never liked me. I know that. I think I always knew, deep down, that I was the odd one out. The other two only put up with me because of Charles. I wasn't daft. I knew that, really. And I knew that this book would bear that out. Patrick warned me, too. He said that I would have to be prepared to read and hear some rather unpleasant things said about me. So I was ready. Or at least, I thought I was. But when I saw the evidence with my own eyes, I was shocked! It shook me rigid, it did; in spite of being warned. I knew they disliked me. At times, I feared they hated me. But I wasn't prepared for the raw truth of their feelings about me, and for the shock of seeing the evidence in print. Let's see that evidence now, shall we? Let's get it out of the way, to clear the air – to give me a chance to say to Jack and Morgan that they don't have to bother any more with the polite noises, because I now know what they *really* thought of me! A few extracts, then, which will let you see what was said about me behind my back:

> Notts is almost like Cambridge of my youth. We (Charles & I) discuss the same dear old questions. Is it better to love or be loved? What are the duties of lover to lover? So far it is in terms of: 'Your and my relationship is the ideal one', though there are excitements in Fucky's (his new b. friend)'s lip.[149]

> I will write to dear Charles. I have, as a matter of fact, been feeling that he 'ought' to have written to me, both after he had my flat with Fucky, and to thank me for the ash tray I sent him. Class feeling again, of course.[150]

> I do not suppose you want Shread Ted back, and I have not got him down here. The fact that he has no 'case' makes him difficult to handle. You feel sorry for him, I know. I think it

is for Charles to deal with him. Neither your kindness nor your firmness are likely to quiet him.[151]

I have come across Shrit Tit's letter which may instruct you.[152]

Charles' visit was very successful; at least I think you will hear so from him. We did not have any 'serious talk' until the end, but he professes to have grasped the position properly, and has agreed that you and Ted had better not meet or pretend you can get on, and I encouraged him to bring Ted to your flat as little as possible . . . William Plomer writes this morning that Charles impressed him – I assume favourably.[153]

I was glad to hear that I need not write to Shredded Ted after all. Or should I? I do trust that Charles has the mastery. Such awful fates await him if he doesn't.[154]

Dearest Jack. Do you think Charles and Shredded Ted will mind sleeping in sheets which have been used for two nights by two other clean gentlemen? I thought it would be all right, but Bob thought they mightn't like it.[155]

I greeted the lads this morning. Charles as sweet as ever, Ted quite monumental in his tediousness and meanness. I had been meeting people to whom it has come quite [the word 'quite' is crossed out] natural to behave nobly, and the change was more impressive . . . Oh how *can* Charles.[156]

But I don't want to see other people who have no nobility in them, was even irritable with mother, mother, endless mother, and contemptuous of a sly shit like Shredded Ted.[157]

Charles must be in a sad state [his mother had died] . . . (Discourage Shredded, by the way, if he develops a tendency to head a party up. I don't feel I want them, even if I am not there!) . . . Much love to yourself and to dear Charles.[158]

Give me Shredded news.[159]

Best love to Jack, much to Charles, and really none to Ted. Why should I pretend to like him?[160]

I keep good health, though, except for deafness. I hope that you are well and that Ted [written upside down] is not behaving too topsy-turvy. Much love dear Charles from Mature Morgie, who now retires to roost.[161]

Seen enough? Had enough? I know I have. It doesn't make pleasant reading, does it? And that's me they're talking about! But it does bring out some very interesting points, mind you. Take the first two letters. They put the record straight, don't they? First, Jack's been calling me 'ducky' all this time – when really it should have been 'fucky'. Charming, I'm sure! On this one, Patrick's been keeping things from us, hasn't he? But I'm sure he meant well. He did it to spare my feelings, he said. And to spare his readers' feelings as well. He thought some of you might be offended if that 'f' word kept cropping up. So he had me referred to as 'ducky' instead. The interesting thing is, though, that if anyone should have been called 'ducky' it's probably Charles, not me. Not in the nasty way it was used in my case, of course, but as a term of affection – a bit like the way it's often used in Nottingham, where everybody's 'me duck'. There's proof of it in one of Jack's letters to Morgan:

> My ducky is coming to see you. Give him my love, and tell him to look after himself and you.[162]

The letters also show, don't they, how Charles managed to charm everyone? Like I was saying, he was everybody's blue-eyed boy. A bit different to me, eh! Going back to the comments, I was surprised to find almost all of them written by Morgan; in fact, there was only one from Jack. I would've expected the opposite, because Jack never left me in any doubt that he couldn't stand me. He was often horrible to me – even to my face, which I suppose was honest of him at least – whereas Morgan was never rude like that. So I would have expected most of this hatred to come from Jack, not Morgan. But Patrick has explained that very few letters from Sprott to Forster have survived, so perhaps we're left with a false picture. When you think how Jack put me down in public, Christ only knows what rotten things he must have said about me in his private letters! And it must've been him who poisoned Morgan's mind against me, because I didn't deserve all those horrible comments. I can't understand it, really. What did I ever do to Morgan Forster – apart from love Charles, that is? It must have been Jack who stuck the knife in. I mean, in some of his letters to Jack – and we'd better see these, to be fair – Morgan could be almost nice to me:

> Is Ted all right? I have had a line from Charles and want to meet their wishes if I can. I must send them to a hotel if I want the flat at the moment – Let me know whether all is well.[163]

Explain to Charles with my love that I shall be very pleased to
meet Ted during my stay [in Nottingham], but don't want to go
to the Empire with them on Saturday. Honestly (as your mother
might further say) the fact is that I shall be pretty dead with the
early start and long motor drive, and I would much rather stop
quiet in the flat that evening. You and Tom will assumably go out,
and Charles and Ted might call on me after their show and find me
in authentic deshabille.[164]

I was so glad to find things going better. Charles is transformed and
if he can keep at that level there will be no more trouble for either
of you. That business of my letter is very funny, but it might have
been an awful nuisance – Let me know whether there is anything
I can do. Ted has sent me the socks with a dignified note.[165]

Dearest Jack. Have at once written off a line to Charles . . . Is
there anything I can do or send. If so, please inform me. I expect
Ted is all right on these occasions.[166]

Thirdly – this question, almost looming into a problem, of the
china for Ted and Charles. I have some very pretty blue stuff – 4
big cups and saucers, 4 small dishes, tea pot, coffee pot, milk jugs,
jam jars, all matching – which I am prepared to present to *Charles*.
Offence? If so, I have bits and ends which I will discharge upon
them both. What do you advise? Ted did all the asking, of course,
doing it very nicely. I suppose bits and ends are the wiser, since if
ever they part their establishments Charles will give Ted anything
he has. But it would have been a pleasure to present him (Charles)
with something worth using.[167]

Dearest Jack. Glad to get your letter. I ought to begin with
hapless Shredded, but proportion will out and I turn to the play
. . . Poor Ted, I really must add. But I do hope it's not going to
make trouble for Charles.[168]

These last two letters are probably the most interesting. They
get closest to the truth, I reckon. In other words, they show that
Morgan could write about me almost kindly – or, at any rate, that
he was prepared to put up with me. Far more so than Jack. But –
and this is the point – when you get down to it, he only put up
with me out of the love and respect he had for Charles.

All in all, they don't present Morgan Forster in the best light, do
they, these references to me? I mean to say, up to now he's come
over as very gentlemanly, hasn't he? Patrick's had to show him as
very civilised, very tolerant, very ready to see other people's point
of view, always anxious to make the peace and avoid trouble, and
so on, because that's the way he was ninety-nine per cent of the

time. And that's the way he was, most of the time, when I was in his company.

But there was another side to Morgan. There is to all of us, isn't there – whether we're great or small? For example, he always seemed to be looking down on the lower classes – whereas somebody like Joe Ackerley never even mentioned class. People were just people to him: class didn't come into it. Also – and this may surprise some of you – Morgan was capable of making you feel small. It wasn't his normal way, it's true; but he was capable of it. For example, I'll never forget an occasion when he made me feel a complete idiot.

It was towards the end of the war, when we lived on Welbeck Street, and Morgan had come over for the day with Jack. He'd noticed an old chess-set lying under the coffee-table, and he said, 'Oh, I didn't know you played chess, either of you. Who plays? Is it you, Ted?' 'Yes', I said, with some pride, adding foolishly – because I'd only recently been taught the game, by one of the two German POWs we used to have at the house for a few hours some weekends – 'can I give you a game?' I remember, as if it was yesterday, Morgan smiling as I made a bit of a mess of setting out the pieces. He kindly came to my rescue, though, getting everything – whites and blacks, kings and queens – on the right squares. He let me have black, too – which I thought was very generous of him at the time: I always preferred black – and when I made my first move he seemed to nod encouragement. Then I made my second move, and suddenly – fool's mate! – it was all over. Prat that I was, I'd walked right into it. It was very embarrassing. I went as red as a beetroot. But Morgan, he loved it! Chuckled and shook with delight, he did. Jack, of course, thought it was marvellous, and even Charles joined in the fun. Everybody thoroughly enjoyed themselves at my expense. Perhaps I deserved it. I was always too keen to show off any bit of knowledge or skill I thought I had. But Morgan could have spared me, couldn't he? He didn't have to make a fool of me, did he? In those days I was a big enough one to start with. So yes, he could be a bit cruel sometimes.

He liked to name-drop as well, did Morgan. Not loudly and boastingly, but quietly, almost modestly – slipping them in as if by accident. But he wanted you to know, all right. He wanted you to know that he had met royalty, that the Queen had ordered his books to be put in her library, that he had lunched the week before with Churchill, that a police inspector had saluted him and waved his car through when he attended a big society 'do' in London, that a big meal had been arranged in his honour and around the table were earls and countesses, and so on. There were many more examples, too. But these are the ones that stick in my memory.

Morgan could be a bit spiteful, too, if people upset him or things didn't go his way. I remember Charles telling me something about an occasion – and I hope I've got this right – when Morgan donated some portraits to be hung in the art gallery in Nottingham Castle. He wanted to see them during one of his flying visits to Nottingham, but it couldn't be arranged for some reason. I forget the exact details. Perhaps it was outside normal hours? Or maybe the curator wasn't available? But anyway, Morgan was furious – so angry, in fact, that he withdrew the pictures from the gallery, denying Joe Public the pleasure of seeing them! So you see, he wasn't all sweetness and light, the famous writer, and it's only fair that the record should show it.

Which brings me to another thing I want to mention – something I wanted to come in on at the time, but for some reason didn't manage to. You remember Patrick being puzzled by something which had been written in one of the letters – that bit about Morgan not getting an 'emotional kick' out of Brian's visit because Brian had refused to go and meet him? Well, I want to say something about that, linking it to what Charles told us about the photograph we took of Patrick lying on the bed, the one we gave to Morgan. It raises the whole question, you see, of how much pleasure some homosexuals can get out of being with young boys, or just seeing pictures of them in some cases. Here, I've had to admit certain things to Patrick – things that I've never admitted to anybody before – and I have a feeling he didn't like what he heard. Like our reasons, for example – Charles' and mine, that is – for bringing Brian up during the war. Let's set the record straight on this one to start with.

When Charles's sister, Dorothy – Patrick and Brian's mother – came crying to us in the early years of the war saying that she couldn't get Brian to do as he was told, we agreed to take him in. It must have looked as if we were right do-gooders – and it's true that we did take pity on Dorothy, who was at her wits' end, she said – but secretly we had other reasons that were more important than simply helping somebody out.

First – and it's one of the things you miss, you know, when

you're like us – we had the chance of becoming parents, of bringing a child up. Well, a boy anyway. We wouldn't have had a girl! And we thought we could make a success of it. We had ideas, you see. Dorothy had failed, we reckoned, because she hadn't used the right psychology. Charles had discussed it with Jack, and he'd agreed. Also, of course, she was a woman, alone without a husband. That was another reason. Anyway, we got Brian to do as he was told by promising to treat him like an adult, like a man; and by promising him little treats, like letting him go camping and swimming and ice-skating. We also hoped – and I don't think Patrick was too pleased to hear this – that we could bring Brian up to be like us. To prefer men to women, I mean. And of course, to get to the point, it gave us pleasure just having Brian around – in the same way that straight blokes would get a bit of a thrill seeing a girl about the place, I suppose. It was no different, and it was innocent enough. I swear to God nothing ever happened – like, you know, there was no abuse; nothing like that.

Mind you, to be honest, it mightn't have been quite so innocent if Brian hadn't been Charles' nephew. For example, I caught him wanking in his room one afternoon – and he didn't stop, either, though he knew I was looking on from the landing, I'm sure – and that really excited me. I went straight to my own room, lay on the bed, closed my eyes, and with that picture fresh in my mind I too began to masturbate. It gave me a real kick to think that we were doing it at the same time. After that, I wanked a lot over the thought of Brian. And just thinking about Brian helped Charles to masturbate as well. He told me. We talked about things like this. But we never touched Brian. I swear it. It was just innocent thoughts.

We had them about Patrick as well. We liked it when he came to the house, as he often did to listen to the wireless – 'Appointment with Fear', with 'The Man in Black', and 'Saturday Night Theatre', stuff like that: he liked listening to plays and stories, did Patrick – because even if we went out for a drink and left him by himself, listening in the dark, it was just nice to think that he'd been there. For the same reason, Charles used to like to take Patrick with him to Portland Road when he went to do for Jack. I reckon he got a lot of pleasure from seeing Patrick lying around there reading – and from thinking about him naked in the bathroom. Yes, that for definite. And when Brian and Patrick weren't around, photographs would sometimes help.

It's a strong bet in my opinion that Morgan was a bit like Charles and me. He didn't do things with small boys, I'm not suggesting that. All of us – and all of Morgan's group, I think – were much more interested in grown men. Benjamin Britten was perhaps the only exception I can think of. Although he lived with that singer – what was his name? oh, yes, Peter Pears – Ben had a reputation for being a bit too fond of the boys in his operas. Or so people said. Charles probably knew more about that than me. I only met Ben once, and that was just to say hello. It was on Shaftesbury Avenue, I remember, as Charles and I were coming out of a restaurant. But Charles met him a couple of times, I believe, through Morgan. No, Morgan wasn't like Ben Britten, I'm sure. Like us, though, I reckon he'd have got a lot of pleasure out of the thought of Brian and Patrick being in his flat, out of feeling a young boy's hand warm in his, out of photographs of pretty boys, and things like that. Innocent things, really – leading to nothing more than masturbation alone in the privacy of your own room – but things that wouldn't occur to someone who wasn't homosexual. They certainly hadn't occurred to Patrick.

And the fact that you're a famous writer, or whatever, doesn't put you above these things. Just as it didn't put Morgan above going on about crabs and piles, and things like that. Things that we don't normally let on about, that we manage to keep secret and private most of the time, though there's no shame in them. We all have these little secrets. But if you're famous enough for people to want to write about you, then you have to expect some of these things to come out, I suppose. For example, Morgan liked dirty stories. He didn't tell them himself in public, mind you. In fact, if anyone was smutty with him in public he soon let them know with one of his looks that he didn't want it. But in private it was quite a different matter. It was the same with swearing. You hardly ever heard Morgan swear in company. Or Jack. In fact, any of that lot, really. Yet in private – in their letters, for example, as we've seen – they often used bad language . . .

Patrick

---◆❋◆---

... I only ever heard uncle Jack swear on one occasion. It was at Kenilworth Castle. I was twelve or thirteen at the time. Uncle Jack had taken uncle Charles and me out for the day in his car. We had been to Stratford-upon-Avon to see Shakespeare's birthplace and Anne Hathaway's cottage. It was a hot day, I remember. My uncles kept pushing their trilby hats – the sort Humphrey Bogart wore on the pictures – to the backs of their heads and mopping their brows with large handkerchiefs. Uncle Jack bought me a Henley ice-cream – a great dollop of it, lovely and creamy and smooth, in a big crispy cornet. I enjoyed that. I liked the river, too, with the willows trailing their branches in its slow-moving water, and the old stone bridge straddling it. Better than the cottages. I couldn't imagine anybody living in those: they were like museums. And the furniture in them looked improbably uncomfortable. Like Shakespeare's 'courting settle', for example. I couldn't imagine anybody kissing and cuddling on that! Obviously uncle Charles thought so, too. He made a joke about it which I didn't quite catch, but it made uncle Jack laugh.

Anyway, detouring, we'd called at Kenilworth on the way back. Uncle Jack had obviously been there before – several times, I kept thinking, unless he had an incredible memory – because he guided us round, going on about Edmund Crouchback and John of Gaunt and the Earl of Leicester and the Roundheads, without once having to look at the pamphlet he'd bought at the gate. It cost three pence, I remember, that booklet. I looked after it as we walked round, keeping it open at a plan of the site so that I could keep track of where we were on the tour.

I liked the keep best. The wall was missing on one side – the north side, I think it was – but it still had its big turrets, and looking down through the arrow-slits you could imagine what it might have been like defending it under siege. When we came to

111

one of the turrets – one next to the missing wall – we suddenly found ourselves looking down into a deep pit. It was so deep that you could only just make out the stonework at the bottom. I wouldn't like to fall into that, I was thinking: you'd never escape up those vertical, stone sides.

'What do you make of this, then, Patrick?' uncle Jack asked, cutting into my thoughts. 'What do you think this was for?'

Normally, I was rather nervous when uncle Jack asked questions. In fact, to be honest, I was a little bit afraid of him. In some ways he reminded me of my headmaster – and headmasters didn't like wrong answers! But this question was easy, surely? I relaxed.

'Well, it looks like the dungeon to me', I offered, confidently.

'Yes, that's a good observation', he responded. He seemed pleased with my answer. I smiled with pleasure.

'And what about you, Charles?' he said. 'Do you agree with Patrick?'

Uncle Charles nodded; then he cleared his throat extravagantly, in that funny way of his. 'Aah', he ventured, 'it sounds reasonable to me.'

It was at this point, offering no hint of what he was leading up to, that uncle Jack came right out with it – the swear-word, I mean.

'Yes, it is reasonable', he said, 'most reasonable. But I'm afraid it had quite a different function. A man down there would have died faster and more wretchedly, I fear, than any man in a dungeon. You see, this was one of the privies, or garderobes as they were called. In other words, this was the castle shit-house.'

He said it just like that! Right out of the blue. Cool as you like. There was no intention to shock, it seemed. It fell from his lips quite naturally, neither more nor less measured or stressed than the other words. For a second or two I was shocked. This was my posh uncle Jack speaking: the learned gentleman, the professor, with whom I'd been warned to mind my p's and q's! However, my shock gave way quickly to giggles – inward ones, of course – as I said to myself, over and over again under my breath, trying to capture the long 'a' in castle, trying to imitate uncle Jack's frightfully plummy voice: 'This was the castle shit-house, don't you know? This was the castle shit-house'! . . .

Uncle Ted

... Now, where was I? Oh yes, that business about Forster
not liking any kind of smut in public, but being quite partial to
it in private. Charles told me once that Jack Sprott used to keep
Morgan amused with all kinds of tales – and the filthier they were
the better he liked it! He used to send Sprott little ditties, too,
Charles used to tell me. This sort of thing, for example, which
comes from a letter in which Morgan describes someone visiting
his flat and reciting:

> 'Seated on the closet what bliss
> Now you hear the noise of a piss
> Now a rumbling fart is heard
> Now here comes the thud of a turd'
> – Tennyson ... as it well may be.[169]

So that's another thing about Morgan, then. He had a bit
of a dirty mind. Not that that puts him down, in my opinion. Far from it. It makes him human, like the rest of us.
Apart from his genius as a writer, Morgan wasn't that much
different – no better, no worse – than you and me, as far as
day-to-day living's concerned. Most of us like a bit of smut, if
we're honest. Even someone like Sprott, who always managed to
look down his nose at common people like me as if we'd invented
it!

Ah, I expect you were wondering, weren't you, when I was
going to get round to Professor Sprott? After all, I've had a go
at everybody else – so I'm hardly likely, am I, to spare the bloke
who hated my guts? Well, I hate to disappoint you, but there's
not much more I want to say about Jack. I've had several goes
at him already, and the picture he presents is largely an accurate
one as far as I can see. I don't want to make things up just for
spite. Mind you – going back to that business of homosexuals

and young boys – I was tempted a bit when Patrick asked me
to comment on something he'd come across in a couple of letters
written by Lytton Strachey's brother. The first one included the
information:

> Sebastian is stopping here & is now immersed in the Mass Murderer.[170]

This sounded promising! But according to Patrick, it was
simply a reference to a man named Haarmann who was on
trial at the time, accused of twenty-seven murders, all of them
involving young boys. It was claimed that he had lured the
boys into sexual relations with him before killing them by
biting through their throats. He was eventually found guilty,
and was hanged in 1925. It was no more than he deserved, by
the sound of it, the vile bogger. The thing was, though, that
Sprott was apparently so fascinated by this case that it was still
very much on his mind when the second letter was written five
months later:

> To escape this, I went out and called on Sebastian . . . I always find
> Sebastian most soothing, & we discussed as usual the Haarmann
> case.[171]

Patrick said he was sure that Sprott's unusual interest in
this case was to do with his work as a psychologist. Even so,
he said he had to ask me whether or not Jack, in all the years
I'd known him, had ever shown any interest in young boys. As
I say, just for a second I was tempted! But no, Jack wasn't like
that, I'm sure. The only time I've ever known him to be mixed
up with anybody underaged was back in 1952.

I have good reason to remember it because Charles and I
were involved as well. In fact, it was me who first met the
youth. I was working as a porter at the Flying Horse hotel
at the time, and he came to one of the Christmas parties we
used to have for needy children. I felt sorry for him – like me,
he came from a very poor home – so I invited him to come and
have tea with us. He came a few times. Then Charles took him
to Portland Road to look round the house – which must have
looked like a mansion to him – and to meet Jack. Like Patrick, he
couldn't get over seeing all those books! He seemed a nice lad, and
we enjoyed having him around. We wanted to help him to better

Patrick, aged 11, in Trafalgar Square on the day he met E.M.Forster.

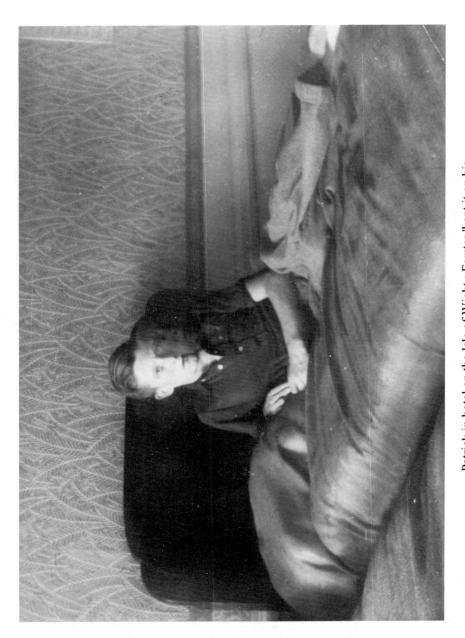

Patrick in hotel on the Isle of Wight : Forster 'kept it on his mantelpiece, he did, for ages afterwards. Or so he said ...'

'Sebastian' Sprott, the image maker.

'Sebastian' Sprott, lecturer in psychology,
University of Nottingham, c. 1928.

Ted Shread, aged 16 : 'proud as a peacock', in Sprott's Clumber Street flat, 1929.

Charles Lovett at the time he met Jack Sprott.

Charles Lovett (extreme left) at the wedding of Patrick's
mother and father, 1931.

Ted Shread, hotel porter, c. 1952.

Ted Shread in his Sneinton flat, two months before he died.

Charles Lovett during his convalescence, 1964.

Bob Buckingham, Jack Sprott, May Buckingham, Morgan Forster, Robin Buckingham.

himself, to see a different side to life. It was all very innocent. We weren't conscious of it at the time, but I suppose he was helping to fill the gap left by Brian. By this time, you see, Brian had left us to become a steward in the Merchant Navy. We missed him a lot.

Anyway, all went well with this youth until one day, shortly after we had moved into Dryden Street, Charles and I suddenly had the police banging on the door. At exactly the same time – though we didn't learn this till later – an unmarked car arrived at Portland Road and Jack was escorted to an interview with the Chief Constable. There was the bleddy class system at work again, you see. Professor Sprott was invited to make a private statement to the Chief Constable, while Charles and I were interrogated in separate rooms by burly detective constables. Sprott was probably given tea and biscuits: all we were given was a bleddy rough time! They made it very clear what they thought of 'perverts who messed about with young lads', as the big bastards who pushed me about put it, and we nearly shit ourselves, the pair of us. We hated the police after that. Looking back now, though, I suppose you couldn't altogether blame them. They threw their weight about, it's true – and mine said he hated 'bum boys', as he called us – but they probably thought they were doing their duty, protecting the public from the likes of us. There was a lot of fear and prejudice about at the time – there still is, I suppose – and, especially if they had sons of their own, they were hardly likely to give us the benefit of the doubt, were they?

It turned out, you see, that our young friend had failed to go home a couple of nights earlier; and when asked where he'd been, he'd told everybody – his family, and the police when they were brought in – that he'd spent the night at Portland Road with Jack Sprott! He hadn't. He couldn't have done, for the simple reason that Charles and I went to Jack's for supper that night. We were there till nearly midnight. But the youth had convinced the police that he was telling the truth by giving them a detailed picture of Jack's bedroom – remembered, I suppose, from his tour of the house – and for a while it looked very black for us all.

We were involved, me and Charles, because the lad had also described how he had been 'entertained' in our house on a number of occasions. The police said there would be a prosecution. There was a big clampdown on homosexuals at this time, you see, following the Burgess and Maclean case. Police forces all over the country had been asked to tighten up. We were worried to death, naturally. Jack, though, was in a far worse state. He really panicked – thinking of his job, his reputation, I suppose – and he asked to see the Chief Constable again, hoping to pull strings. Our hopes were raised. But it was too late, the Chief Constable told him: it had already gone 'above his head'. As you can imagine, we were really sweating by this time. Then quietly, secretly, Jack saved everybody's bacon by using the old boy network. As luck would have it, the then Master of the Rolls – I think it was him: somebody like that, right at the top, anyway – had apparently been at Cambridge with Jack. There was a telephone call – and a trip to London, I believe – and suddenly Jack was all smiles again. Our case was never called!

It was a strange business. We never saw the youth again, of course, so we never did find out where he'd spent that night. He must have been protecting somebody. But I'm sure Jack wasn't guilty of any funny stuff. And we were very grateful to him, me and Charles, for getting us out of a real hole. He could be all right over things like that, could Jack, because he always knew what to do and who to have a word with. In fact, for all he couldn't stand me for some reason, I've got very little to say against him really.

The only thing in his piece that doesn't ring true to me is where he talks about having an open house for down-and-outs, ex-convicts and the like. I don't remember seeing people like that – either in the Clumber Street flat or, later, at Portland Road. Of course, I was always there with Charles – and usually when Jack was away! – so that could explain it. It's strange, though, that I don't remember Charles ever mentioning it. Also it seems out of character, somehow. To me, Jack never seemed that interested in the lower classes – apart from his affair with Charles, that is. Unlike Joe Ackerley. Now, he was a different kettle of fish altogether. When we went down to Joe's, Charles and me, we actually met the sort of people we're talking about in his flat, or in the local pubs when he took us for a drink. We met his burglar friends, and some other shady characters, too. Most of them, though, were ordinary working-class blokes like us. But I never met people like this at Jack's. I wonder if he might've made them up, some of them, to amuse Morgan? Or at least, he might have exaggerated a bit for Morgan's benefit – because we've heard how much Morgan used to love reading in Jack's letters stories about the seamy side of life. I don't know. But it's a thought, I suppose.

So that's that, then. I hope the reader doesn't mind me getting all this off my chest. It's well and truly put the cat among the pigeons, I'm sure; but I want us to get things right. As I see them, any road. Just to set the record straight.

Now, getting round to the story at last, I thought you might be interested in this. It's my own account, exactly as I wrote it – spelling mistakes, grammar and everything – of how I came to meet Charles and Morgan. Patrick asked me if I would do it. He said it would help him to capture my way of putting things – my 'voice', as he put it – as well as telling my bit of the story:

I've always said that I was 17 yrs old when I first met Charles but on reflection I could only have been 16. and the reason for me thinking this is because I was in the 20th Nottingham Boys Brigade for quite a long time, maybe a year after the first meeting and as one had to terminate ones membership of the Boys Brigade at the age of 17 it is obviouse I was much younger.

At this age I was expected to do menial jobs one of which was taking the rent to the rent office in St Peters Gate on Fridays simply because my mother had to wait for my sisters pay packets.

On taking the rent I got into the habit of going down St Peters church steps where I found that men stood around and it was quite easy to be picked up and maybe earn yourself sixpence which in those days was quite a large amount and it was here that I first met Charles

I was immediately attracted to him. He was good looking and well dressed and he suggested we both went to his place which I later learned was not his flat but that of Sprott a freind of his.

It was a spaciouse flat two floors up over a tailors shop in the centre of the city and only a few minutes walk from St Peters

After a very pleasant evening he decided that he would walk me home. As I lived in the slums I felt ashamed and told him I lived in Bridgford. He left me at Trent Bridg.

We arranged to meet the following evening at the same place and much to my amazement he turned up and once again had a marvelouse evening

It was during this evening that he told me it was not his flat and that it belonged to a freind who I was later to meet. It was Jack Sprott who at that time was a lecturer at Nottm University

He also said he lived in Muskham St with another of his freinds Boyd Jephson and his sister Miss Jephson known as Dickie an abbreviation of Hickman

On the following Sunday morning I went to 16 Muskham St. I

was greeted by Miss Jephson and introduced to Boyd who to my astonishment was sufering from sleepy sickness and had to have everything done for him.

Miss Jephson was pleased when I suggested I take Boyd for a walk. She was later to be my greatest freind. When I was 21 I left home & took a unfurnished room at Wellington Sq.

After about 6 months Miss Jephson decided she would rent a large house in Wiverton Rd. I could then have the upper floor & she & Boyd the rest of the house

During all this time Charles and I were getting closer and closer and we were more or less inseparable except that Charles saw Jack each Tuesday and Thursday and it seemed that Jack had a very big hold on Charles.

Miss Jephson told me then that Jack was a possesive man and It was about this time I first met Morgan.

One Sunday about 12 noon Charles came to see me to say he had brought a freind to see me from London and he was famouse but he waited to see me and was waiting at the bottom of the street and we then went to Jack's flat for lunch and this was the start of a long freindship. Everything went well I had a good job and I led a much better life due to mixing with a nicer type of people

I was spending more time with Charles but when in 1939 war loomed ahead Miss Jephson said she would have to take Boyd to Southwell to her mother and it was decided Charles and I look for a small house to rent which was quite easy and it was the reason Charles and I rented no 46 Welbeck St a parlour kitchen scullery type and from this we lived together until Charles death. Jack interfered with what we did and for some time before Charles death Jack had a horrible dislike to me for no reason at all but I did not dislike Jack. When Charles died Jack took over and arranged for him to be cremated. I never saw Jack again.[172]

That's it, then. What do you think? I know what I think. I could kick my bleddy self, that's what I think, for looking so bleddy ignorant! I mean, I do know the rules you know. Christ, I ought to: we had them drilled into us often enough at school! I should know about 'i' before 'e', except after 'c', and about ending a sentence with a full stop, and all of that. Because in those days if you couldn't get it into your head, you had it well and truly caned into your arse! It's just that when the words start falling off the biro you get flustered, don't you? If you'd *asked* me about those spellings and that, I could have got them right. I know I could. I'm just a bit out of practice at writing, that's all. Yes, I know what I think all right!

I know what Patrick thought of it, too. Of course, he was very polite when he thanked me for it on the telephone. But I could tell he was disappointed. He admitted it later. It was nothing to do with the spelling and what have you. That didn't really matter at all, he said. What mattered far more, he said, was the fact that it just wasn't Ted Shread, that piece of writing. That was why he was disappointed. His bright idea had failed. It hadn't allowed him to capture my voice, as he'd hoped. Or little else about me, either, for that matter. He should have known, he said. He shouldn't have asked me to do it. It had only succeeded in embarrassing me. Then he cheered up a bit. Some good had come out of it, he thought. It had at least helped to show some of the problems writers have when they're writing about people's lives . . .

Patrick

... Initially, it all seemed very straightforward. I had a story to tell; a true story, about events and relationships that preoccupied a small group of people over sixty years ago. It was a history, in other words; and one that could be authenticated, for there was a substantial body of primary and secondary evidence on which I could draw.

But what are the problems of writing history? And what would be the best way for me to recreate this particular piece of history? Could my story be presented in standard biographical form, for example? If so, to what extent would I compromise the genre by introducing, almost at the outset, a device allowing the living and the dead to become reunited? Was my evocation of the Celestial Omnibus an irreversible stroke of liberty-taking? From the moment it came silently on to the scene did this book begin to slide into fiction? If so, how much does it matter? What indeed, I asked myself, would be gained and lost if I took the basic facts from my research and bedded them into a novel? The main gain would be, I suppose, that I could circumvent the problem of any gaps in my knowledge of the main characters, and at the same time be as imaginative as I pleased. It was very tempting! The main loss would be, of course, that in a historical novel, or a *roman-à-clef*, the reader could have difficulty separating fact from fiction – separating what really happened from what might or could have happened, or from sheer invention. Also, as Virginia Woolf once wrote, 'no one takes a character in fiction quite seriously'.[173] This would be the clinching point for me, surely?

However, the problem was that even if I eschewed fiction, and attempted to interpret and present my research evidence in the manner of a formal biographer, I would still not be able to guarantee delivery of the truth. For biographers reserve the

120

right, do they not, to select from their source material, to filter information, and to place their own individual interpretation upon the evidence before them? Take Forster, for example. A writer of great integrity, would we not agree? But wait. In the preface to his biography of Goldsworthy Lowes Dickinson, he claimed solemnly:

> I have not tried to exclude facts about him with which I am not in sympathy or which might be held to decrease his reputation. To do so would be to pay him a poor compliment, for neither did he care anything for his reputation, nor was he dazzled by the reputations of others.

However, this claim was only partially honoured. He went on to write a life which, though honest in other respects, failed to refer overtly to his subject's homosexuality. This left him culpable, critics agreed, to the charge of constructing an imperfect portrait and an incomplete narrative. Not surprisingly, he was accused of casuistry. Of course, Forster's motives for drawing a veil over the sexual side of Dickinson's life were entirely laudable. He was, it should be remembered, very close to his subject; too close, perhaps, giving rise to a strong conviction that his story would have to be told sensitively, almost reverently. The thought of sacrificing in any way the respect which 'dear Goldie' commanded and deserved would have been unthinkable. Let it not be forgotten, too, that his account was written in a pre-Wolfenden era; it had to be presented without implicating the biographer and other close friends. In more enlightened times, one would like to believe, Forster would have displayed greater courage and frankness.

Biography, then – indeed, all history as it is written or told – is not the final word on lives and events, not a pure distillation, but a version of the truth based on selection and interpretation. 'History isn't what happened', writes Julian Barnes:

> History is just what historians tell us. There was pattern, a plan, a movement, expansion, the march of democracy; it is a tapestry, a flow of events, a complex narrative, connected, explicable. One good story leads to another ... all the time it's connections, progress, meaning, this led to this, this happened because of this ... And while we fret and writhe in bandaged uncertainty ... we fabulate. We make up a story to cover the facts we don't know or can't accept; we keep a few true facts and spin a story around them.

Our panic and our pain are only eased by soothing fabulation: we call it history.[174]

All attempts to present a true picture of human character and behaviour are destined to fail. Sadly, inescapably, I have to come to this conclusion, because the process by which our intelligence operates is inherently flawed. We cannot get inside the heads and hearts of other people; therefore we cannot know what really moves people, what drives them. We only know what they want us to know, and what our own inadequate intelligence tells us. In fact, as Forster himself wrote, the irony is that if we really want to know a character inside out we must turn not to fact, but to fiction:

> In daily life we never understand each other, neither complete clairvoyance nor complete confessional exists. We know each other approximately, by external signs, and these serve well enough as a basis for society and even for intimacy. But people in a novel can be understood completely by the reader, if the novelist wishes; their inner as well as their outer life can be exposed. And this is why they often seem more definite than characters in history, or even our own friends; we have been told all about them that can be told; even if they are imperfect or unreal they do not contain any secrets, whereas our friends do and must, mutual secrecy being one of the conditions of life upon this globe.[175]

This is why the biographer may have to rely on what one might call the 'truth of circumstance' – or may feel the need to lean, like Dr Aziz in *A Passage to India*, towards the 'truth of mood' – in certain situations where, due to a paucity of conventional evidence, or a reluctance to take such evidence at face value, the actual truth seems impossible to get at. When this happens, the biographer is beginning to operate like a novelist; and at this point the ground between fact and fiction becomes swampy and treacherous. Here is a no man's land in which it is easy to become disorientated – and a biographer behaving as a novelist, or a novelist behaving as a biographer, offers no firm footing or direction to the traveller. Nor does a life that seems to behave like a novel, or a novel that seems to behave like a life.

Virginia Woolf would have coped in this terrain, of course. Indeed, she might even have wondered what all the fuss was about; for this was the woman who wrote: 'There is a virtue in truth; it has an almost mystic power', adding that unfortunately pure unselective truth may fail to transmit personality, and that 'in order that the light of personality may shine through, facts must be manipulated; some must be brightened; others shaded; yet, in the process, they must never lose their integrity'.[176]

Woolf agreed with Sir Sydney Lee's view that 'the aim of biography is the truthful transmission of personality', but confessed that she was always going to have a problem with the truth ('something of granite-like solidity') and with personality ('something of rainbow-like intangibility'), concluding that the formidable task of the biographer was 'to weld these two into one seamless whole'.

She admired greatly Harold Nicolson's book *Some People*, seeing it as a seminal work which made 'the best of both worlds'. She wrote of it:

> *Some People* is not fiction because it has the substance, the reality of truth . . . [and] . . . It is not biography because it has the freedom, the artistry of fiction.[177]

Will my book, I begin to wonder, be similarly difficult to classify? If so, will it matter? Perhaps not. Perhaps I ought not to worry about method and presentation. But I do worry about 'the reality of truth'. Take my portrayal of Ted Shread, for example. I choose him because he is my only living character. Surely I should be able to get him right? But no, it is not that simple. For there is more than one Ted Shread.

The first one – the one given the chance to write about himself – is not the real Ted Shread, I can assure you. He simply does not come alive in his writing. This is because Ted is essentially a talker – and a highly animated and engaging talker – not a writer. I've spent hours and hours in entertaining conversation with this second Ted Shread – the real Ted, I am tempted to call him – and some of our talk is recorded on tape. So I think I know my subject. But I can't reproduce him for the reader. I can give you the facts, of course, recorded with scrupulous attention to accuracy; and I can attempt to authenticate my writing with a few verbal mannerisms. However, I can never capture the way he laughs and cries and smiles and takes in his breath and holds his head – and the hundred and one other things that make the man what he is – because it is not possible. No, this third Ted Shread is at best an approximate. He is at least once removed.

He has to be presented through my writing; he is my creation, in effect. It would take a video recording, filmed with a hidden camera, to bring anything approaching the real Ted Shread into the reader's sitting room.

Indeed, does anyone know the real Ted Shread? For inevitably there is a fourth Ted Shread: the Ted Shread that Ted, as I know him, is not letting on about – to me, or to anyone else! It is true of each and every one of us. A part of us, varying in amount from person to person, is always kept private. We, all of us, keep secrets from one another . . .

Uncle Ted

———◦❈◦———

... Christ, I feel sorry for Patrick – but not half as sorry as I feel for you, the reader! After all, you're supposed to trust the word of someone who confesses that he can't even get me right – me, and I'm alive! – so what chance does he stand with the other three boggers who can't speak for themselves? You can't believe in anything after this, surely? As Patrick says, can you really expect people to tell the truth, the whole truth, and nothing but the truth, about themselves? And even if they do, there's still the bleddy biographer to worry about! He can tell what he wants to tell, to suit his own purposes. I wouldn't like the biographer's job, mind you.

Take Patrick, for example. Having let me write my own account he still had to come back at me with questions about it. Questions, he said, that the reader might ask. What did I mean, for instance, when I said that a lad could earn himself sixpence near the rent office in St Peter's Gate? Well, as you might guess, it wouldn't be for running errands! It was easier work than that. You just went off somewhere quiet with the bloke who'd called you over, and there he'd open his flies and get you to play with his cock. Often he'd put his hand on your leg and ask if he could play with yours. Most of them liked that: wanking you while they were being wanked. You ended up tossing him off, usually. And often he'd do it to you. But if he didn't, you were usually so excited that you'd come anyway. Perhaps it sounds dirty to you? And you probably think that these blokes were evil for leading young lads astray? But any lad who went off with them knew what he was letting himself in for. I certainly did, and I enjoyed it – as long as the blokes were clean, and as long as there was no rough stuff, no attempt at buggery, that kind of thing. I never went in for buggery. Nor did Charles – not with me, at any rate. We lived together all that time without ever going further than what they call mutual masturbation. It was enough for us.

It was certainly an easy way to earn sixpence. I quickly learned how to please those men, and they were grateful. Far from corrupting me, or even using me, they usually gave as much pleasure as they got – often without realising it – and I got paid into the bargain! No wonder I used to linger there, waiting for a call, looking for a signal.

By then, as you've gathered, I'd known for a long time that I was homosexual. I'd known since the day my brother Bobby touched me between the legs one night in bed. Perhaps it was accidental, I don't know – the bed we shared was small, after all, and Bobby wasn't queer: he was courting Bertha, his wife-to-be, at the time – but I do know that it gave me a thrill. It made me go all tingly. And after that I'd often snuggle up close, or even start wrestling matches with him, in the hope that he would touch me there again. He never did. But I enjoyed the closeness of his body all the same – whereas I'd never wanted girls anywhere near me.

Patrick also wanted more detail about those early years with Charles. He was right to ask. I'd forgotten to include all sorts of things that I meant to at the time. Like that first meeting with Miss Jephson, for example. My knock on the door of 16 Muskham Street was answered by a thin, bird-like woman. She looked rather severe. I wasn't expecting this, and there was an embarrassing pause before I managed to introduce myself as Charles' friend.

'So you're Edward, are you?' she said.

'No, Miss', I replied, 'my name's Ted.'

'Well, I shall call you Edward', she insisted.

And she did, throughout her life. She was the only person I let take liberties with the name my dad had deliberately given me. I didn't like the name Edward; but it sounded right, somehow, coming from her. She had a very posh voice, and quite a commanding way with her. She was not to be argued with, I thought – though I soon discovered that underneath she had a heart of gold. Yes, she was very good to me, was Dickie. From that very first day – when she discovered I was wearing two pairs of trousers, the arse out of one, the knees out of the other – she took pity on me. Right there and then, as you've heard, she sat down at her old treadle machine and altered a pair of Charles' old plus-fours for me to go home in. Somewhere there's a snapshot of me looking as proud as a peacock in that suit; it was taken in Sprott's Clumber Street flat one weekend when he was away. I was wearing a pair of checky socks – right bobby dazzlers, they were – that Charles bought me to go with the suit, and I was smoking a fag to make me look more grown up and sophisticated. Yes, I thought I was the bee's knees, I can tell you, posing in Jack's chair that day. Now when I look at that photo, it makes me laugh. 'Christ! Who's that lairy bogger?', I ask.

Anyway, getting back to Miss Jephson, it didn't stop at the suit. The next week when I went – having had a birthday in between – there she was at the tea-table with another lovely surprise: a special cake she'd baked, which had 'Edward' written in icing on the top. I was touched – almost in tears – at the trouble she'd gone to. For some reason Dickie and I seemed to hit it off from the word go. She wanted to mother me, I think, and she liked the way I took to Boyd. Not everyone was able to do that. People were put off by his slavering and choking; and it needed time and patience to get to know him, to understand him, because he wasn't able to talk.

It was Dickie who lent me money in 1933 to set up the first place of my own, an unfurnished room in number 19 Wellington Square, near the old drill hall, off Derby Road. It hadn't been easy up to that point for Charles and I to be alone together. Occasionally we managed it at my house: if we turned up unexpectedly, for example, we would sometimes be lucky and find everyone out. The same thing sometimes happened at 21 Westgate, which was no longer the crowded place described by Charles. By the time I was making regular visits to the house with Charles there was only Mrs Lovett, widowed in 1929, and two of her daughters, Win and Gwen, living at home. Dorothy, you see, had left to get married in 1931. So it was now possible to get some privacy at Westgate, though never for very long.

Incidentally, I remember Dorothy's wedding very well. She and Tom, Patrick's father, were married in Basford – at the church of St Leodigarius, it was – with the reception afterwards at the Vernon Arms public house. Charles was there, of course, giving his sister away; and the best man was the groom's brother, Eddie Belshaw. Charles' sister, Gwen, and Tom's sister, Ella, were the two bridesmaids, I remember. There's a photograph of it somewhere. I'm not on it: I was just one of the guests. But Charles is – and looking a treat he is, too. In his spats, and wearing a brand new trilby hat, he was the best-dressed man at that wedding. Mind you, the groom and the best man looked very smart and handsome, too, with their bowler hats. I wouldn't have said no to any of them! It was a good do, with plenty to eat and a non-stop flow of ale. They liked their ale all right, did the Belshaws. I think the Lovetts looked down on that a bit. I'm sure they thought it was a bit common, and that Dorothy was marrying beneath her. But everybody seemed to enjoy the day. I gave the happy couple a set of curtain hooks, crocheted by my mother.

A few months after the wedding Charles and I had a good evening to ourselves at Tom and Dorothy's, where we had volunteered to keep an eye on baby Brian while they went out for a drink. That was the sort of thing we had to do to be together. But you couldn't keep offering like this, in case people twigged. It was the same at Muskham Street. From time to time we used to persuade Dickie to have a break while we looked after Boyd; but it was hard work getting her to go out – and even when she'd gone, we didn't like to do too much in front of Boyd. After all, he'd once been very close to Charles, and we didn't want to upset him.

Our best opportunities to be alone came at Jack's flat when he was away for the day. Better still, he was sometimes gone for a night, or even a whole weekend. That was marvellous – though I always felt that Charles held something back when we were at Jack's, as if he thought that somehow Jack could see what we were doing! It all came to an end one day, anyway. Jack found out that I'd spent the night there – something had made him suspicious, and he'd wheedled it out of Charles – and there was one almighty, blazing row. You've seen in the letters the trouble I was causing between Charles and Jack – quite innocently, as I saw it – and that was often just through Charles *seeing* me, let alone sleeping with me in Jack's bed!

Charles and I had to manage like this in other people's houses – always listening, or keeping a look out, in case someone should burst in on us, and forever feeling guilty – for about four years. So you can imagine what a great relief it was to have a place of my own, however small, where we could feel safe together. It was the move to Wiverton Road, though – and again, I had Dickie to thank for that – that gave Charles and me the chance to live together permanently. Except for Tuesdays and Thursdays, that is! Yes, except for Tuesdays and Thursdays – and his occasional weekends with Morgan, though I never resented those as much – Charles and I were very happy at Wiverton Road. If we wanted company there was always Dickie and Boyd living below, and we now had room to entertain our friends.

We had two particularly interesting visitors during this period – one who came to see me, and I knew him well, and the other who came to see Charles, though Charles himself didn't know it! I'm sorry if I seem to be speaking in riddles. Let me explain about these visitors. Mine was my father. He came to see me one night when Charles was away at Jack Sprott's. I was very surprised. He was still wearing his working clothes: dirty trousers, old jumper – the one with the elbows out – and heavy, dusty boots. That was strange: why hadn't he bothered to change, I wondered? It wasn't like him – unless, of course, he'd had to come straight from work? Then suddenly I came to my senses.

'Hey, wait a minute', I said, sitting bolt upright in bed, 'what are you doing here? We buried you on Monday: you're supposed to be dead! What's going on?'

'As long as you're alive, my lad', my father replied, 'I'll be alive to look after you.' Then he vanished.

Charles' visitor never actually came to Wiverton Road, but he turned up elsewhere on two or three occasions. It came about this way. During this period of our lives, leading up to the outbreak of war, Charles and I – perhaps influenced by the Cosmo, but mainly for somewhere to go until the pubs opened – used to visit different religious organisations to find out what they believed in. We'd been to the Catholics, the Baptists and the Jehovah's Witnesses, and we were now having a go at Spiritualism. Halfway through the first session we went to, one of the leaders – a woman claiming to be a medium, who said she could get in touch with those she called 'the dear departed' – suddenly turned her attention to Charles. She asked him if he knew anyone who had once been a soldier – because she said, as Charles stood there shaking his head, she could see one of the 'departed', dressed in full uniform, standing next to him! Well, nobody else had seen anything in what she called the 'aura' surrounding Charles, so we left killing ourselves with laughter at the thought of this batty old dear trying to get Charles off with a soldier boyfriend. But in the next few weeks, in different establishments, two other mediums picked Charles out from a large gathering, claiming to see a figure

– again described on each occasion as a soldier in uniform – standing next to him!

It made a big impression on us, I can tell you. Charles said it felt weird, the thought of this spirit following him around everywhere. He obviously discussed it with Jack who, in turn, must have mentioned it to Morgan in one of his letters. I say this because Patrick has been able to show me a reference to it, taken from a letter which Morgan wrote to Jack from Dover. There's no date on it, but it must've been written between 1936 and 1938 when Morgan and Joe, and lots of their friends, were often in Dover. They had lodgings there – well, Joe certainly did, because Charles and I stayed there with him one weekend. I remember it well. He took us to a pub called, of all things, the British Queen! It was well-named. The place was full of queens, young and old; it was marvellous for pick-ups. They were soldiers mainly; but there seemed to be a lot of blokes down from London as well, looking for a bit of rough. Back to the letter, though. Morgan had written:

> The psychic experience is very odd. I suppose Charles is rather a 'subject'. The ghost sounds to have been dressed more provocatively than is usual beyond the veil.[178]

Well, I think I'd better start winding up now. We've got to the outbreak of war, just before which Dickie took Boyd to live in Southwell where she thought there'd be fewer air raids and less chance of bombs falling on you. It was to prove a wise move. After she and Boyd left, Charles and I didn't stay long in the Wiverton Road house – it was too big, and too expensive to keep up – and by the time we moved into Welbeck Street in 1940 the war had really hotted up. The sirens went nearly every night. Dickie had been right. It was the city the Germans were after – or rather, the munitions factory at Chilwell – not small villages like Southwell. Thank God she was out of it. She would never have coped – not with Boyd to look after, and everything. It was such a long way to the shelters for most people; and even if there wasn't an actual raid, you didn't sleep for worrying, or false alarms, or the ARP wardens shouting up about your blackouts. Nobody got a decent night's sleep for months. We did better than some round our way, mind you, because we'd moved into a house next door to a pub – the Zetland Arms, it was called – and we were able to shelter in their beer cellar.

I could do with that shelter now, I reckon. I've stirred up too many ghosts, I think, so stand by for bombs of a different kind to start falling! . . .

The Celestial Omnibus

JACK: . . . Villain! 'Treacherous, lecherous, kindless villain!' Now we see you in your true colours, ducky – or should I say 'fucky'? I see no reason why not, since you have seen fit to lower the tone with your tasteless revelations. Now we can all see you for what you are: a charmless, mean-spirited, vindictive shit.

CHARLES: I say, Jack, steady on! That's a bit strong, isn't it?

JACK: Not at all. Morgan was right. You're a sly shit, Ted Shread: there isn't an ounce of honour or loyalty in you. And, to return some of the honesty for which you appear to be claiming a monopoly, it's about time you understood how much we all despised you.

CHARLES: No! I'm sorry, Jack, but I'm not having that. Ted's had to have his say – just like he used to: he always had to get things off his chest – and yes, he's hurt me with some of the things he's said, but I don't despise him. I've never despised you, Ted. In all sorts of ways, I loved you. I want you to know that, in spite of your bitterness and the cruel things you've said about me.

MORGAN: 'Despise' is not the word I would use, either. Contempt is not an emotion to be admitted lightly, Jack. You risk the charge of appearing 'holier-than-thou', surely?

JACK: Maybe, Morgan dear; but rather that than hypocrisy. Or do you now deny saying those things about Ted?

MORGAN: Oh dear, my worst fears are being realised. I can't recall who said something to the effect that biography brings a new terror to Death; but he was right. Inevitably, I suppose, one stands trial for the things one has said. And I plead guilty. How can I deny the contents of those letters? They were written in my hand. But I claim to have been under a great deal of stress at the time. The war was eating into me – into my heart, I fear – and during that period I may well have said a number of things I did not mean. Certainly, I regret calling Ted a shit. Hitler was a shit, I thought. My crude verdict on him remains unchanged. But thankfully there were few human beings I would have been prepared to write off completely like that. No, let us keep things in perspective. Ted wasn't a shit. But he did irritate me – immensely, on occasions. And if that happened when I was tired and depressed, my reaction could be extreme, as we have seen.

JACK: Well, I thought you were being impressively perceptive at the time, and I still do. Don't you see, both of you? Nothing's changed: the sly shit is still at work. He has inveighed against our reputations, throwing up all these scurrulous charges, and all we seem to be doing, by way of response, is disagreeing with one another. You are not suggesting, I hope, that we should take these libellous attacks without defending ourselves? It would be outrageous, surely, to allow this mendacious little runt to get away scot-free?

CHARLES: Calm down, Jack dear, please. I don't like it when folk get angry like this.

TED: Yes, less of the abuse, Professor, if you don't mind. Charles is right: you gain nothing by losing your rag. And I don't understand what *you're* getting so het up about, anyway. The others, yes; I might have expected some flak from them. But I've said very little against you.

JACK: Oh, yes? What about that snide reference to my interest in the Haarmann case? And that innuendo regarding young boys? You were right off course there, as you well know. You simply hoped that some of the muck might stick.

TED: Come off it, Jack! I never actually accused you of messing about with small boys, did I? I didn't, did I, Charles? Morgan?

MORGAN: Perhaps not in so many words, Ted. But there was perhaps a hint of possible impropriety.

JACK: Yes, and hints sometimes damage more than outright accusations. Apart from that issue, you were wrong to question my account of the company I used to keep in the early days. There is plenty of evidence, I would have thought, to support my position. For example, you will remember that Dora Carrington showed great interest in what she called my 'low life'.[179] Joe Ackerley noted it, too. He once speculated:

I wonder why S [Siegfried Sassoon] won't have a chap like that

133

to tea, mix with his local labourers like Jack [Sprott] does, who goes to tea with them and they with him. 'They aren't my mental stature', said S. when I hinted as some such cure for loneliness. He isn't really interested in people, I think.[180]

Then there was the time I was burgled. Do you remember that, Morgan? I wrote to you about it at the time:

> At 3.15 I entrained for Notts, being met by Charles in a crisis. The flat had been burgled – a clock and some china images and my rings had been taken. I consulted Alice and Charles and we thought it best not to call in the Police.[181]

And the reason why we didn't want to involve the police, Mr Know-it-all Shread, was that we thought the perpetrator could have been one of the dubious characters I was befriending at the time.

Yes, there is evidence enough of the company I kept. Not that my motives were entirely altruistic, of course; first-hand encounters with the criminal mind were helpful to my understanding as a criminologist. But I was quite fond of some of those men – and I certainly didn't want the police in my flat, poking their long truncheons into my affairs.

TED: Well, here's a turn up for the books. By all accounts, Professor, it must've been a rare thing in those days for any of your lot to turn down a policeman with a long truncheon!

JACK: Oh, very funny, fucky!

MORGAN: And rather tasteless, if you ask me.

JACK: Quite so, Morgan. You're thinking of Bob, of course. Well, this is what I was about to say. It isn't so much for myself that I'm angry. It's for you, Morgan, for the affront to your sensibilities, and for the scandalous way he has attempted to damage your reputation. And for you, Charles. Particularly for you, because for some reason – which I confess I have never been able to understand – you once loved and trusted this Judas. That's why I'm so disappointed that we three seem to be disagreeing, when we should be uniting against this little shit, against this misanthrope who has betrayed us.

MORGAN: Oh, come now, Jack: can't we forget it? What does it all amount to now? It is history. So surely we can be civil with one another? And if not, perhaps we should be silent.

CHARLES: I agree. I can't do with name-calling, and all this bad feeling. It upsets me.

TED: That's right, you two; you tell that stuck-up bogger where he gets off!

MORGAN: No, Ted, please. Let us all try to display a little chivalry. If I may say so, this was always part of the problem with you. Ah, you look a little puzzled. Would you like me to explain? It will call for a certain frankness.

TED: Be my guest. And be as frank as you like. I don't think I can be hurt much more than I was when I first heard what you'd written about me.

MORGAN: Yes, I'm sorry about that. You were correct, of course, in suggesting that my first-hand knowledge of you was such that I had no right to be anything other than tentative in my judgement of your character. Most of what I knew of you came from Jack. I trusted his judgement on this, as I did on most things. I begin to see now that this may not have been wise. On this subject, at least, due to his strong attachment to Charles, Jack was probably incapable of complete impartiality.

Sadly, however, on the several occasions when we did meet, your behaviour tended more often than not to reinforce the prejudices put there by Jack. I could reason that it was not your fault, but I found you rather too vulgar, too brash, too cocky, for my taste. Much of this I could put down to insecurity; you were with someone of another class, after all, and you were trying to make an impression.

Perhaps, like Jack, I was rather jealous of the special place you clearly occupied in Charles' affections; and perhaps as a consequence I was looking too hard for evidence that would justify the privileged position you seemed able to command. I don't know. I tried to make allowances for your deprived background, but really I could find in you very little of what one might call natural nobility – nobility, that is, of the kind that transcends class. Perhaps I expected too much of you. The quality to which I refer is not easy to define; and few men have it in abundance. Charles had a great deal, I thought. But there: it seemed to me that you and he were different in so many ways. He was quiet where you were loud, he was self-effacing where you were immodest, he listened where you talked, and he had a natural reticence where you rushed in. Where angels feared to tread, indeed! I was surprised that you stayed together for so long.

Obviously you must have had qualities that endeared you to Charles – indeed, in retrospect, I see some of them now: tolerance, I suppose; and generosity; high energy; a sense of fun; hard-working – but at the time my prejudice was blinding me to these. I am sorry if I was harsh in my assessment of you, Ted. To be frank, though, you were simply not my cup of tea. I tended to warm to people who were more restful to the spirit – but I recognise that this quality is not within the gift of everyone.

TED: Well, people are what they are. The leopard can't change his spots, can he? But I tried hard to please you, Morgan. And all of Charles' friends, for that matter. Even Jack. That's what got my goat. I couldn't understand it. No matter what I did, I just couldn't win. It's clear enough to me now, though. I was always going to fall short of the high and mighty standards set by you and the Professor here, wasn't I? But there's no point in falling out over it now. It's all water under the bridge, as far as I'm concerned. It was me who wanted to get at the truth, to set the record straight; and I still don't regret bringing these things out into the open. It's a pity we couldn't have done it fifty years ago.

CHARLES: Yes, but it's easy to say that now, isn't it? With hindsight, I mean?

JACK: Yes, and it's easy for any one of us, fucky, to talk about the truth as if there is only one truth, our truth. You are entitled to your narrow little view of things, I grant you; but by the same token, we are entitled to dispute that view.

MORGAN: Granted, Jack; and we will, perhaps – just as soon as you are able to refrain from being abusive . . .

Patrick

... You have now heard from each of my four main characters.
They have spoken, it seems, freely and independently, with no
chronological restrictions. For it has to be admitted that I have
taken liberties with chronology – perhaps with similar excuse to
that once used by Joe Ackerley?:

> The apparently haphazard chronology of this memoir may need
> excuse. The excuse, I fear, is Art. It contains a number of surprises,
> perhaps I may call them shocks, which, as history, came to me rather
> bunched up towards the end of the story. Artistically shocks should
> never be bunched, they need spacing for maximum individual effect.
> To afford them this I could not tell my story straightforwardly and
> have therefore disregarded chronology and adopted the method of
> ploughing to and fro over my father's life and my own, turning up
> a little more sub-soil each time as the plough turned. Looking at
> it with as much detachment as I can command, I think I have not
> seriously confused the narrative.[182]

Of course, it may be that I am simply not good at handling
chronology. If so, I may take some comfort from the fact that I
am in illustrious company. Proust thought it 'a labour in vain'[183]
to attempt to recapture the past in sequential fashion, and Forster
once wrote:

> I can't myself manage chronology. The River of Time must be
> left to historians and Matthew Arnold. Most of us see the past
> as a swamp. Events do not flow past us; they neither go down
> to the mighty ocean nor are they lost in the sand.[184]

But the time has come, I fear, for me to attempt to impose
some order. There is a need to begin to pull a few threads together.
So where to begin? Well, let me take you back to the late
'twenties and early 'thirties, to a time when the strange affair

between Morgan Forster and the lover on loan to him, Charles Lovett, was entering a crucial stage. I refer to the intrusion into their lives of Bob Buckingham and Ted Shread. Buckingham and Shread arrived on the scene at approximately the same time; and after a somewhat unpromising start in each case, strong, loving relationships developed from their respective liaisons. However, as we are about to see, the relationship between Forster and Buckingham did not signal the end of the affair between Forster and Lovett. On and off for several years to come, undeterred by the novelist's obvious love for Buckingham, Forster and Lovett continued to spend time alone together; and the special friendship they had formed was to last to the end of their lives, some thirty years after their physical relationship came to an end.

We have learned how and when Ted Shread entered this story. But what of Bob Buckingham? Well, as far as I have been able to establish, the first mention of Buckingham is to be found in a letter from Joe Ackerley to Morgan Forster, dated 3 October 1929, which concludes:

> Harry [Daley] took me out last night – he thought it would be good for me – to The Seagull! and then, when I was very tired at about 11.30 p.m. and on the way to bed at my flat – I met a friend of his, Bob Buckingham, another P.C. and rashly I asked him in and he stayed till 2 a.m. – just talking – at a distance. I enjoyed having him there.[185]

Inevitably, perhaps – it happened to most men who took Ackerley's interest and fancy – Bob was invited to Joe's annual Boat Race party in the spring of 1930. It was at this party that Forster and Buckingham first met; and, as usual, it was only a matter of days before Forster was confiding in Sprott:

> I have got a new friend – at least it feels like that, though we have only spent one evening together so far. He is Bob Buckingham, from Harry's [Daley] Section House . . . very intelligent and affectionate and we thought well of each other.[186]

Over the next twelve months, a growing friendship slowly developed into an intimate relationship. The following two extracts from his letters to Sprott seem to indicate that during this period Forster's feelings for Buckingham changed from mere physical attraction – and what stood for lust at this time of his life – to an appreciation that something rather more spiritual was happening between them:

> I wrote to Charles at Muskham St. yesterday and mis-spelt it. I asked him if he'd come for part of Easter to me at Brussels – arriving Good Friday evening or any time Saturday ... Bob b [*sic*] is the goods though.[187]

> I'm quite sure that his feeling for me is something he has never had before. It's a spiritual feeling which has extended to my physique – pardon, cher maitre, such nomenclature; I desire to convey that it's something he calls MORGAN he's got hold of, so that my lack of youth and presence, which in other relationships might hinder or depress me, are here no disadvantage, in fact the reverse.[188]

Up to this point – and even beyond, as we will see – Forster was enjoying a warm, sweet relationship with Lovett, albeit saddened by Morgan's realisation that Charles really belonged to Jack Sprott. The strength of the friendship between Forster and Lovett has already been demonstrated by numerous extracts from the Forster–Sprott correspondence, and it is confirmed in many other letters, too:

> Dear Charles, Please give Jack my love and tell him I will write. I am so happy about Sat. but you will have to act the nurse, boy, as I have sprained my ankle and can hardly walk: lucky I managed to get up here for here I shall stick. I will meet you at St Pancras if I can, otherwise come on straight here, please. I am trying to get us tickets for something Sat night – do hope you'll enjoy yourself Charles, but you must expect rather a quiet time – also taxis! ... Have got my mother up here now and wanted to give her a nice change, but she has to go out alone. It's a damned nuisance ... I look forward to seeing you, and also my socks and handkerchiefs, which I had long mourned but I knew not where they were buried. Your affectionate Morgan dear.[189]

> Dear Sebastian, I miss Charles dreadfully: spoilt is what I should be called. Well you know what he is and I needn't go on, so clever, too, at massaging my ankle. We were lucky boys at 'Lucky Girl' and at the Film Society, suddenly laying his head on my shoulder, he observed 'Care to come away, kid?'[190]

> Dear Joe ... The only person I haven't to take trouble over is Charles Lovett, he's a great comfort, and I shall dine with him next Sunday I hope.[191]

> Dear Joe ... Well to run on. Charles Lovett was for the night on Sat. the 25th to G. Sq. [Gordon Square] and if you have time to

take us two seats for an evening performance anywhere I should be grateful . . . He arrives at 4.0 on Sat. and leaves by the 9.25 PM Sunday.[192]

Dear Joe . . . It is possible I might get Charles Lovett to meet me in London Saturday (12th) if we could have your rooms. Would you let me know and then I will tell you definitely. We should both be there for the Sat. night and I for the Sunday.[193]

Dear Joe . . . Are you sure it will be convenient for me and Charles Lovett to be at H [Hammersmith] Terrace on Sat. night? You said it would be, but as he and Sebastian were there last Sat. you may find it too great an interference with your weekends.[194]

Dear Joe, Charles and I are going to the Italian pictures and the pantomime on Sat., and shall not reach our abode until late.[195]

. . . only Joe I'm not romantic, not like you – at least not so any more. I like these flowers, and life would be lovely if a new one sprouted every day, but I've learnt how they wither. Here and there stands something solid and conscious, like Charles, but the rest wither, whether I pick them or not.[196]

Dear Joe . . . Charles has written me the most affectionate letter I have ever had from anyone. I meet him at 4.0 St. Pancras, theatre in evening, probably staining floor Sunday morning. I suppose you couldn't lunch with me in town – he would love it too.[197]

To town and my sweet Charles – Sebastian cooked us supper.[198]

Dear Joe . . . Had a lovely weekend in Notts – Charles just perfection.[199]

Dear Joe . . . What are you doing at Easter? I shall be on the loose, either alone or with Charles Lovett whom I have invited to the flat. He'd like to see you.[200]

Dear Joe . . . Charles comes from Saturday to Tuesday at Easter, so if you would like to see him will you make some suggestion. Sunday and Monday I have tickets for shows, but those are the only engagements.[201]

Dear Sebastian . . . So Les may be in Norfolk on the 17th! Oh, indeed. Very nice, I am sure, and what about me? What, that is to say, of the hopes held out by C., I must say . . . Charles and I had a very nice Easter, and usually a gay one, though there were tiny threads of sadness. I am afraid he must know what bad times are.[202]

These last few extracts reveal that Forster's growing relationship with Buckingham did not deter him from spending Easter 1931 with Charles Lovett. And by so doing, a pattern for the future was set. For example, in the summer of 1931 we read:

Dear Sebastian . . . He (Bob B) and I are getting domestic . . . also, yesterday, a plighting of troths. Can't tell you how happy I am.[203]

followed in the late autumn by:

Dear Sebastian . . . Charles was invited by me to spend the weekend after next at B[runswick] Sq[uare]. Has he answered? No. Will he come? Probably. Let me know his opinions.[204]

This invitation was obviously favourably received:

Dear Sebastian . . . A nice visit from Charles. Bob must — [indecipherable word] blow in at Joe's at tea time – a thing he never does. I don't think it will matter.[205]

Thus it was, by accident, that Lovett and Buckingham came to know of one another. Given his sensitivity to the feelings of others, Forster must have found this situation more embarrassing than he here seems willing to admit. However, three weeks later it must have amused and pleased him to receive, by kinder chance, matching Christmas presents from the two men in his life:

Dear Sebastian . . . The blue tie from Charles goes splendidly . . . [with] a shirt received from Bob.[206]

There are a number of reasons, I suggest, why Forster was tempted to continue his relationship with Charles Lovett after he met Bob Buckingham. First, he was very fond of Charles, whose gentle, easy-going nature he probably found soothing and relaxing. This would have meant a great deal to Forster, because from what one can gather regarding his rather complex sexuality, he needed to feel at ease and in control of the situation in order to achieve a satisfactory sexual climax.

Secondly, despite the fact that Charles belonged to Jack Sprott – and indeed that he had now taken up, it seemed, with Ted Shread – he was readily, almost instantly, available. Forster had only to lift his pen to procure, through Sprott, a familiar, friendly, accommodating partner for a weekend of whatever he had in mind. It was as easy as that. No mess, no fuss, no complications. A request was made, the parcel was delivered and its contents enjoyed; then the parcel was rewrapped and returned to sender. Furthermore, it was easy to keep the Nottingham and Hammersmith connections apart – most of the time, at least! – and he could rely totally on Sprott-the-provider's discretion. It was an ideal set up.

A third reason relates to the complicated nature of Forster's relationship with Buckingham. Unlike Lovett, who was a declared homosexual ('I'm not one of them', he would occasionally tease, 'but I love what they do!')[207] Buckingham was apparently a heterosexual who just happened to be 'between girlfriends' when Forster first met him. Indeed, it was not long after this meeting that Buckingham found another girlfriend, a nurse named May Hockey. Thus it was that Forster, right from the outset, found himself involved in yet another of those emotional triangles which had dogged him for most of his life.

Not surprisingly, Forster found it very difficult initially to accept the woman in Buckingham's life. And quite early in the relationship, true to form, he discussed the problem with his trusted confidant:

> What think you of Maisie her letter as apart from her handwriting? Like you, I am not much worried over the thing except by its being there, which one resents, and it is annoying to think that I have enhanced him in her eyes. Such a thing to get to know a writer! On the other hand this sort of thing is inevitable for him, and I got to know him just when, and only because, he had broken off an engagement [with previous girlfriend]. So the class of events one calls Fate have worked more for me than against . . . He must be made to see that there can't be a menage à trois, which I think is his dream, and, for the moment, possibly hers too; but he should easily see this when told.[208]

On this occasion, he sounded hopeful and philosophical – but in a letter written the following day his mood was quite different:

> I wish there wasn't this horrid nurse – I assume she's horrid . . . At present she is longing to meet me, but one knows what that means and how it ends.[209]

However, when the encounter eventually took place, Forster was forced to admit that May was probably 'a good sort'. According to Furbank, he even went as far as to concede that she was nice-looking! 'But oh the voice!' he is reported to have said to Sprott. 'Oh the proprietary screams at Bob!'[210]

One of Forster's early letters to Buckingham nicely reflected the position in which he now found himself. If he wanted to cultivate Bob's friendship, he had to address himself courteously to a matched pair:

> I am writing to send you both my very best wishes for your happiness. I shall be seeing you on the 31st.[211]

The date referred to here is 31 August 1932. This was the day Bob Buckingham married May Hockey. It must have been almost as symbolic for Forster as it was for the Buckinghams. May was now legally joined to Bob, who in turn was joined to Morgan – leaving Morgan with the daunting prospect of having to reach out to touch May's side of the triangle. His task was not made any easier by the fact that after the wedding he was unable – somewhat understandably! – to command as much of Bob's time and attention as he would have liked:

> I can hardly ever see him ... it is as I feared, only worse – the woman is domineering sly and knowing and at present she seems to have got him down ... and even if Bob gets the woman under control when his seed comes out of her next year – shall I be in a state to profit?[212]

The baby that May Buckingham had on 21 April 1933 presented a further complication to a relationship which must have appeared to be developing rapidly along bizarre lines – even for someone like Forster, with his knack of straying into sticky, tangled webs. First it had been a matter of take *me*. Then, take *me and my wife*. And now it was *take me, take my wife and child*! No, this was nothing like any of the relationships that had gone before. Forster hadn't simply found himself a new man: he had found himself a family. Small wonder, then, that from time to time he sought to escape to a situation which was less complicated, less demanding, less committing and – almost certainly – more satisfying physically and sexually. He certainly permitted himself such an escape two months before Bob's baby was born:

> I must catch the post with this and, if possible, with one to Charles, too – I am telling him to consult you as to our meeting ... As for dear Charles, I don't know whether he comes for a night or not. I am just telling him I must have a nice time alone with him.[213]

Indeed, as the following extracts testify, over the next eighteen months Forster continued to correspond with, convey messages to and (on one occasion, at least) meet Charles Lovett. Except for the last snippet, which comes from his diary, the extracts are taken from his letters to Sprott:

> Tea with Leo, Christopher Isherwood, et al ... Have had a line of thanks from Charles to which I will reply.[214]

> Such a nice visit from Charles, and I found it easy to talk about Ted and I think I may have done some good ... Charles and I agree with advanced unctiousness that it is a most inconvenient time for you to lend the car, but that cannot be helped.[215]

> ... my love to Charles as soon as you see him. Piles bleeding less.[216]

> Did you know that I sent Charles my photo and that he has thrown me into a faint rage by getting Miss J[ephson] to thank me for it, instead of not thanking for it at all or sending a message by you.[217]

> I had a lot of news, but except that Charles has written me a nice letter, it has run out of my head.[218]

> Dearest Jack – Only that I have asked Charles to stop for the weekend June 2–3rd. Do make him come over.[219]

> I have written to Charles and asked him for the 9th instead. You might kindly see I get a reply as soon as may be.[220]

> I am going to the flat tomorrow with my mother, who has to go to the dentist, and I shall remain there until Charles arrives. If he wants anything special Saturday, he or you should send me a line at once. If I don't hear, I shall get tickets for the Comédie Française performance of 'Le Cid' as I know Charles enjoys being abroad.[221]

> My next care is to see what money I've got. I wish I had a lot in order to help Charles, but some investments have stopped paying and I have sold out of others. I do not have anything to spare for my own comforts this winter, esp. if I go to France ... Love to Charles to whom I have written.[222]

> Thanks for your letter ... and I have had one from Charles too. I mean a letter.[223]

> I have had some nice letters from Charles.[224]

Charles Lovett was not the only person, either, that Forster was seeing outside his relationship with Bob Buckingham. A chap needed a bit of fun, after all. Variety was the spice of life! So yes, Forster did indeed go to France in that late autumn of 1934, ostensibly and mainly to see his good friends, Charles and Marie Mauron. But he had been corresponding sporadically with his old sailor friend, Achille, who, for some time, had been pressing him for a reunion. Since Achille lived in a town which was conveniently *en route* to the Maurons, it was hardly surprising that Forster found the invitation irresistible! An undated entry in his diary for 1934 records his unabashed fall from grace:

> Spent two happy nights with Achille at Forbach, and a week in the south with Charles and Marie.[225]

The episode – which was not without humour, drama and a strong whiff of farce – is recorded with some relish by Furbank in his biography of Forster:

> To explain Forster's presence to his friends, Achille passed him off as an uncle in the clothes trade, long domiciled in England – in a small way of business, Achille added, to account for Forster's dowdy appearance. Achille relished the drama of the occasion. He put Forster up in a hotel but made rules, such as that they must never leave the hotel together, or look out of the window, since the restaurant opposite was kept by a cousin. Forster, enjoying himself, reflected that nothing like this had happened to him in his youth.[226]

There seems to be little doubt that Forster needed such light relief from time to time: the escapade with Achille was probably not the first during the Buckingham era, and it was certainly not the last. He needed, too, as we have seen, someone like Charles Lovett in whose company he could feel at ease, and with whom he could achieve sexual satisfaction. Sex for Forster, as he once revealed to Furbank, was 'a kind of private magic'; and although it did not necessarily require the physical presence of another person, it was all the more magical when it could be conjured up in partnership with a loving, reciprocating friend. In Charles Lovett he found someone who was gentle, unvexatious to the spirit, accustomed to physical intimacy, and sexually accommodating. All these, without being sexually demanding. This is an important point to make. Lovett did not go to Forster 'hungry' for sex; he had frequent and ample outlets through his relationships with Sprott and Shread. He went, almost always at Forster's request, to provide satisfaction, to be whatever his illustrious friend wanted him to be – companion, cook, lover, sounding-board, masseur, handyman – so that he was unlikely to be unduly put out if Forster found it enchanting, at one extreme, just having him near. Equally, if Forster wanted them to make magic together, whatever the degree of intimacy, there is little doubt that Charles would have been ever willing to oblige.

Forster may have needed diversions – sexual ones, particularly – but he was not unhappy with the developing relationship with Bob Buckingham. On the contrary, he was fast discovering that there were new satisfactions to be gained from the strange triangle of which he was now a part. For example, almost in spite of himself initially, he began to warm to May Buckingham. She had aspirations to better herself and her husband, and was flattered to be playing hostess to such a famous literary figure. Forster began to appreciate that she was making remarkably few difficulties for him regarding his demands on Bob's time and affections. Was his luck about to change, he perhaps wondered? Was the 'wonderful chariot' (that marvellous phrase) 'ready to move'[227] for him at last? He must have felt hopeful, for he ended the year feeling pleased with life, as the following entry in his Commonplace Book testified:

> Happiness. I have been happy for two years. It mayn't be over yet, but I want to write it down before it gets spoiled by pain – which is the chief thing pain can do in the inside life: spoil the lovely things that had got in there first. Happiness can come in one's natural growth and not queerly, as religious people think. From 51 to 53 I have been happy, and would like to remind others that their turn can come too. It is the only message worth giving.[228]

The year that followed certainly gave the chariot a little nudge and added another dimension to his relationship with the Buckinghams. Forster was not looking forward to the birth of May and Bob's baby. It would surely mark a further consummation and cementation of the marriage, not to mention an increase in Bob's domestic responsibilities: in short, it would present a threat to his own relationship with the husband. However, when the event actually took place he seemed mightily pleased. The day after the birth he asked Bob Buckingham, Joe Ackerley and Christopher Isherwood to his Brunswick Square flat to 'wet the baby's head' with champagne,[229] and he was delighted to hear that the Buckinghams intended tactfully to name the boy 'Robert Morgan', and that he was invited to be godfather. He had always wanted a son, he said. Two days later he described the baby's arrival, selecting typically colourful language for Sprott's benefit:

> Bob's baby's head appeared through May's what d'ye call it, and following it, a prick. Bob called in the afternoon and we went down to see the object, which was the colour of a raspberry and not unfavourable.[230]

The Celestial Omnibus

MORGAN: ... Welcome aboard once again, Ted. We are gathered, and ready, I think, to conduct ourselves with dignity this time. Is that correct, Jack?

JACK: Yes, indeed, for my part. Or at least, as long as Mr Shread promises to behave unprovocatively.

TED: I do. There are more important things on my mind than crossing swords with you, Jack. I've just come from the hospital, and – well, let's just say that I don't think you'll have to go to the trouble of stopping the Omnibus for me much longer.

CHARLES: Oh, Ted dear, you don't mean ...

TED: Yes, I do. But please don't upset yourself. It's got to be faced, like everything else in life. That's what Death is really, isn't it? A part of life. The final part. It's cancer of the lung, you see. And they can't operate. I'm too far gone. So there it is. It won't be too long, I reckon, before I join you three for good. Oh, Charles, if only this meant that you and me could be together again, I would welcome it. But there, I know there's no hope of that. That sort of thing only happens in books, doesn't it, Patrick? No, you only get one chance, I reckon. I think I've gathered that. That's why I'm grateful to this book, and to Patrick – for asking me to go over my life again, I mean. It's been a bit like living it twice over! And I'm glad Patrick seems to be getting a move on, too. I got a bit impatient at first. Almost as if I knew. I do hope I'll see the book finished before I go. Before I swap this cheap day-return for a one-way ticket!

CHARLES: Oh, Ted, I am so sorry. And there were we, a short time ago, having a go at you like that!

JACK: Yes, perhaps if we had known ...

TED: Hey, come on! I hate hypocrites. And there's no sense in anybody floating around looking mopy. There's work to be done, I presume – else, why are we summoned? Let's get on with it, shall we?

MORGAN: Yes, you're right, Ted. I, too, am saddened by your news; but if it's any consolation I should confess that I personally have found oblivion quite agreeable. Not that I haven't found our little diversions here enjoyable. Mercifully, the remembrances have been sweet, for the most part. And where they have been unpleasant I have found myself coping tolerably well, comforted by the knowledge that my torments were to be short-lived. For I know that all pain will cease when the curtain is finally lowered on this pageant. We could all be summoned again, of course. There's something to look forward to, everyone: another attempt to harm us with light and a song!

JACK: Really, Morgan dear, you are the Devil's own! Don't even think of it.

CHARLES: No. It's been nice in some ways. But too sad. Happy-sad, usually – though all that bitterness and bad feeling, that's been awful! I thought that might have been forgotten by now, but it's obviously going to take an eternity.

MORGAN: A sombre warning, indeed, against careless and uncaring relationships – which is why I hope that this gathering will be more constructive than the last, attempting to get at the truth rather than at Ted.

CHARLES: Here, here! Agreed, Jack?

JACK: Yes, we should always seek the truth – even though, as Oscar Wilde declared, it is 'rarely pure and never simple' – and unless I am mistaken, Morgan, you have a questing look about you at this moment. Is there a subject you would like us to pursue?

MORGAN: Yes, I do have something in mind, prompted by Patrick's account of the birth of Robin. In a sense, it returns us to an earlier topic: namely, the question raised by Ted about the place of young boys in the sexuality of homosexuals. I presume that the reader would expect me to confirm or refute any reference to myself in this context. Indeed, I wanted to come in the last time we were gathered, but we seemed to get ourselves side-tracked by the reference to that grisly Haarmann case. Also, tempers were out of control. The moment simply wasn't right.

JACK: I can only apologise again. Please proceed.

MORGAN: Thank you. First, may I say how pleased I was to hear Ted make that point about our kind being unable to have sons of our own. For some of us, this was a source of considerable regret. Thus, despite his sometimes foolhardy indiscretions, one always felt some sympathy for Ben Britten. He would genuinely have loved a son of his own, I'm sure. It was common knowledge.

He always had boys around the place; one or two of them were mentioned in his letters to me. For example, I remember a reference to a boy named Roger Duncan, whom Ben 'shared' for a while with the full permission of the father, Ronald Duncan, the librettist. In that letter, I recall, Ben was complaining that Roger, whose innocence had so delighted in earlier years, had been transformed at Harrow from a 'lively, intelligent and tender little boy' into a youth now possessed of an unbecoming 'glossiness'.[231] I felt at the time that Ben sounded just like a father expressing a natural concern for his child; in effect, he was regretting the loss of innocence. It was the view of most of those who knew him, in fact, that with many of his boys Ben was simply seeking a substitute for the son he could never have. He once said as much, I believe, when writing of John Newton, the singer who took the part of the boy in *Curlew River*:

> He is a sweet affectionate child – makes me feel rather what one has missed in not having a child . . . Johnny is a little bit of a substitute, and I'm really lucky.[232]

In your case, Ted and Charles, this need for a substitute may not have been as strong as Ben Britten's. But I would have thought that it partially explains your attempt at surrogate parenthood – which incidentally was more laudable, I am sure, than you were willing to admit, Ted – and also, perhaps, your befriending of the hapless youth who embroiled you and Jack with the police. The need was not as urgent in my case either, but it probably explains the strong feelings I developed for my godson, Robin.

JACK: My apologies, Morgan. I am not smiling because I doubt the truth of all this. It's simply that I have just remembered a little ditty that Lytton Strachey used to recite. I was reminded of it during Ted's piece – when he said that he and Charles, though more than happy to foster Patrick's brother, Brian, would not have considered a little girl – and I have been trying to bring the words to mind ever since. Now, suddenly, they've come to me. It's just a bit of nonsense really, but I thought you might find it amusing:

When I'm winding up the toy
Of a pretty little boy,
– Thank you, I can manage pretty well;
But how to set about
To make a pussy pout
– *That* is more than I can tell.[233]

MORGAN: Oh, lovely, Jack dear! But to return to the topic, I can't confess that I ever experienced powerful emotions about boys. Mostly I liked them, I think. Their appeal had something to do with innocence, and with the excitement to be derived from speculation about their potential. Each one, nature and nurture permitting, was a possible influence for good in the world. But if I liked them at all, it was always in the singular, never in the plural. Groups of boys can be most unrestful, not to mention disruptive; they bring out the worst in one another. What say you, Jack, from your encounters as a teacher?

JACK: From my limited experience, I agree. But I am no expert, you know. As a teacher of the young I was a dismal failure, I fear. Not surprising, really. My motives were suspect, for one thing. I had no sense of vocation. I was simply looking for something to occupy me, and provide me with a living, between leaving the army and going up to Cambridge. Something not too exacting, which wouldn't soil my hands and break my back; and something that would keep me vaguely in touch with Academe. Teaching, I thought, would be an easy option. Of course, I don't deny that the thought of working in an all-male environment was not without its attractions.

TED: A-haa!

JACK: The reality, I can assure you, was more appalling than appealing. It was ghastly. Schools at that time were much as Evelyn Waugh described them in his novel *Decline and Fall*. The boys weren't so bad – on their own, that is: Morgan is right – and one or two of the masters were quite fetching. But therein lay the main problem: there were so many opportunities, so many temptations. Yet the consequences of yielding to temptation were too dire to contemplate. The frustration became unbearable. It drove one to the very edge, to the point where discretion was threatened. To be frank, this was the main reason why I left my first post.

CHARLES: I guessed as much.

JACK: What did you guess, Charles dear? To a degree, all of

us are tempted by the fresh-faced innocence of youth. But don't jump to false conclusions. I left that school to avoid scandal, not as a result of it. Enough of me, however. Please continue, Morgan?

MORGAN: Well, as I say, I can't claim that my emotions were stirred strongly by pretty boys. Or if boys occasionally had that effect on me, it usually came from my imagination. I could control the situation then, you see. I found boys in the flesh too challenging, I think. Not perhaps in the way that you did, Jack dear. It wasn't the fear of yielding to temptation so much as the fear of betraying their trust. Or, put another way, it wasn't a fear for myself – for what might happen to me as a consequence – but more a fear for them: a fear for lost childhood, for lost innocence, if you like.

This was why, perhaps, I was so fascinated by George Crabbe's poem 'Peter Grimes', the one upon which Ben Britten based his opera. Here was a story in which homosexual, paedophilic urges – which in themselves, without the element of sadism, might have been harmless enough perhaps – went tragically wrong. To be honest, yes I think I was attracted by the idea of a relationship between a man and a succession of young boys – only to be shocked and sickened by the degenerate conduct of Peter Grimes. I think I experienced similar feelings of attraction and repulsion when I read James Hanley's *Boy* – Jack will remember the book: it was declared obscene in 1934 – and again when I worked on the libretto of Ben Britten's *Billy Budd*, another tale of sadism on the high seas, though not explicitly pursuing a homosexual theme, based on Herman Melville's novella. And I am left wondering, dear Jack, whether or not there was something of this conflict in your fascination for the Haarmann case?

TED: Ah, now we're getting down to it!

MORGAN: No, Ted, I am not suggesting anything improper.

JACK: Thank you, Morgan. I am sorry to disappoint the prurient appetite of Mr Shread – or, indeed, that of Patrick, claim though he might to be acting on behalf of the reader! – but I repeat that my interest in Haarmann was academic. Having said that, it is true that I experienced feelings similar to those stirred in you by the character of Peter Grimes. The procurement of boys for the purpose of sexual practices was never my ticket – to borrow a phrase from you, Morgan[234] – but it was fascinating to read of it on such a large scale. So yes, the case did have an element that was quite titillating in a way; but one felt ashamed of such thoughts as more and more evidence of Haarmann's grossly deviant behaviour came to light. At the time, of course, I was far from alone in my fascination with the case. The gruesome facts which emerged during the trial made compelling reading in clubs and drawing-rooms across western Europe. The general public's craving for gore and sensation was apparently insatiable. 'Tis ever thus, I suppose. We're all guilty of this, though few of us are made to feel guilt in this context. Perhaps this is because the situation becomes unreal for us. When a human being malfunctions so dramatically, so extravagantly, so outrageously, as Haarmann did, pushing the boundaries of behaviour well beyond the comprehension of ordinary people, a feeling of unreality is created. And once we feel that we have lost touch with reality, our own behaviour – no matter how morbid, or lascivious, or voyeuristic – becomes acceptable.

CHARLES: Crikey, Ted, it makes you feel thankful, doesn't it, listening to what can happen when things go wrong with relationships, that we never allowed our feelings for boys – particularly for Brian and Patrick – to lead us into temptation?

JACK: Oh, very biblically put, Charles. But it couldn't have happened to you. With someone like Haarmann one was staring in disbelief at a spectacularly deranged mind. And Grimes, too, I think Morgan would agree – though much less evil, and his decline much more comprehensible – was a man with a disturbed mind and a tortured soul. With all your faults, Charles dear, I don't think you could be mentioned in the same breath.

MORGAN: Jack's right, Charles: despite our little peccadilloes, we were almost virtuous by comparison. Listening to this, I can't help thinking how innocent after all – though in part it may have been sexually derived – was the simple pleasure I obtained from that afternoon with Patrick in the National Gallery. And how harmless it was, some time later, to have a photograph of him to remind me of our innocent connection.

I have been thinking, too, that although I was never obsessional about boys, nevertheless if they were more than usually on my mind around this time it would hardly have been surprising. They had been kept well to the fore of my consciousness in a number of ways. By the *Peter Grimes* theme, certainly – Ben Britten's first production came just after the war – and also by my artistic collaboration and friendship with Ben, which was to culminate in *Billy Budd*. I remember, for example, going out in a boat with Ben and one of his boys – 'Nipper' he was called, though that wasn't his real name – together with a fisherman named Billy Burrell, the boat's owner.[235] A photograph was taken, I recall; it appeared later in *Picture Post*. The outing showed me how good Ben was with young boys – in Nipper's presence he seemed to become a boy himself almost – and it gave me something of an insight into how much enjoyment and satisfaction might be gained from their company. This could explain the mysterious 'emotional kick' reference (though I still can't remember writing that about Patrick's brother: the context seems to have been lost in the mists of time) and indeed it might explain how I came to encourage Charles to bring his nephews to stay in my flat in the first place. It is not easy always to explain one's behaviour – particularly fifty years later, with half that time spent *post mortem*! – but, as with one or two topics discussed aboard the Celestial Omnibus, we are at liberty to offer reasonable speculation . . .

Patrick

... As godfather to baby Robin, Forster had almost become one of the Buckingham family; and with May preoccupied with her son, and her movements restricted by motherhood, he was pleasantly surprised to find that he was able to see more, rather than less, of Bob. He took advantage of the situation to organise a holiday with Bob in the West Country, and for this purpose he requested the use of Sprott's car:

> ... to roll about in for a rather indefinite period ... we should arrive on the 16th or 17th. If we arrive latish ... we should very much like to stop the night with you – Charles gave me your very kind message on that point. If it is a morning arrival I think we should go straight off, hoping to make Shrewsbury.[236]

After the holiday he wrote:

> Dear Jack ... The car has gone marvellously. I fear it will return none the better, but I think none the worse. You really have provided a grand opportunity and holiday.[237]

> Dear Isherwood ... The bother of talking and of moving increases as I get older, so I would rather talk English [Isherwood had been to Greece] to Bob even though my mother does think his voice common, and be driven round the western counties by him in a car, advancing to be sure into Wales, but retreating from it on the grounds that it was un-homey, and that the Welsh did not wash. We were away for a fortnight.[238]

Clearly, Forster had regarded the holiday as a 'grand opportunity' to have Buckingham to himself for a while. Beforehand, he had told Sprott:

> I have been 'watching' him over this holiday, but he advances

blandly towards it, apparently not thinking it will be too long with me or wanting to be with his wife.[239]

Despite the attraction of this enjoyable jaunt, Forster obviously treasured far more those moments of intimacy that he and Buckingham were able to snatch from time to time at home:

> My ever dear Bob ... Yes – there will be our holiday, I know, but the happiest hours of my life will always be the short hours we can spend together in the flat ... Talking to you alone every now and then about the little things that happen to me – that's what I like.[240]

In this touching letter we gain an insight into the innocent pleasure that Forster derived from his meetings with Buckingham – and a clue, perhaps, to the need for periodic diversions that would satisfy the carnal side of the writer's nature? He ended the letter in nostalgic and sentimental mood, displaying not only a fine sense of history, but also the extent to which he now felt part of the Buckingham family:

> I walked on Clapham Common instead and found the house where I used to stop with my great aunt [Marianne Thornton] when I was a little boy. She was born in 1798! It seems incredible. Here is your baby, who is in a little way mine, because he bears my name, and he is born in 1933: one hundred and thirty five years later, and I have lived to see them both.[241]

Sprott, as we have seen, supported Forster's holiday enterprise. He appeared pleased to see that Forster was prepared to scheme for a share of Buckingham's time and affections. In a letter which offers further insight into the frustrations of triangular relationships, he offered the following somewhat subversive advice:

> He must not become the slave of his wife ... he must live his own life – all that sort of thing. I believe that the lower orders couch their tendencies in the form of principle, and that the principle gains a certain force of its own, like a habit. I am sure all that works with her. What you have to do is fight against anything that savours of fidelity to his wife. It can't crop up in such old-fashioned dress as 'FIDELITY' – nous avons change – but there's a nice line in fancy dress at its disposal. 'It wouldn't be fair ...' 'If one builds a home, it's only right that one should stop in it.' 'She is so miserable when I am away.' And so on. Well

then, you have a nice line in counter-arguments, and among them
FREEDOM, which is much thought of by any who want to appear
modern.[242]

As things turned out, Buckingham was soon to have more
freedom than Forster could have wished for. It arose from
adversity. Early in 1935, May Buckingham took ill and tubercu-
losis was diagnosed. For several months she was hospitalised in a
sanatorium, leaving young Robin in the care of one of her sisters
– and Buckingham senior with time and opportunity to be with
Forster. Fate's beneficence did not end there, however. May was
concerned for the welfare of her husband, and she made Forster
promise to keep an eye on Bob in her absence. Needless to say,
Forster did not find this a difficult promise to keep!

By all accounts, though, this turn of events brought Forster
not only closer to the husband, but also closer to the wife, to
whom he wrote many letters. True to Forster's promise, this
correspondence included regular reports on Bob's welfare; in
addition, May Buckingham was offered advice on what she
might read in order to further her literary education. For example,
Forster suggested:

> The other two you will want to read are *Jane Eyre* & *Wuthering
> Heights* which some think one of her greatest novels, though it is
> really more like a poem than a novel.[243]

And less than a fortnight later he was recommending Jane
Austen (*Emma* and *Northanger Abbey*), George Eliot (*The Mill on
the Floss*) and Tolstoy (*Anna Karenina* – 'not as good as *War and
Peace* but of manageable length' – and *The Death of Ivan Ilych*).[244]

Interestingly, Forster was to confirm his respect for two of these
writers in a memorable broadcast for the BBC's Home Service in
1949 entitled 'In My Library'. Talking about his love of books –
always to be treasured for 'the words, the wine of life' ('an uncut
book is about as enspiriting as a corked-up bottle of wine') – he
revealed that, together with Shakespeare and Gibbon, Jane Austen
was his favourite author. He would have these three on his shelves
in every room, he declared – 'so that I can stretch out my hand
for them at any moment'. Of course, he would also have some
Tolstoy. 'But one scarcely wants Tolstoy in every room. A short
walk to Tolstoy seems preferable. He is too prone to overwhelm
one at close quarters, is Tolstoy.'

May Buckingham was indeed privileged to have her tutelage in the hands of such a discerning reader – though whether, in her convalescent state, she was able to cope with a diet so rich in cultural fibre is another matter. One wonders, too, how punctilious she was in returning the books on loan to her. It is curious how many people, otherwise quite irreproachable, are careless or unscrupulous over books. Forster himself took no high-minded stance on the subject. In fact, he had a charming confession to make to his Home Service listeners:

> 'Do you ever lend books?' someone may say in a public-spirited tone of voice at this point. Yes, I do – and they are not returned; and still I lend books. Do I ever borrow books? I do – and I see some of them unreturned around me. I favour reciprocal dishonesty.[245]

In addition to his interest in her education, Forster became genuinely concerned for May Buckingham's physical welfare, as the following ingenuous advice to Bob reveals:

> You'll be careful over the intercourse won't you, unless of course you both wish to have another child, but I should think it would be bad for her health.[246]

Also, very significantly, he began to confide in her, sharing confidences about close friends in a way he was never wont to do unless he felt he could really trust someone:

> Jack Sprott arrives tomorrow – for six weeks! (that is to say he will be here when I don't want it [the flat] for any other purpose.) He is doing a special course on Vocational Training at some Institute of Psychology. He is awfully good at his work, but doesn't get recognition because he doesn't or can't produce a book on it. I hope this specialised study will get him some recognition in Nottingham – Robert & I think he must jolly well lend us his car when we want it, since I've lent the flat . . . Joe is off on holiday to Malta.[247]

Sprott, incidentally, had changed his address that summer, moving from his flat on Clumber Street to the house on Portland Road which he retained for the rest of his life:

> Dear Jack . . . I had hoped to see you at *the* dinner, but saw Guy Burgess instead . . . I am glad you moved. Although

I have spent so many happy times in Clumber St., I can't by any stretch of my nerve regret it. I look forward to coming to see you.[248]

But to return to May Buckingham. She had from the beginning desired Forster's friendship; and she now began to respond 'with great good will', as Furbank puts it,[249] placing fewer and fewer difficulties in the way of Morgan and Bob's relationship. The more reasonably she behaved, of course, the greater grew Forster's respect for her. In fact, respect for the couple, and a regard for their child, developed quickly to a point at which Forster would do anything rather than jeopardise the mutual love and trust which had been built up. More about this later.

There has been much speculation about the precise nature of Morgan Forster's sexual relationship with Bob Buckingham. As late as the 'sixties, Buckingham himself added to the obfuscation by protesting that he was even unaware of Forster's homosexuality, let alone willing to admit that they were lovers in the physical sense. Now, what are we to make of this? It is surely highly improbable, if not impossible, that a worldly-wise policeman, possessed of at least average intelligence, could fail to recognise the sexual proclivities of such a close friend – especially when that friend consorted with so many self-confessed homosexuals? No, this is a blatant challenge to our credulity – explainable, perhaps, as a knee-jerk response to an understandable reluctance on Buckingham's part to make public the bisexual element of his own make-up.

However, the notion of a chaste relationship between the two men may perhaps be less difficult to accept, though it is not a view shared by Nicola Beauman. Writing in her biography of Forster, she claims:

> That Morgan and Bob were definitely lovers is clear from the intimacy of their letters, from their loving pose in photographs, and from other details such as Morgan reassuring Bob that he did not have venereal disease.[250]

Beauman may be right, though it seems to me that her evidence is far from conclusive. Regarding her first point, she concedes that Forster's letters to Buckingham were usually 'relatively circumspect in case May read them'. In fact, their contents were usually inclined more towards the trivial than the intimate. On her second point, Forster and Buckingham do indeed sometimes appear to adopt loving poses when photographed together; but this you would expect, for their love for one another – particularly Forster's for Buckingham – is not in question. Whether that love found frequent physical expression is quite another matter. Thirdly, the reference to venereal disease cannot be counted as reliable evidence to support the case. If the inference here is that Buckingham was worried that he may have acquired a sexually transmited disease from Forster, it should be remembered that Buckingham was bisexual and therefore may well have had opportunist affairs, male and female, outside his marriage and his relationship with Forster. Indeed, Beauman recounts one such affair – involving a 'girl' named Muriel – describing how Morgan consoled May and then had a 'breakdown of grief' himself.[251]

My own view of the sexual relationship between Forster and Buckingham occupies the middle ground. That it was a completely chaste affair is unlikely, I feel. There was physical contact between the two men, I am sure. But to me it seems likely that it was largely confined to kissing and touching. Forster was middle-aged when he met Buckingham, and by his own admission his sexual power was very much in decline. By this time in his life, his was 'an elderly man's love'.[252] By contrast, Buckingham was young, lusty and athletic. I cannot believe in their physical compatibility; not enough certainly to support the notion of sustained love-making over a period of many years. It is more likely, I think, that Buckingham may have preferred to keep their physical relationship at the level I have suggested, and that Forster, too – perhaps uncertain of his own powers – may have been content with this arrangement. Forster would certainly have been sensitive to Buckingham's feelings, and to his position as a married man; and to avoid any possibility of jeopardising a precious friendship, he was quite capable of sublimating his own sexual impulses. At times this may not have been easy for him, but he was hardly unpractised in the art. He was able, as we know, to channel some of his urges into the imagination, chiefly into fantasy, while others could be satisfied through physical relationships elsewhere, mainly with Charles Lovett. In this respect, in the early days, Charles Lovett may be seen to have provided a valuable service. If Forster's long-standing liaison with Buckingham was the most important friendship of his life – and, on balance, in a long life dedicated to the cultivation of friendships, it probably was – it surely owed much to other relationships, like the ones with Lovett, Sprott and Ackerley, which offered outlets of a different kind denied him in the rather conventional, bourgeois world created by his adopted family.

So it was, then, that at a time when Forster was particularly close to the Buckinghams, he continued to make contact with Charles Lovett:

> Dear Joe . . . Next weekend I hope to be in the flat with Charles Lovett.[253]

> Dear Jack . . . Much love to Charles, so looking forward to seeing him.[254]

> Dear Jack . . . You are the only person I can write to on it . . . Then Charles – did he tell you of my suggestion that he should come for a night in the middle of the week – possibly for two nights? He liked the idea. Do you think it is safe for him – I mean as regards the Labour Exchange? We thought of a Thursday, and if that is kept to I don't think I've got one before Dec. 12th.[255]

Forster, it seems, was here attempting to arrange a meeting with Lovett before he went into hospital on 18 December 1935, for part one of his prostate operation. Regarding this forthcoming surgery, he wrote to Buckingham:

> Dear Bob, Operation at 9.0 A.M. tomorrow . . . This is written in Joe's hole. I go in in about ½ an hour. I feel gay and calm, but have an open mind as to whether I shall get through or not. I don't say this to anyone else, but I love you too much to say anything but the truth. I don't feel afraid of anything and it is your love that has made me be like this. I hope to come back to you and everything and be as before, and I will try my best to do so. If I should go under or come out as an unattractive invalid, it can't be helped. Some things in my case are against me – e.g. the distended bladder may have [been] worrying the kidneys. On the other hand I'm young for the thing and blood pressure is all right.[256]

– and after the operation, during recuperation at West Hackhurst, he wrote to Forrest Reid:

> Thanks for your affectionate letter. My latest news is . . . I have been sent down here to get fit for the second part of the operation – it's not to be for a month at earliest. I feel all right,

but my blood-test is unfavourable ... I miss Bob dreadfully –
he came to see me almost every day in the Nursing Home for a
month and did countless jobs. I do feel very grateful to his wife
for making it easy for him. Joe came constantly too; my mother
& aunt occupied my flat.[257]

Shortly after writing this letter, Forster was making plans
for Buckingham to come to see him at West Hackhurst:

– come booted and spurred for a country walk ... Will you
go to the flat and bring down with you here my moth-eaten
bed jacket which I forgot, also that pair of blue bed socks which
Charles Lovett gave me.[258]

But the visit had to be called off:

My darling Bob, tomorrow is off, and I feel somewhat depressed.[259]

It seems likely that Buckingham's visit was called off because
Forster was summoned to hospital in mid February for the second part of his operation. The operation was successful, but the
wound took a long time to heal and he remained incarcerated in
the nursing home throughout the month of March, with a long
period of convalescence about to follow.

This was not a good time for Forster. His long convalescence,
and its inhibiting effect on his social life – particularly, his relationship with Buckingham – made him very depressed from time
to time. He confided in Buckingham:

I seem to get on all right without you for about a week, but
when it is for longer I start moping.[260]

And to make matters worse, he had hardly left the nursing
home when he was informed, in April 1936, that he was to
be sued for libel over an article which had been reprinted in
Abinger Harvest. He and his publishers, Edward Arnold, suffered
quite heavy damages and costs, not to mention the expense of
withdrawing and reissuing *Abinger Harvest*, minus the offending
article. Discouraged by this, and debilitated by his state of health,
he withdrew from the task of editing the letters of T. E. Lawrence
– a project which had up to this point greatly interested him.[261]

Looking back on those months, he lamented in a letter to
Buckingham:

I have had altogether too much bad luck for a whole year or more, Bob. I don't notice it between times, but it is because of you, dear.[262]

If adversity seemed to be bringing Forster and Buckingham closer together, their intimacy did not deter the writer from arranging to meet Charles Lovett:

Dear Joe . . . Later on this week I may have Charles Lovett to stay, and perhaps with or without him we might meet.[263]

Dear Jack . . . If still available the 18th or 19th will suit me, and it will be nice being with Charles. I have never been to Southwell. Perhaps he will take me there . . . I look forward to coming to Nottingham as a pure man of genius very much, and do hope it can be arranged.[264]

Charles did indeed take Forster to Southwell to see the Jephsons, with his mother, Ada Lovett, and Ted Shread, accompanying. The excursion led to an amusing incident which Shread remembered well. Forster had expressed a desire to see Southwell Minster – a good example of Norman architecture, he was able to assure them from his reading; though the Jephsons, at least, would have been well aware of this – so off they set on the ten minutes' walk from the little cottage in West Thorpe Lane. Forced into pairs by the narrowness of the pavement – Ted at the front, pushing Boyd in his wheelchair, Charles behind, making conversation with his mother, and Dickie Jephson caringly bringing up the rear with the convalescing writer – they must have made a rather strange group. *En route* they met a free-ranging billy goat who, it seems, had shaken off his tether; he was now systematically demolishing a villager's flower border. Fearlessly, Forster stroked the animal and congratulated him on his new-found freedom. Everyone was greatly amused. The party then turned into the Minster, and the incident was soon forgotten as the church began to make its impact on the visitors. Much of the time, heads were uplifted; either that or turned towards Forster, to whom, for the most part, if sometimes out of deference, they looked for information. Then suddenly there was a noise behind them, and Charles Lovett was laughing and pointing towards one of the aisles. It was Forster's friend, the billy goat, who must have followed them into the building. Solemnly, he was now about to make a start on the books of Common Prayer!

During July 1937, as part of his convalescence, Forster took his mother to Dover for a change of scene. They stayed at Joe Ackerley's lodgings:

> How I do like this place. My mouth needs a lot of looking after, so I haven't had a specially good time, but Christopher [Isherwood] is round a corner, and Leo [Charlton] and Tom [Wichelo] next door.[265]

Forster was to sojourn in Dover quite often during the following twelve months. However, despite his fondness for the place, less of his time than might have been imagined was spent there alone with Bob Buckingham. Perhaps he sensed instinctively that Bob's professional and domestic reputation – indeed, his very livelihood – could be jeopardised by the potentially scandalous goings-on within the growing homosexual commune which was now camping (as Leo Charlton almost put it!) 'beneath the lintel of England's continental doorway'.[266] If so, he had no such qualms regarding Charles Lovett, whose several visits – one accompanied by Ted Shread – included 'crawls' from one notorious pub to another:

> I tried to take Charles Lovett there for Whitsun, but he couldn't come, and there won't be time to organise Johnny Fisher. So I shall be alone.[267]

> Towards the end of July I might ask to bring Charles Lovett for a couple of days if you had no other plans, though I could easily entertain him in London instead.[268]

> Dear Jack ... the pubs [in Dover] are the British Queen and the Prince Regent and I think it's called the Invictor ... Hope to get Charles up before the end of the month. Which are his periods. Tues. and Thursday isn't it?[269]

This particular plan obviously came off, for in a letter to Ackerley, dated 18 July 1938, he advised him that he might not reach Dover until the 25th 'when Charles comes'. Later, following the visit, Forster gave Ackerley an interesting description of the few days spent with Lovett, painting a picture of touching domesticity:

> Charles' visit has gone off all right – though he hasn't the physique and the deportment which are at the present moment convenient to me [EMF still convalescing]. We walked to St Margaret's Bay in the morning, glorious weather, bathed, at least he did, in the afternoon,

and he has cooked me a delicious supper of hake, parsley sauce and potatoes. He departs by break of day tomorrow. Bob should arrive Friday.[270]

Yes, it seems that Forster thought nothing of having Charles Lovett one week and Bob Buckingham the next! This is confirmed in an earlier letter to Ackerley:

I want to take Charles Lovett for a couple of nights to Dover between July 18 and July 25th, and think it convenient to do so irrespective of your convenience. We shall not be there at a weekend and should not want the large room. I should also like to bring Bob for Friday 29th to Aug 1st.[271]

Sadly, Dover was soon to become – in Forster's words to Sprott, reported by Furbank – 'a Closed Port'.[272] The behaviour of the Dover coterie – and chiefly that of Joe Ackerley, it seems – had become more and more indiscreet, culminating in an incident which had led to Ackerley being asked by his landladies to vacate his lodgings. Forster rightly thought it prudent that he, too, should leave the scene. He saw the episode as a warning; it made him realise how close he had come to embarrassing Buckingham:

Dearest Christopher . . . I wish it [the novel, *Maurice*] could be published, especially after getting your letter. But it isn't so much my mother now – it's Bob. Everyone connects him with me, and this Dover muddle showed me how careful I must be not to bring bother or harm his way. My 'Life' if briefly and blazingly written, might be worth doing after my death, but that's ruled out too while he lives.[273]

This letter serves to emphasise with some poignancy the point made earlier that Forster was ready to do and sacrifice anything, almost, in order to spare Buckingham's feelings and protect his reputation. To a degree, of course, it was a case of enlightened self-interest: he did not dare to put at risk a special friendship which now embraced May and Robin as well as Bob. Forster had always displayed a strong sense of duty regarding his mother: he was now demonstrating a similarly unswerving loyalty and commitment to his new family, the adopted Buckinghams. There were mutual benefits to be gained, of course. Forster was always generous with those he loved, and his gifts of money to the Buckinghams are well documented.

For their part, then, Bob and May Buckingham hardly needed reminding that it was in their interest to cultivate Forster's friendship. Nevertheless, there is a letter in which Forster – showing unaccustomed worldliness, perhaps? – appeared to encourage the Buckinghams to cherish their relationship with him for material reasons:

> Dear Bob . . . It is 2.0 A.M. and I must really go to bed instead of continuing to write what may be a very interesting letter, and which Robin after the next great war may be able to sell for a considerable sum.[274]

Further extracts from this long letter are worth quoting because they confirm Forster's deep regard for Buckingham, and reveal that in the months leading up to the outbreak of the Second World War the two men were seeing little of one another – or at least, not nearly as much as Forster would have liked:

> If you call living a full life seeing me once a fortnight, I don't. So please look ahead over the next few weeks . . . And in particular fix up when you can come for the night, which you have not done since our walking tour . . .
> . . . An absolutely bloody day, still it keeps me feeling important. Was very pleased to see you win your little piss-pot [a rowing trophy]. That made me feel important too, and in a better way . . .
> . . . It (the war) is to start during the next few weeks (?) – the period which at the beginning of this letter I have bidden you consider. Truly we live in strange times, Bob, and the only thing which is really real in them is love.

They were indeed strange times, bringing humour mixed with depression:

> Germany has attacked Poland. Depressed and weepy, not afraid . . . About 30 nice rough boys [evacuees, obviously] have come from E. Dulwich . . . Not an apple will be left in the village soon.[275]

– and finding Forster in nostalgic mood, reciting a selection from a litany of lovers past and present:

> Dear Joe . . . Fortunately I have no important commitments here,

but I feel at the bottom of a well when I see, ringing the sky, the heads of Johnny, Reg, Charles Lovett, Charlie Day, Harry Digby, George Dowsing, Achille, Mohammed and Bob himself. To those whom I can I am sending money[276] . . .

The Celestial Omnibus

MORGAN: ... Good morning, Ted. It's nice to have you back on board again. We apologise for the early call – the sunrise service is frightfully unsocial, we realise – but your recent experience of hospitals has probably made you all too familiar with disturbances at dawn. How are you, anyway?

TED: I'm fine, thanks. I'm in no pain, at least. They're going to give me some radio-therapy, they tell me – just enough to stop the bleeding, as far as I can gather. Then it's best to leave me alone, they think, and let nature take its course. For me that means taking each day as it comes, and trying to make the most of it. I'm still enjoying my pint, anyway.

CHARLES: You're taking it very well, Ted dear; but then, you always did manage to put a brave face on things.

JACK: One of your nobler characteristics, obviously. It is good that you are taking it so philosophically.

TED: Well, I don't really have too much choice, do I? But how about changing the subject? For example, I'd like to ask a question about that long list of Morgan's lovers.

MORGAN: Oh, spare my blushes, Ted. One's life appearing like a laundry list! And, sadly, by no means a definitive one: there are several items missing, I fear.

JACK: Careful, Morgan dear: we don't want to make Charles weepy again.

CHARLES: Please, don't mind me. I've got over that, now. And I had no right to get upset, anyway. My own list wouldn't be much shorter.

MORGAN: But we would want to say, would we not, Charles dear, that some names in the roll call strike a truer, warmer note in one's heart than others? And rest assured, dear love, you and Bob made the sweetest music for me.

CHARLES: Thank you for that, Morgan – and for everything

you gave me. You opened doors for me, you know, you and Jack. You let light into my life. Don't be jealous, Ted; that was before I met you. You gave me other things. We laughed a lot, Ted, you and I. I think you brought a lot of sunshine with you. Some showers, too, perhaps. But, all in all, I was a very lucky man.

TED: I'm glad you think so, Charles love. But can we turn to that list of Morgan's? It suddenly struck me that there was nobody on it from what you might call his own background. Am I right, Morgan? Weren't they all working-class blokes, your lovers? And if so, isn't that strange? I mean, it's not as if there was any shortage of queens from your own class, is it?

MORGAN: You are quite right, Ted. Your point is well observed, though you might guess that you are by no means the first person to focus on the subject.

JACK: Yes, I suppose it was dear old Oscar Wilde, about a hundred years ago, who did more than anyone to draw attention to the phenomenon. 'Feasting with panthers' was the colourful metaphor he used to describe the practice of seeking sexual gratification with members of the lower orders. I believe he once said that to lie with a member of one's own class was too much like lying with oneself! And some of the ungrateful cats he had lain with were not slow to give evidence against him at his trial. Poor Oscar was but one in a long line of those who have suffered for the cause. In a society that is class-conscious, if not class-dominated, and geared to the comfort and convenience of heterosexuals – it has to be, you might argue, to safeguard the institution of marriage, and to ensure the propagation of the species – our kind have always had to face up to a number of problems. First, we have had to recognise and come to terms with our inverted sexuality; then, again early on, many of us have had to wrestle with guilt, and sometimes shame, regarding onanism.

TED: Ona-whatsit! I'm sorry, Professor: you'll have to explain. What is onanism?

JACK: Masturbation, ducky. Remember Onan in the Old Testament, the son of Judah? No? Well, it is written that Onan's married brother, Er, 'was wicked in the sight of the Lord; and the Lord slew him. And Judah said unto Onan, go in unto thy brother's wife, and marry her, and raise up seed to thy brother. And Onan knew that the seed should not be his' – for, the truth be known, he was not drawn to women! – 'and it came to pass, when he went in unto his brother's wife, that he spilled it on the ground, lest that he should give seed to his brother. And the thing which he did displeased the Lord: wherefore he slew him also'.[277]

MORGAN: Yes, incredible, isn't it? The good Lord you were brought up to worship, Ted, slew Onan because the poor man didn't show a preference for women – because he would not have intercourse with his brother's widow, but instead chose to waste his seed upon the ground!

JACK: Hence, onanism: to waste your seed, to masturbate. So you see, we have been marked men from earliest times. And what a stigma to have to bear: to be wicked in the sight of the Lord! No wonder we have been hounded – in Nazi Germany, for example, we were almost the lowest of the low: along with the Jews we were forced to wear distinguishing marks, in our case a pink triangle – and no wonder that our embarrassed society has created such pressure to find euphemisms to describe our sexual nature, using phrases like 'the third sex', the 'intermediate sex', 'the other love' and 'the love that dare not speak its name'.

MORGAN: Yes, and in addition to being regarded as traitors to our sex – threatening, as Jack has pointed out, important institutions like marriage and family – we of the upper orders, by our practice of consorting with those below us, were seen by some to be traitors to our class. I don't think we were. On the contrary, we worked endlessly and conscientiously at the maintenance of fine friendships with our peers. It was simply that we tended, most of us, to turn to a lower class for physical and sexual relations. Such relationships were of enormous interest to me artistically – in *Maurice*, with Scudder, for example, and in some of my short stories, like *Dr Woolacott* and *Arthur Snatchfold* – and of course in my later fiction I was able to draw on experiences from my own life. And yes, I do remember quite clearly writing, in 1935, that oft-quoted personal memorandum:

> I want to love a strong man of the lower classes, and be loved by him and even hurt by him. That is my ticket, and then I have wanted to write respectable novels.[278]

JACK: Hearing that again, Morgan, I am reminded of the preference – attributed to Duncan Grant, I believe – 'I like a completely uneducated intelligent person as a companion'. This moves us on, perhaps, to make the point that some of our peers were looking for a more permanent relationship. You and I steered clear of homosexual marriage – perhaps because we never found the ideal, or even thought the ideal was possible? – but you came quite close with Bob, even though it meant taking on his family, and Charles and I also enjoyed long-lasting companionship. Joe Ackerley was certainly searching for it – to fulfil a need which was stronger than ours, I venture – and there is an early indication of this to be found in a reference to the theme of his unfinished play *Judcote*:

> A young, upper-middle class, intellectual homosexual (myself of course), lonely, frustrated, and sick of his family, especially the women, his feckless chatterbox of a mother, his vain, quarrelsome and extravagant sister, and the general emptiness and futility of their richly upholstered life, becomes emotionally involved with a handsome young workman . . . Jude falls in love with him and, after various other happenings which I never got right, runs away with him into working-class life and they live happily together as mates ever after.[279]

CHARLES: I'm finding this very interesting – and who am I to complain! – but why did you and your lot want to go 'feasting with panthers', as you put it? I mean, by and large, we working-class chaps seemed to be quite happy with lovers of our own class, so why weren't you?

TED: Yes, where's the difference? Why doesn't it work both ways?

MORGAN: Ah, explanations! It is invariably easier to state the *what* than the *why*.

JACK: Quite so, Morgan. But we might try. For one explanation, we could turn to Christopher Isherwood. Remember what he said of himself in his autobiography:

> Other experiences followed, all of them enjoyable but none entirely satisfying. This was because Christopher was suffering from an inhibition, then not unusual among upper-class homosexuals; he couldn't relax sexually with a member of his own class or nation. He needed a working-class foreigner.[280]

That was true to a degree in your case, was it not, Morgan? Without the foreign element, I mean?

CHARLES: Yes, but the foreign bit would account for Achille, wouldn't it? And what's-his-name – Mohammed?

MORGAN: Well, Charles, they were working-class foreigners, certainly. But consider: if you are abroad, and seeking a working-class partner, you are more likely than not to land a native, surely? In any case, there was more to it than that. Joe, you may remember, used to advance a very interesting argument: he claimed a need to work out the 'shame' of his condition on somebody who was outside his own class – a need, perhaps, shared in varying degrees by a good many of us, if we are prepared to examine ourselves?

JACK: Yes, though when Joe talked about his 'condition', he meant not only his homosexuality but also his tendency to *ejaculatio praecox*[281] – premature ejaculation, Mr Shread! – which brought a shame of a different kind. It embarrassed him greatly, he once confided, that he would often reach his climax well before his lover could even achieve tumescence. He saw it as a cruel and gross handicap to what was, I am sure, a genuine desire for sensitive, mutually satisfying love-making. This perhaps leads us to another reason why some men dropped a class or two when seeking sexual satisfaction, for you can understand a certain reticence among upper-class equals for displaying any sort of behaviour that contained an element of grossness. The interesting thing about Joe in this context, though, was that he also hoped to avoid the gross and the distasteful in his contact with working-class partners. This was hardly realistic, surely? He himself, you may recall, was very fastidious in his younger days, once confessing amusingly:

> I have never been able to enjoy other people's smells – farts, feet, armpits, semen, unwashed cocks – as I enjoy mine.[282]

Unfortunately, his standards of personal hygiene would have been neither understood nor achievable in respect of some of his pick-ups. He must often have been disappointed – haven't we all! – which perhaps accounts for the emphasis on youth, health and hygiene in the criteria he once listed for his elusive 'Ideal Friend':

> ... he should be physically attractive to me and younger than myself – the younger the better, as closer to innocence; finally he should be on the small side, lusty, circumcised, physically healthy and clean: no phimosis, halitosis, bromidrosis.[283]

TED: Christ, here we go again! I may not understand some of those long words, but I certainly recognise another insult to the working classes when I hear one.

CHARLES: Yes, the uneducated are not always the unwashed. But even if Jack's right – and I suppose he meant that the lack of facilities in those days was against us – then surely in Joe's case that would have been a strong point against taking working-class lovers?

MORGAN: Quite right. We begin to see just how complex this subject might be. We are not looking for single motives; nor are we suggesting that one particular motive can apply to everyone. We recognise, too, that there will be inconsistencies in some men's behaviour. All we are trying to do, I suppose, is peel back a few layers. It isn't easy – and we seem to have saved till last what is possibly the most complicated of all the arguments: namely, the Classical one, the one that explores the nature of 'the love that dare not speak its name'. Would you like to pick up on this one, Jack?

JACK: If you insist, Morgan – though you are the real classicist, not I. Well, the phrase Morgan has just mentioned featured in the second trial of Oscar Wilde at the Old Bailey in 1895. Dear Oscar was asked by the prosecuting counsel what it meant, and he gave this impassioned reply:

> 'The love that dare not speak its name' in this century is such a great affection of an elder for a younger man as there was between David and Jonathan, such as Plato made the very basis of his philosophy, and such that you find in the sonnets of Michelangelo and Shakespeare. It is that deep, spiritual affection that is as pure as it is perfect. It dictates and pervades great works of art like those of Shakespeare and Michelangelo, and those two letters of mine, such as they are. It is in this century misunderstood, so much misunderstood that it may be described as the 'Love that dare not speak its name', and on account of it I am placed where I am now. It is beautiful, it is fine, it is the noblest form of affection. There is nothing unnatural about it. It is intellectual, and it repeatedly exists between an elder and a younger man, when the elder has intellect, and the younger man has all the joy, hope and glamour of life before him. That it should be so, the world does not understand. The world mocks at it and sometimes puts one in the pillory for it.[284]

MORGAN: Yes, who could forget that marvellous speech.

173

I remember reading that it produced a 'spontaneous outburst of
applause from the public gallery, mingled with some hisses'.[285] I
thought it a plucky, if theatrical, attempt to defend his life style
by the use of Classical allusion. But really, it was sheer humbug
– for his account of a purely spiritual and intellectual relationship
failed by a mile to match the emerging evidence of the way he was
actually conducting his love affairs.

JACK: Rather! He was not deluding himself, I'm sure, so much
as indulging a weakness for hyperbole. But he stood no chance
of deluding the jury, that was certain. What did he say in *Lady
Windermere's Fan*? – 'I can resist everything except temptation'!
Dear Oscar, he was quite incapable of Platonic love.

MORGAN: Yes, poor Oscar was never able to control the
wonderful chariot. He let it run away with him most of the
time, due to a serious impediment: his lack of discipline.

CHARLES: My turn, I think, Ted, to confess our ignorance.
What's all this 'wonderful chariot' business, Morgan? You've
mentioned it before, if I'm not mistaken?

MORGAN: My sincere apologies, Charles dear. It comes
from a book by Plato, in which we find man in the image of a
charioteer trying to control two horses. 'One of the horses', Plato
tells us, 'is good and one not.' One is 'upright and clean-limbed',
and his 'thirst for honour is tempered by restraint and modesty':
the other is 'crooked, lumbering, ill-made', and 'wantonness and
boastfulness are his companions'. The first horse represents a
regard for 'absolute beauty', the second 'the stings of desire'
for the 'sweetness of physical love'.[286] It was the prancing of
this second, lustful horse that Wilde couldn't control.

JACK: Few men can, surely? Indeed, it seemed to me that
Wilde's trial raised again the question of whether Platonic love has
ever been – indeed, can ever be? – anything more than an ideal. We
have here, perhaps, an explanation which applied to a good many
educated, upper-class men of our time? They clung to a lovely
ideal – as we ourselves did, Morgan – but one that could only be
kept intact by turning elsewhere for sex. And by so doing, men
from our background were often judged to be enjoying the best
of both worlds: maintaining chaste friendships within their own
class, according to the Platonic ideal, whilst slumming it elsewhere
in the social scale in order to satisfy the shameful, erotic side of
their nature? Idealism and lofty debate on the upper floors: lust
down in the basement!

MORGAN: Oh, I think we probably did have the best of both worlds. And we could always justify the lower-class connection, remember, by arguing (to ourselves, at least!) that if the Platonic ideal was unattainable for ordinary mortals, then a complete relationship – one that admitted physical and sexual elements – could only be achieved if the partners involved had unequal status. In Classical Greece, after all, a loving relationship met with approval only so long as the 'eromenos', or young lover, remained a pupil, and therefore an unequal. The moment he graduated, thus acquiring equal status with his former teacher, an erotic relationship could no longer be condoned. No, our consciences were clear, weren't they, Jack? We were doing nothing reprehensible. Far from 'slumming' among unequals, we could persuade ourselves that we were acting in the best Classical tradition!

CHARLES: You were enjoying yourselves, you mean! Just like old Oscar. And why not? I never blamed you. We all of us had to find our pleasures where we could in life.

TED: That's right. You don't have to justify yourselves. Why the hell do you need to cover everything with words? You fancied a bit of rough, all of you! That was at the bottom of it – if you'll pardon my cheek! Because, if I may say so, Morgan, the only snag with your argument is that you and me, and Charles and Jack, we're not unequal. Not in my book, we're not. I'm as good as you lot, any day!

JACK: But perhaps not as bad, ducky!

MORGAN: Well said, Ted. And you, Charles dear. You are right, of course, both of you. You have seen through us. You have got in behind (so to speak!) our pomposity. I can remember being much more honest and down-to-earth in some advice I once gave to Joe Ackerley. 'Joe', I said, 'you *must* give up looking for gold in coal mines – it merely prevents you from getting amusement out of a nice piece of coal.'[287] Of course Jack and I were more fortunate than Joe, I believe. We enjoyed many a fine lump of coal – with here and there a gold nugget or two in addition. Would you agree, Jack? We are referring to you, of course, Charles.

CHARLES: Yes, I know, you flatterers. Are you sure it wasn't fool's gold, though?

JACK: Excellent! Could it be, Morgan, that our teaching is paying off? Ducky could have a point, after all. One, at least, of our pupils may have graduated to a position approaching equality – though if that's true, Charles Lovett, just remember, before you start celebrating, what Morgan was saying about equality and love-making.

CHARLES: In that case, Jack, I for one will swallow pride and principle. If equality means no sex, I will settle for inequality any day! . . .

Patrick

... In that letter to Ackerley, dated 8 September 1939, in which he listed his working-class lovers, Forster had added, you will remember, 'To those whom I can I am sending money'. And with one of these men, at least, he followed up this intention:

> Dear Jack ... Will you buy something for Charles with the enclosed – shirts, socks. It will go in infernal neckties if I send it to him direct. I am writing to him.[288]

The nightmare of war had now begun, and Forster went on to arrange what he feared might prove, perhaps, to be a last fling with Charles Lovett:

> Dear Jack ... I have just had your letter, and should very much like to have Charles up in London once more before he is swallowed up – that is to say if it is possible and if it is not imprudent and 'unsettling'. You will now, I dursn't, write about it direct to him. I go to the above address on Wed. Will you let me know whether Charles could come on Friday the 17th for one night. I could meet him at St Pancras at whenever he wished and take him back to it on the Saturday. Please send me a wire to above address and finance him if he comes.[289]

He also sought a little light relief from the horrors of war by arranging to meet his old friend, Joe Ackerley:

> I shall be delighted to see you dear Joe and to talk freely and dirtily with you. I do hope you'll be in good spirits.[290]

Clearly, like everything else, good times were not easy to come by in the early years of the war. In a letter from Forster to Buckingham, written in February 1940, familiar frustrations re-emerged:

Dear Bob, By Jove I'll try a little hitting back, and will take a piece of Refugees paper for the purpose. You scoffing at me because I'm not master in my own house and making out your own position is so different! Now look here – you never come and stop with me in the flat these days, though I would have come up any day you named for the last 5 months. May has never suggested you should come (now has she?) and she has got you placed just where you don't like to suggest it, yourself, as being unfair on her. I am very fond indeed of May as you know, indeed I love her, and I do not blame her, but I do blame you for not standing up against feminine techniques better than this . . . This may seem a silly fuss to make considering we are just as fond of one another whether you come to stop or not, but I'm not all that spiritual and unselfish, whatever you are, and I don't intend those visits of nine or ten years' standing to come to an end for want of a little arranging.[291]

This rebuke appeared to have the desired effect, for three months later he was writing:

Dear Bob, what a lovely day we spent together. I don't think I have ever been happier with you, the weather, the rowing, the flowers, all made it into a sort of poetry. Siegfried's poem 'Everyone suddenly burst out singing' came into my mind at Kew, and I felt the trees etc were all taking flight into a better place and taking us with them. I don't often feel like that at my age.[292]

Such meetings, however, were infrequent. Mostly there was depression, alternating with disgust, in those early, dark days of the war:

. . . but, at bottom, I don't belong to this terrible world and all my efforts to take part in it are half-hearted.[293]

. . . London burning! I watched this event from my Chiswick flat last night with disgust and indignation.[294]

It's a dim battle for the most part: ignorant armies clashing by night, I suspect. The bad news so frightening, the good news enough to make any decent person sick, and yet no possibility of recommending peace.[295]

However, despite his despair, he kept in touch with old friends:

Dear Jack . . . This is not so much a letter as a line of thanks for your news, and an enquiry as to what I could do for Christmas for my always dear Charles. I want to spend about £2 on him, but it is no use sending it to him. Could you possibly take him, sword drawn, to a shop, and get him what most he is in holes over, leaving a shilling or so over for nonsense. I shall be very grateful. Let me know what I owe you.[296]

Dear Joe . . . Thank you for your letter, and I do hope you are having a good weekend at Notts. It's very pleasant there as a rule.[297]

Dear Jack . . . The socks fit perfectly and the defective rib, though perceptible to the female eye, is invisible to mine . . . How most vexatious for you and for poor Charles how shattering! Please let me know what has been lost. It is a comment on the 'situation' that people will thieve for food . . . The coat I meant to offer Charles has already been given to Bone [his gardener] or Scarecrow. Joe likes his new flat in Putney.[298]

Dearest Jack . . . I am glad that in an England so morally lawless more should not have been stolen from you. How very mysterious, and how upset poor Charles must have been? I want news of him. I never sent a coat, because the coat I had thought off [sic] has disappeared, either on to Bone or on to a Boggart, no one was sure. But now I fear he [Charles] is in some sort of uniform.[299]

Now for the enclosed – which does look like a Christmas present. It is not really. At least £1 of it is, but that is for Charles, and I want you to get him something really needful with it. I am sending him under another cover, 5 shillings for the purpose of something needless and presumably — [word indecipherable] and am telling him of the division. The £20 is for you, with usual love.[300]

Do you want any clothes coupons with a view to you or Charles? I will leave you my book which is almost full.[301]

Have also been thinking what I could give Charles for Christmas. I say to myself 'No presents this year' – then start wanting to give something to Charles. Have you any ideas? My 1942–3 Clothing Book is untouched so far.[302]

Will you kindly wire Charles' size in shirts if you know it – 15? Very sorry to bother you, but there is no changing things these days and I shall be shopping on Tues.[303]

I popped straight into them. Just like a real marriage, and we shall never be parted. Now as for your visit to town. Ah! not such a good fit . . . Many thanks for wire about Charles' neck. He has by the way sent me such a nice tie for mine, kind boy.[304]

He continued to meet Buckingham as often as the latter's

professional and domestic duties allowed, and the letters reveal
a continuing intimacy:

> Dear Bob . . . I wish we talked seriously more often, but probably
> it comes only when it has to come. I liked what you said about
> 'Blessed are the Meek' . . . Let me know as soon as possible whether
> Fri. or Sat.[305]

> Dear Bob . . . I felt a bit sad at some of the things you said
> yesterday, not that you meant to make me sad, but you made
> me think of my limitations whereas generally you make me forget
> them . . . I did enjoy the food and the champagne (though not the
> red wine) and woke this morning without a headache for the first
> time for a week . . . I find myself awfully indifferent to my own
> death, but easily upset when people I love are threatened: I suppose
> most people, shits excepted, feel like this.[306]

By this time, Charles Lovett had been working for over a year
on the railways – for the LNER company in Nottingham – doing
unskilled general maintenance work. He had been forced into this
regular occupation in order to avoid being drafted into 'some sort
of uniform', as Forster had put it. One night, towards the end
of the 1942–3 winter, he lost his footing on the iced rungs of a
signals-post ladder and fell several feet to the ground, straining
his back and generally shaking himself up; luckily, he escaped
serious injury. His dear friend, Morgan, was quick to enquire
after his welfare:

> Dearest Jack, Have at once written off a line to Charles. What a
> catastrophe, and what an escape. Is there anything I can do or send?
> If so, please inform me. I expect Ted is all right on these occasions.
> They were to have come to the flat on the 20th. I wonder whether
> Charles will be able to make the journey by then? Please write
> again. Do I gather that something has been displaced or broken?
> With love and sympathy. Morgan.[307]

> I am so glad he is progressing: what a good thing you were
> so tidy and middle class about his bladder.[308]

Within a month Charles had recovered sufficiently to make
that journey, as recorded by Forster in his diary on 21 April 1943:

> I am terrified of losing Bob . . . for the memories of those one
> loves are all alike: crumpled paper, charring . . . yesterday I lunched
> for 10d. at the British Restaurant, Chiswick, received Charles Lovett
> and his Ted at the flat and had tea with Joe at his flat.[309]

It was during this visit to London with Charles that Ted Shread had shocked Morgan with his account of how cleverly – declaring himself a 'queer' – he had managed to get out of khaki:

> I quite gasped when Ted detailed how neatly he had got out of the army, and he desired no better audience – Charles giggling delightedly the while in the back-ground. Oh, how *can* Charles.[310]

As a registered conscientious objector Shread had been drafted first into the Pioneer Corps, and assigned to non-combatant duties, then into No. 9 Company of the newly-formed Non-Combatant Corps, stationed at Ilfracombe in Devon. He was given compassionate leave to come home at the time of Lovett's accident – and it was the plight of Charles, laid up with his bad back and managing to look suitably pathetic, that had spurred him, he claimed, to attempt the stratagem which Forster had found so distasteful. To be more accurate, it was Shread's braggadocio performance, surely, which had offended Forster's sensibilities, rather than the ruse itself? After all, Forster was no admirer of the sort of blind patriotism, or stupid machismo, that sends men hurrying off to war. In 1937, when asked by someone why he wasn't going to Spain, he had replied in a mild, cheerful voice, 'Afraid to' – a response of such simplicity, recalled Christopher Isherwood, that it rebuked his own posturing, though it was done 'without a hint of malice'.[311] No, as a conscientious objector himself, Forster might have been expected to applaud Shread's courage in sticking to his principles, and to admire the ingenuity which had enabled him to avoid any further contribution, however indirect, to the war effort.

In fact, poor Shread had caught Forster at a bad time – for by now Bob Buckingham, 'sick of hanging about'[312] and ready to declare that he would never forgive himself if he didn't go, was determined to enlist. Forster argued against it. He worried for Bob's safety, and also for May's peace of mind. May had recently found out about Bob's affair with Muriel[313] and she feared that her husband wanted to join up because he was unhappy in his marriage. Forster attempted to comfort her, and then to seek consolation himself:

> I console [May] and next have breakdown of grief myself . . . Ap. 29 in my flat am consoled by Jack Sprott. I feel after it as before; sad. All this may read foolishly soon. Better to chronicle

dinner of asparagus soup, cold pork, stewed currants with sherry, two bottles of vin rosé and nearly a bottle of curaçao drunk. It was grand. After which Bob and I; – felt a bit sick next morning.[314]

If Shread had been able to tell his tale – however immodestly – a few weeks later, when Forster was in a quite different frame of mind, it might have been received more sympathetically:

> Wire from Bob: 'Failed RAF'. It is almost too like life, which, if it displays any principle, dislikes the heroic.[315]

> Charles wrote me a sweet letter, I think with my troubles in view though I did not mention them. I replied to it yesterday. Please tell him the latest news.[316]

In 1944 the progress of the war allowed people to hope once again. Forster received good news from France. Charles Mauron – who, it was said, had been working for the Resistance – and his wife, Marie, were reported to be alive and well. A more relaxed Forster resumed an interest in a not-unfamiliar theme:

> Jack Sprott has written a randy tale in the style of Henry James. I am sure he would be glad for you to see it if you'd like to. But it is rather too much in H.J.'s style to be rude.[317]

However, such are life's vicissitudes, the following year brought sadness again. Forster's mother, who was ninety and had been ill for some time, died on 11 March 1945:

> Much love to Charles. I am sure of his sympathy ... [at the end of this letter, before posting, he adds another date, 12.3.45, then continues] ... Mother died very peacefully yesterday. Was giving her her lunch. So all is at its best.[318]

> Yes, sad news. My mouldy mother, as you once called her, is dead, and I expect now to start mouldering myself, in accordance with the laws.[319]

> Dear Bob, You may have gathered from the p.s. on my last envelope that mother is dead. Peacefully, while I was spooning her some lunch on Sunday, and the famous death-rattle wasn't too bad. I said 'Can you hear me?' and she nodded. I think there was something deeper between us than I knew, for the shock is worse than I expected. I can't explain – or could explain all too well, being a writer – but it has to do with the greatness of love and one's own

smallness. I have had that feeling sometimes – only happily – when with you . . . You must expect to find me a bit altered.[320]

Forster was now faced with the harrowing task of clearing his mother's house. Not surprisingly, his spirits were up and down during the following weeks – as Furbank, with access to the novelist's diaries, was able to record:

5 April.   Churchyard with blossoms. Broke down returning.
6 April.   Bob to W.H.[West Hackhurst, his mother's house]Happy.
10 April.   Broke down returning to W.H.
13 April.   Went to Dorking. Broke down.
11–13 May May and Robin here. Happy.[321]

With the end of the war in Europe, things began slowly to return to normal. Visiting and travel became easier:

Dear Jack . . . Joe returned in ecstasies from his visit – had much enjoyed, among other things, his time in Welbeck St. I come Friday the 15th. don't I?[322]

Dear Bob, the Maharajah's guests, we sit in the red sandstone court of his modern palace, looking over the marble pavements . . . we see a good deal of His Highness, who is one of the leading Indian Princes, frank and easy to talk to, and good to his people in a patriarchal way, I should think.[323]

Relationships, too, became more relaxed, and life could once again be observed with a touch of whimsy – not to mention fantasy, into which Forster could escape cathartically from time to time:

Sun, sex and a little pain because Bob was rough and sarcastic to me on his boat. Over in a flash for him. Otherwise, flowers and trousers opening . . . Don't ever look back at the sun and the sex. Get them into your blood, and they will shine in your eyes.[324]

It was about this time, as we have seen, that Lovett and Shread took my brother, Brian Belshaw, to stay in Forster's flat. My own visit followed a couple of years later:

Dear Jack . . . Yes – flat for Charles and Co. from the evening of the 17th – 20th will be all right. I should be back [from America] on the 14th (or 15th at latest) which should give time for key.[325]

By the time I met Morgan Forster on that July day in 1947, he had been forced to give up West Hackhurst and was living sometimes in his London flat and sometimes – increasingly, as he became more comfortable with the situation – in the accommodation which had been made available to him by King's College, Cambridge, when they made him an Honorary Fellow in 1946:

> Agreeable news. King's offers me a large room facing south and fitted with bookshelves. I go up for the day on Thursday for a squint.[326]

> I am (today) back from a night at Cambridge, slept in my new rooms, and if I am to live that sort of life things couldn't be nicer.[327]

By that time, too, my father had been returned to us from the 'forgotten Army' in Burma. After demobilisation he had worked for a few months at his old job, cleaning Nottingham Corporation buses. It was not work for returning heroes (not that the reality of my father's 'war' had elevated him to this category, it should be said) nor for ex-sergeant majors who, far from being used to taking orders, had become accustomed to giving them – and, indeed, having them obeyed instantly. My father was looking for an alternative, preferably one which would offer him some semblance of the status, power and responsibility he had enjoyed in the army. He sought a post as head porter in a hotel – a position which he thought would not only meet these criteria, but would carry the added attraction of a smart uniform on which he could pin his medal ribbons – and Professor W. J. H. Sprott of the University of Nottingham (wouldn't that sound impressive!) was approached, via my uncle Charles, for a character reference. Uncle Jack duly obliged:

University College
Nottingham
September 12, 1947

I have known Mr T.B. Belshaw and his family for upwards of ten years. He has always struck me as a man of high integrity and competence, and I feel sure that he would do his best – and do well – in any employment he was offered. His war record is a proof of his organising and administrative ability, and I was by no means surprised to find him given posts of responsibility of which he found himself worthy. W.J.H. Sprott.[328]

Patrick

When my father died in 1985, I found this somewhat flattering reference – along with a photograph of Vera Lynn, and two or three letters I had written to him during the war – in his wallet. It was one of his few treasures. The crested notepaper on which it was written was rather grubby and heavily creased. Goodness knows how many times he had taken it out to read those reassuring words! Jack Sprott, you see, was not only instrumental in securing a suitable position for my father: more importantly, his testimonial had almost certainly helped to restore a man's pride.

To return to Forster, he was nearing his seventieth birthday and feeling rather low during the autumn of 1948. Joe Ackerley helped him out of this period of depression by arranging for him a birthday celebration in a Soho restaurant. Forster was asked to think about his guest list:

> An inveterate fiddler with my private part-y, I have amused myself by working out the following suggestion for seating the 13 acceptances:

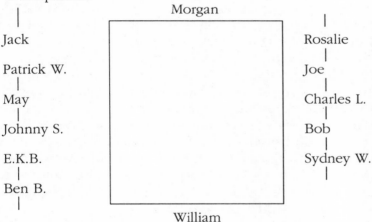

> I have put lines between people who are known to like one another, and in the two cases where there are no lines there is no reason to suppose absence of liking.[329]

In the event, the guest list had to be altered. Furbank offers the revised version in a footnote to the event, reference to which was made earlier when I was describing the genesis of my research. These changes did not detract from the success of the proceedings. Forster was hugely pleased by the occasion, apparently, and by the many other private and public tributes paid to him.

185

He was secretly delighted, too, to be offered a knighthood the following year – even though, as the following extract from a letter to Ackerley reveals, he turned it down!

> Yesterday I was offered a knighthood. And ever since refusing it have been wondering whether to have been called Sir Edward Forster or Sir Morgan Forster. I was very pleased to be asked . . . Suppose I ought not to mention this except to 'friends'.[330]

During the remaining years of his life Forster maintained his close relationship with the Buckinghams. Indeed, it was to their house in Coventry – where they had moved when Bob retired from the police force and took up his new career as a probation officer – that Forster was taken to die after his final stroke.

Typically, though, he had kept up his other friendships, including the one with Charles Lovett. He saw Charles periodically. For example, they would meet when Charles went down to London with Jack Sprott or Ted Shread; also when Forster came to Nottingham, to stay at Sprott's house in Portland Road, or to attend lunch or dinner gatherings – with meals always cooked and served by Charles – at Welbeck Street and, later, Dryden Street. And of course he kept in constant touch by letter, usually through Sprott.[331] However, weekends alone together – quite common, as we have seen, throughout the 'thirties – had become a thing of the past; there is no reference to meetings of an intimate nature in any of the post-war correspondence. The reason seems obvious enough. After all, Lovett – who was in his mid-forties by the end of the war and had long since lost the bloom of youth – had set up a home with Shread, and despite his continuing intimacy with Sprott had apparently 'settled down'. Forster, too, had settled for domesticity, if of a different kind. He had become increasingly content with the close friendship he had developed with the Buckingham family, particularly the intimacy he shared with Bob. It is important to remember that Forster was twenty-two years older than Lovett. He was an old man when the war ended (he was sixty-six in 1945), though because of his great spirit, it was sometimes easy to forget his advancing years:

> . . . he always looked younger than his age. And he never ceased to be baby-like. His light blue eyes behind his spectacles were like those of a baby who remembers his previous incarnation and is more amused than dismayed to find himself reborn in new surroundings.

He had a baby's vulnerability, which is also the invulnerability of a creature whom one dare not harm. He seemed to be swaddled, baby like, in his ill-fitting suit rather than wearing it. A baby with a moustache? Well, if a baby could have a moustache, it would surely be like his was, wispy and soft.[332]

Despite the fact that he never quite lost the baby-like quality observed so accurately in this description by Isherwood, in his general demeanour Forster was now beginning to look and move like an old man. Periodically he may have felt the urges of youth, but the inclination and energy to satisfy them was surely diminishing. Like Lovett, he seemed happy to settle for what he had. Not that his relationship with Bob Buckingham ran continuously smoothly by any means. We have seen examples of this already. Here are one or two more, starting with an extract from a letter written a few weeks before the celebrated 'flowers and trousers opening' fantasy:

It's YOU Bob, not the boat. When the boat is finished and put away you'll concentrate in the same way on something else, unless you decide to stop yourself. You have always cared more for things than people, and now this is rather running away with you, so much so that at present you do as little for other people as you can. My own faults lie in the opposite direction. I am too unselfish and soppy. So I suggest that from now onward we each try to occupy a more central position. This will do neither of us any harm.[333]

You were too sharp with me over West Hackhurst. I made a half-humorous reference to Fanny Farrer, to find myself instantly in the dock for harbouring class-limitations and obsessions. No doubt our feelings about house etc differ – if I hadn't mine I shouldn't have written *Howards End* – but there's no reason we shouldn't talk about them mildly. Don't throw your weight about so.[334]

I have been annoyed with you for planning to go to the Boat Race without me. We have seen it together, when we could, since 1930, and this sort of thing hurts . . . Don't do it again, please, if there is an again. Life is never very long[335] . . .

The Celestial Omnibus

MORGAN: . . . Hello, Ted. Can we help you?

TED: I hope so. I hailed the bus because there's something I want to bring up. It's something we've touched on before under different headings, so it shouldn't take long. At least, I hope not, because I'm not sure how long I've got. It's this class business. It was mentioned again in that letter we've just seen – the one from you, Morgan, to Bob Buckingham in February 1953 – and that's about the umpteenth time it's cropped up in this book.

JACK: So? Go on.

TED: Well, two things, really. One, as I say, that 'class' crops up so many times that you must've been conscious of it practically all the time. And two, stemming from that – your lot may not have minded a bit of slumming when it suited you, but you never really became one of us, did you? When you get down to it, you always looked to your own, didn't you? You thought yourselves a cut above the rest of us. We were just a pastime for you – your toys, something to play with. What do you say, Charles?

CHARLES: Aah, that's right. I don't remember Jack or Morgan rubbing our noses in it, mind you – you know, because we were working class – but there's no doubt that they thought themselves superior. Sometimes you treated me as an equal, Jack; but mostly you gave me the impression, you and Morgan, that you were looking down on us a bit – not deliberately to make us feel inferior, but patronisingly, even pityingly. And I didn't want your pity.

JACK: I'm sorry you felt that way, Charles dear. It was so difficult for us, as I am sure Morgan will agree, because our upbringing tended to develop in us a feeling of superiority. We grew up with the belief that we belonged to an élite ruling class, and that the lower orders were ill-educated and rather feckless, and therefore in need of our constant guidance. In general our class took a similar stance, I'm afraid, regarding native colonials – because we still had an Empire in those days, remember – but I hope we won't be judged too harshly. We, too, were victims: victims of indoctrination. Blame Plato, if you like, for his notion of a guardian class; and then the Romans, perhaps, for their system in which the patricians lorded it over the plebeians.

MORGAN: Yes, it is a powerful influence – tradition, upbringing, education, class mores: all of that – and one from which it is more difficult than you think to escape. But we were not as clear in our class-consciousness as Jack's deliberate simplification might suggest. There were tensions for many of *us*. My own insecurity arose, perhaps, from a strong sense of the past, through which I was pulled this way and that between the affluent Thorntons and Forsters on my father's side of the family and the socially inferior and impecunious Whichelos on my mother's side.

JACK: That is interesting, Morgan. It's another oversimplification, perhaps, but does that not explain what many of us suspected of you – namely, an inner struggle between Forster the Tory and Forster the Liberal?

MORGAN: Perhaps, but we are touching upon 'profound and complicated class feelings' here, as I once explained to Nick Furbank.[336] To understand my attitudes to class – which I hardly understand myself, I warn you! – you would need to consider factors other than my awareness of the social differences between the two sides of my family. My education, for example. Remember that I was a Kingsman, and as such I adhered to the view of 'King's' values:

> ... really there are as many classes as there are human beings ... We care for what we call 'character'. I think we care for it more than intellect. I believe that ... our refusal to sacrifice everything to intellectual qualities, our faith & sympathy for the so-called 'stupid' man, even our morality ... helps us to appreciate better on the whole.[337]

JACK: Yes, Morgan dear, the appeal of this notion that each man is a class unto himself, and should be judged merely upon his character, is obvious. We wanted to believe in it. And in your case, it must have helped the desire you had to extend your capacity for loving your fellow man. But it was never going to lead to a belief in a classless society, was it? Man's character is partly inherited and partly formed. We are what we are, not merely because of our genes, but because of education, training, upbringing, value systems – the whole environment in which we develop – and that's where you and I, and Joe, all of us, found tensions. Our better instincts may have been to knock down class barriers and deal with all men on an equal footing, offering love and sympathy and understanding, but in practice we were so often disappointed to find that our precious values, standards and sensibilities were not shared by the lower classes.

MORGAN: That's true. I know that you, Ted, admired Joe Ackerley for being a man of the people; and there was no doubt that for a time Joe attempted to translate his intellectual socialism into practice. For example, I remember that he once asked his father to reduce his allowance to £6 a week. Yes, he actually pleaded for a reduction! It was almost unheard of. At the time, however, he was genuinely embarrassed by the unfair wealth and privilege which an accident of birth had given him. But even Joe's ideals were tarnished somewhat by the reality of rubbing up against the working classes for prolonged periods. I recall that eventually he came to complain:

> How irritating and unsatisfactory the so-called working classes are seen to be, with their irrationalities, and superstitions, and opinionatedness, and stubbornness, and food foibles, and laziness, and selfishness, the more one knows of them.[338]

TED: I can't understand that. It doesn't figure, somehow, that Joe would ever say things like that about us.

MORGAN: Well, he did, I assure you. And more, too. In his diary he once wrote of a man named Freddie: 'His hair is a typical example of working-class vanity and ineptitude and propriety.[339]' Earlier he had complained of Freddie's 'Silly boring stories about himself', adding, 'how the working classes do love to describe and repeat their physical reactions to things . . . over and over again, as though one couldn't be expected to take them in the first time'.[340]

CHARLES: No, that doesn't sound like Joe – unless it was written later on in his life, after he got Queenie, in which case it could well be true. I mean to say, he began to get a bit crabby about most things round about that time, didn't he? And I don't think any man, from whatever class, was ever going to match Queenie in Joe's eyes, was he?

JACK: Charles may have a point there – though, as I recall, Joe was annoyed essentially at the way the working classes treated their dogs. Wasn't that the main issue? Didn't he go on to say in that memoir something like, 'If I were a dog, God shield me from a working-class master, like Freddie or anyone else'?[341]

MORGAN: I believe he did.

CHARLES: I know one thing: he said some rotten things to Ken, later on, about the way he treated *his* dog.

JACK: Understandable, I would judge, in the case of Ken.

MORGAN: Well, I wouldn't know about that, Jack. I know that Joe said some very unkind things about Ken, but at the time I put that down to a disagreement over which dog owners' manual should be consulted – the authorised or the unauthorised version. According to Joe, we all remember, there was only one way to bring up a dog: Joe's way. My own view of the hapless Ken was that he was a kind individual who would never, knowingly, ill-treat any animal. However, dogs apart, I think Charles could be right in another respect. When Joe was younger, he saw the world very differently. In those days, he was naïve and idealistic; it was left to his friends to introduce notes of caution regarding his somewhat romantic view of the working classes. I myself remember counselling him to be realistic. 'Love', I once said to him, quoting from something I had written somewhere, 'doesn't exist in the lower classes. Lust and goodwill – is anything more wanted?'[342] And later, at a time when his affair with a sailor seemed to be breaking up, I advised:

> You must go very easily on Albert. The standards which are so obvious to you are very remote to him and his class, and he was bound to lapse from time to time. And by standards I mean not only conventional methods of feeling. He can be quite deeply attached to you and yet suddenly find the journey up too much of a fag. It is difficult for us with our middle class training to realise this, but it is so.[343]

JACK: I am smiling, Morgan, because I remember receiving similar advice from you on a number of occasions, including the following observation:

> Charles has written to me, too. NO, the dear W.C.s aren't good

at sticking in a job for some reason, though they sometimes do for fear of starvation. I do hope that that letter of mine didn't help to make him softer.[344]

TED: Christ, Morgan, that was a terrible sneer at the working classes – calling us W.C.s! You wouldn't like it if someone called *you* a shit-house, would you?

MORGAN: No, I wouldn't, if 'shit-house' was the term used. But it wasn't. Come now, Ted, you are hypersensitive: it was a joke – a private joke, nothing more.

CHARLES: Maybe. But you can tell something about a chap, can't you, from the sort of jokes he tells, or the things he lets slip? I once heard someone talking about that on the wireless.

MORGAN: Perhaps you're right, Charles dear. I think I was in a bit of a muddle – and I did so dislike 'muddle'! – over this class issue. Joe always claimed that I even looked down on him.

JACK: Well, you did rather, didn't you? As I recall, you once made a reference to his 'ill-bred ancestry'.[345]

TED: Ah, you mean because Joe's father was known as 'the Banana King'?[346]

MORGAN: Well, that too, perhaps – but mainly it was a reference to his great-grandfather, William Aylward, who had married a first cousin of my father's.[347] There was no scandal in the actual marriage, simply in the fact that Aylward owned and worked in a music shop: in short, he was in 'trade', which was more than enough to make him *persona non grata* as far as my family was concerned.

JACK: Yes, Morgan dear, Joe thought a great deal of you, I'm sure. But he used to say jokingly that he never quite forgave you for two things. That was one of them – giving him the impression that you saw him as a social inferior: it seemed to him so irrelevant – and the other was the way you sometimes missed the second 'e' from his surname. If I remember correctly, though, he spared your embarrassment by generously conceding that the second 'e' was rather superfluous anyway!

MORGAN: Quite true. Oh dear, Charles and Ted must be thinking what a frightful snob I was over that business with 'dear cousin Joe'. In mitigation, possibly, I should say that I was also capable of being snobbish towards the land-owning upper classes. Charles will recall that spot of bother I had with Lord Farrer over Piney Copse, the little wood I purchased soon after I moved into

West Hackhurst; and also over the path we used to take from the house to the village, a footpath that crossed Farrer's land. I was guilty of a great deal of ill-feeling towards the upper classes at that time, I am afraid. In the end I came to the conclusion that the ownership of land and property, which I had always thought to be a good thing, did not make people – and I included myself in this generalisation – more tolerant and civilised. I think I wrote somewhere that land-ownership, 'like all possessiveness, does not go down to the roots of our humanity. Those roots are spiritual. The deepest desire in us is the desire to understand'.[348] And I had discovered that ownership does not lead to better understanding!

JACK: I remember those events very well.

CHARLES: I certainly remember you telling me about your precious wood: all about its oak trees, its flowers, and the birds and the bracken – oh yes, and its blackberries, which people would come and help themselves to, leaving behind their litter!

MORGAN: Yes, I liked to bore people with my wood, Charles dear. I am sorry you became one of my victims! But to return to my defence: having admitted a charge of snobbery, I suppose I could say in mitigation that I was also capable of denying my own class. I once wrote to one of my friends:

> That Plato of yours ... was on sounder lines than people who expect life to be like a work of art ... the lines, though he wouldn't recognise them, of the average middle-class man. Talking of whom I have a helpful tip for you. You can remain a patriot if you will become a snob. Realise that the lower class, not the middle, is the typical Englishman, and you can love our race without difficulty. Officers, stockbrokers, politicians, grocers – they run us, but they are not England numerically, and their selfrighteousness is not our national characteristic. Shuttleworth and I have decided to become snobs. We shrink, consciously, from such people, just as they shrink unconsciously from the lower class whom we love. We used to pretend we shrank from no one. But it's no good. Middle class people smell.[349]

TED: Love the lower classes! The middle classes smell! Come off it, Morgan, you must've had to go back a bleddy long way to dredge that one up! The rest of the evidence points the other way, surely? It's no good any of us pretending to be something we're not. Like Charles said in his piece, you didn't really take the trouble to understand the working class. Maybe you found it exciting, or romantic, or whatever, to mix with us sometimes. But you stayed on the outside, really, didn't you? Like an observer. Not that I blame you. Like you say, you and Jack, it was your upbringing. Same with us. If we had little sympathy or understanding for your lot, well, it wasn't surprising, was it, when we didn't even speak the language, or move in the circles, that would help us do something about it? It was a case of different worlds, really – you in yours, and us in ours, with occasional crossings to the other side – so let's at least be honest about it.

MORGAN: I am trying to be, Ted. I am attempting to explore what a complex mix of attitudes and emotions I must have inherited, and developed, regarding class. But I daresay you are right: what snobbery I possessed was probably directed mainly at the working classes. Yes, *mea culpa*. I apologise. However, I don't think I was a culture snob, at least. Partially educated people, usually from the lower middle classes, were the greatest offenders here, perhaps; they thirsted for knowledge and 'culture', not for what it could contribute to their character, or the enhancement of their humanness, but merely in the hope that it might improve their standing in the world. I had little patience with that, I confess.

JACK: I agree with that view, Morgan dear, but I recognise that it was easy for those of us who acquired our learning over many years, in the best schools, the best universities and the best intellectual circles, to look down on aspirants like your Leonard Bast in *Howards End*, who were understandably in a hurry to make up for lost time and opportunity. They were trying to acquire overnight, almost, what it had taken us decades to arrive at – even generations, perhaps, for to some extent we are dealing here with attitudes and assumptions that are inherited and passed down – so it was hardly surprising that they found no time to question the purpose of knowledge.

CHARLES: Yes, and these people were at least trying, weren't they? It seems to me that in those days our sort were never going to win, whatever we did. If we did nothing, we were lazy and feckless; yet if we tried to lift ourselves, better ourselves, we were criticised for copying our 'betters' without understanding the purpose of it all!

JACK: Yes, there's no justice in life, is there? Certainly, there was very little at that time. Christopher Isherwood got it about right when he said that the Poshocracy always wins – though 'in a thoroughly gentlemanly manner',[350] of course! And later, he wrote:

He [Karl] told Christopher that all working-class boys who are homosexual have a natural urge to get themselves educated; therefore they have to climb into the middle class ... Christopher felt shocked ... why couldn't a working-class boy become educated without acquiring bourgeois airs and graces? If his nature required him to be a queen, why couldn't he be a working-class queen?[351]

TED: I could've told him why – because your bleddy lot wouldn't let him, that's why! You couldn't take us as we were. We weren't good enough for you as we were. We had to be improved. So you were always tampering with us. But woe betide us if we began to talk and act like you. No, that would never do! That would close the distance between us – that would close the gap that your lot always relied on to hang on to power, to stay in control. They say that knowledge is power, don't they? Well, your lot knew all about that.

JACK: It interests me that Mr Shread will insist on talking of 'lots' – as if 'our lot', as he puts it, were a homogeneous group. We were not: far from it. Morgan wasn't from the top drawer, you know. He looked up to the land-owning upper classes, almost as part of his upbringing – though as he has reminded us, he subsequently came to look down on them, thank goodness! And you have heard that someone like Joe could be put down for having skeletons in the family cupboard which had a lingering smell of 'trade' upon them. As for me – well, Morgan never mentioned it, but I was always conscious of a certain social distance between us. I came from very ordinary, undistinguished, rather dull middle-class stock. My father was a humble, small-town solicitor; and though we were not poor, my parents had to struggle to keep me at Felsted. By contrast, there were exciting elements in Morgan's genealogy – for example, his great-grandfather, Henry Thornton MP, member of the Clapham Group, second cousin, close friend and fellow abolitionist of William Wilberforce – and there was enough wealth in his family to give him a start in life as a man of 'private means'. Also, Morgan was able to tap into a social network that extended into the upper classes; he had friends in high places, and connections with 'good families'. I developed my own network, of course – I was determined to cultivate useful contacts – but I had to work for mine, whereas Morgan's came with his family. So you see: Morgan, Joe and I may have been equals intellectually; but that apart, there were differences – some subtle, some not so subtle –

195

that pegged us at slightly separate levels on the social scale.

TED: My heart bleeds for you! But none of that surprises me. Life's just a big heap, isn't it? A big, mouldering heap. And guess who's at the bottom of it, Charles love. I was going to say, you and me – but really, the Lovetts were several shovelfuls up the heap from the Shreads, weren't they? I don't think you had much more money than we did – with your father being an invalid most of his life – but you had a piano, didn't you, the one your Gwen used to play? And your father could quote Shakespeare – oh yes, and there were teachers on his side of the family, weren't there?

CHARLES: That's right. And lace-makers on my mother's side, the Dafts;352 don't forget that. For God's sake, Ted, don't forget that: my mother would turn in her grave! She was very proud of it. Whenever she was trying to impress she used to let it slip out that the Dafts owned a lace factory. But they never did. They rented their machine, and the factory floor space on which it stood. However, they were skilled workers, all right.

MORGAN: I never knew that, Charles dear – and to think, I once wrote a story called *Nottingham Lace*. But I think I remember that bit about your father wanting to go on the stage. Well, fancy that.

TED: Yes, fancy that! You weren't really interested enough in Charles' private life to bleddy well find out, were you?

JACK: Temper, temper, Mr Dreaded Shread! No swearing, thank you. Now we know why you wanted to raise this topic: you hoped for an opportunity to be abusive, didn't you?

TED: That's bleddy rubbish! I'm interested in what made you boggers tick, that's all.

JACK: Looking for more mud to throw, more like, you mischievous little . . .

MORGAN: Gentlemen, gentlemen, please! . . .

Patrick

... In the last extract – from the autumn 1956 letter, in which Bob Buckingham got a bit of a ticking-off – Forster mentioned the Boat Race. Interestingly, this event on the sporting calendar had become almost synonymous with the name of Joe Ackerley. Ackerley was not a sportsman, but for some reason – the spectacle of lightly clad, male athletes straining their muscles in front of hordes of pretty undergraduates, perhaps? – the dour struggle between Oxford and Cambridge seemed to capture his imagination, and his annual party to celebrate the occasion was for many years a diary fixture within his social circle.

Forster maintained a close friendship with Ackerley right through to the end, which came when Joe, by far the younger man, died in 1967. As we have heard, their liaison had to survive Forster's early suspicions – not to mention his mischievous slur on Ackerley's pedigree – but slowly, as the years unfolded, affection and trust developed:

> 1924: Your letters (from India) were a godsend to my etiolated novel. I copied in passages and it became ripe for publication promptly. I appreciated them myself very much too.[353]
>
> Your letters are a great joy to me.[354]
>
> 1932: I am lucky to have such friends as you and Jack.[355]
>
> 1956: Dear Joe, I have been thinking odd thoughts, partly because death *cannot* be far away from me, or even you, and one must set things down. It is odd how interesting one is about death. My thought wasn't about that, but about a happier matter ... [goes on to acknowledge the debt he owes to Reg Palmer and to Joe's friendship] ... but for you both I should have passed a much more uncertain and disquieted old age.[356]

Forster was inclined to lecture him from time to time, and

197

Ackerley, though appreciative of his friend's good intentions, must surely have found this irritating. One notable occasion occurred quite early in their relationship. To understand the reference we should first remind ourselves of the entry in Forster's diary for 8 April 1922:

> I have this moment burned my indecent writings, or as many as the fire will take. Not a moral repentance, but the belief that they clogged me artistically. They were written not to express myself, but to excite myself, and when first – 15 years back? – I began them, I had a feeling that I was chasing something positively dangerous to my career as a novelist. I am not ashamed of them – or of my indecent thoughts and acts, or of the indecent writings I get from others, all of which I shall not burn. It is just that they're a wrong channel for my pen.[357]

Over four years later, Forster made reference to this act of burning his 'indecent writings' (in order to finish *A Passage to India*) before going on to say in one of his letters to Ackerley:

> . . . they prevented me from concentrating. You have to make some such sacrifice now. I feel convinced, and what distracts your vitality now is that you are keeping Ernest and about a dozen more on the simmer on the chance of their being useful or exciting some time. An enormous part of your energies go not in lust nor love but in the equivalent of my destroyed MS.[358]

As with all his close friends, though, Forster stuck by Ackerley through good times and lean. Even when Ackerley took his love of Queenie, and of animals in general, to rather tedious and sometimes worrying extremes, Morgan was more patient than most with 'doggy Joe', as he once described him to Jack Sprott.[359] Few people cared for Queenie, and Forster was no exception – he once called her 'that bloody dog', Furbank tells us – but he did not allow his dislike of her to prejudice his literary judgement when *My Dog Tulip* came to publication in 1956. Reviewing the book in a letter to a newspaper, he wrote objectively:

> Of the few 1956 books that I have read, J.R. Ackerley's *My Dog Tulip* . . . is by far the most remarkable. It is a biography of the New Dog – a creature comparable with the New Woman who disturbed our grandparents.

Tulip, the Alsatian bitch in question, does not indeed demand a latch-key; if all doors and windows are left open, all traffic stopped when she crosses a road, and all Guy Fawkes celebrations banned, she is fairly content. Where she innovates, where she rebels, is in demanding to be treated as a creature in her own right, as a dog of dogdom, and not as an apanage of man. This Mr Ackerley affords, with a freshness and innocence of vision that have never before been directed at the canine world.

'Innocence' may seem an odd word for a book which describes excretion, copulation and parturition realistically; but they are part of the outlook that includes the beauty of her fur, the grace of her movements, her happiness on Wimbledon Common, her loyalty and her exasperatingness. She is often tremendous fun . . .

Tulip's biography has shocked some people. Sometimes it shocks me, but much too much fuss is made over feeling shocked. And – as one of its readers has gaily remarked – it will certainly not corrupt any dog into whose paws it is likely to fall.[360]

It is not canine love that shines through this delightful piece, so much as Forster's affection for the dog's owner, and his respect for the quality of his friend's writing. In the same year, in a letter which included a *double entendre* for Ackerley's amusement, Forster offered him a further compliment on his literary talent:

This idea *is* a big solid one, and would that I had thought of it 16 years ago – i.e. at your age, for your writing Joe is now at its very best . . . you should therefore write all you can before the pen, like another weapon s— [word difficult to decipher: possibly 'shrinks'!].[361]

Forster and Ackerley exchanged some interesting and highly entertaining letters from time to time:

Today at his (Francis) advice I have torn up my mother's diaries without reading them or almost without! Thirty or forty years of depression, regrets, feelings of uselessness and wasted life. I don't believe she actually was as sad as all that. And she does say that she was fond of me and that I was a good son. Oh but the women, the women, Joe, how difficult, how irritating they are.[362]

Dearest Morgan . . . We go from 'gay' bar to 'gay' bar of an evening, tiny bar-rooms containing 'gay' boys, sometimes in kimonos. 1 small bedroom at the back to which you can take him if you fancy him. 25 shillings about the lowest tariff. Not really my cup of sake, not to mention my pocket. Bad breath,

I am told, no circumcision. Good torsos, no legs. One sees an occasional handsome face, the Simian look predominates.[363]

Darling Joe ... I did not take to them and they seemed to share my opinion of each other ... I perused her breasts with some care during the meal, and admit that they must be more comfortable to lay the head on or between than the flat and sometimes hairy board that has hitherto been my portion. But I don't wish to change.[364]

Dearest Morgan ... I spent two nights in Jack's house last week ... It was a bitterly cold day and the house like a refrigerator. I entered it alone, for he [Charles Lovett] had Ken's supper to arrange ... I turned on all Jack's electric and gas fires; even so one shivered in the chill ... Charles is an animal-lover without a clue to the animal mind. Needless to say, I don't write like this to poor Jack, nor do I interfere (*Where Angels Fear to Tread*, with its good intentions, has gone home), but I think it right to hint to Jack about the frozen atmosphere in his house and he has now instructed Charles to leave on an electric fire for pussy day & night while the frost lasts 'regardless of cost'! Really, of course, Charles should be lighting a coal fire in it two or three times a week for the good of the house itself (the bathroom-basin pipe was frozen up while I was there) – then perhaps the house would burn down! So I have shifted the responsibility on to Velda.[365]

The background to this letter – and to the following one, which contains a reference to two members of my family – was explained in a letter from Ackerley to Paul Cadmus[366] in which he made reference to the task of looking after 'the domestic affairs of our friend Jack Sprott, who went off to Ghana and that Nkrumah at the end of October for 4 months, leaving behind him in Nottingham, where he lives, two sad hearts, his servant-friend of long standing and his marmalade cat. It is the latter who really touches my own heart, and I go up to keep him company whenever I can':

Dearest Morgan ... I am at Jack's desk in Jack's house in the City of Nottingham. Xmas had to be spent in Putney, but I came up as soon as I could to comfort the cat and arrived by train late yesterday evening, about 6.30, to spend three nights. I had told Charles that I hoped to come during the weekend, unsure of the day and time. I needn't have put myself to such trouble and expense. The house, far from cold & gloomy was ablaze with lights, fires burning in both sitting rooms & kitchen. Charles' sister, Dorothy and her daughter are in residence. They have been here some days, it seems, the caravan in which they normally reside having got frozen-up. Mutual embarrassment: indeed at first I did not know

200

who they were. They said they thought I might come, but since I had not appeared on the Saturday, had given me up; they had been prepared to move out if I did come. Charles had said they should . . . , perhaps they had better go now? Awkward for me. It was dark, late & cold, they were thoroughly settled in, doing their laundry which was drying before the fire. Perhaps I should have turned them out there and then, for I remembered that Jack had told Charles that he did not want them staying in his home. However, Charles had let them in and they had been there several days. I didn't know what to do, it seemed hardly my business, they clearly didn't want to go & the caravan was said to be an hour or more away. So I said they had better stay the night in Jack's room and I would talk to Charles in the morning: he hasn't come yet. I'm afraid now that a drama may arise, that they may never be got out of the house and back to their caravan, and Jack will be *furious*. Yet, if they *can* be got out before he returns, it seems to me a good solution to our troubles, that they should remain at any rate, for a time, the house & cat will be properly looked after and I shan't have to keep popping up in January which I meant to do. Dorothy (who never stops talking) has looked after me like mad ever since I came and since I am not very well with a cold it was very cheerful to find a nice large fire burning in the sitting room when I came down this morning instead of having to light one myself. I intend to stay 3 nights (I don't mix with them, I live in Jack's sitting room and get waited on) and since it has now been discovered that such a domestic situation works, another visit from me will not disturb.[367]

Further extracts from selected correspondence between Forster and Ackerley in their final years may be of interest:

Dearest Joe . . . Being an invalid is a nuisance though. I find I require constant attention and complete independence at the same time. Being a lecherous elder does not however disturb or incommode one in the least.[368]

Dear Joe . . . unlikely that Bob will come up for the Boat Race . . . and I am not interested in watching that outmoded show-off without him.[369]

Dear Joe. . . I look sad too for I have idiotically allowed two German girl students to consult my wisdom at 6.0 p.m.[370]

Darling Morgan just a line of love to say I hope you are well. I expect you will have seen all the notices of your play [*Howards End*], and sadly agreed with the general disappointment and occasional yawns they voiced. Not good box-office notices, I fear; pretty intelligent on the whole in realising that a major novel has made a minor play . . . but the front-page picture, in one of the more popular rags, of Lord —'s new

201

woman entering the theatre in a mini-skirt may sell a few more tickets.[371]

Joe Ackerley made another reference to *Howards End* in an entertaining letter in which he described his 'foster-mothering' of an injured sparrow:

> It is a dirty, tatty, unrewarding little beast, entirely ungrateful but used now to my presence in the room. We chirp at each other. It has a playground by my book-case on the floor, a dish of water to splash about in, an earthy dust-bath in a flower pot, various seeds, ants' eggs (6d. a packet) and bread-crumbs. It lives among the books, hopping from shelf to shelf and shits on them all. *Howards End* seems to be its favourite book for resting (and shitting) on, and I think Mrs Wilcox would have approved of that.[372]

By this point in his life, Ackerley had become more sympathetic to animals than to most human beings. Indeed, he never did find his 'Ideal Friend' in human form, and in a letter to Francis King he appeared to identify a fundamental flaw in himself which might have offered an explanation for this:

> If caution was ever important, I went too fast; we are quite friendly still, but I fancy that now a game of skittles – rather than pocket billiards – is as far as we shall ever get. No matter; I never managed to be considerate in matters of sex and I daresay it is better that I should not start again. I doubt if it is a subject in which one gains wisdom if one has never had any.[373]

In a letter to Sonia Brownell Orwell a few weeks later he offered another fragment of self-perception, this time very touching:

> But I know nothing about happiness, though I get pleasure from time to time ... Many years ago, some forty years ago, Morgan Forster, trying to guide me through some miserable love affair, wrote to me 'But happiness may not be your deepest need'. It was an impressive remark, especially from a man who can't read Freud and generally dislikes what is called 'Psychology'. More recently, indeed quite recently, he said to me 'You don't want to be happy' – not so good, but adding up. He himself is a happy man, he has cultivated his garden. For many of us, at any rate for me, that has not been possible.[374]

202

To the end Ackerley admired, and was rather envious of, Forster's 'cultivated garden':

> Morgan is up at Bob's in Coventry . . . He is wonderfully better. The head of his Cambridge hospital designed a stick for him . . . It is made of steel, and sprouts three legs at the bottom, a tripod. This strange contraption . . . he regards with deep distaste and some apprehension (will he be sent a bill for it?) and has never used. Now, Bob tells me, he is going about without any stick at all. The dear old boy loves life (a thing I can never understand).[375]

This declining appetite for life had become apparent to his friends after the death of his Alsatian bitch, Queenie. He who had once been so gregarious and outgoing became, in his final years, a rather sad, eccentric figure. Ever creative, though, he found a novel way of relieving his loneliness:

> Living as a bachelor in my flat I have got into bad lonely habits such as farting loudly in order to hear the noise – for company. Even with Bunny and Ann here I do it still, without thinking. Do they laugh? They are awfully unobtrusive and good, but must be somewhat taken aback sometimes to hear resounding explosions from my room.[376]

Like many another, Ackerley came to seek a familiar refuge from his growing disillusionment:

> . . . your beautiful bottles are a great pleasure and comfort. I face a featureless Christmas, which booze alone can save, booze inducing sleep. I don't think you go in for that, the afternoon siesta, such a comfort to old geezers like myself who have no future. Though to take a wider sample, in your language, Prof. Sprott, who is endlessly busy, can't do without it either, but, having sipped gin from 12 to 1.30 and cracked ½ bottle of claret at lunch, dozes in his armchair with pussy-cat on his knee in front of a large coal fire beneath a portrait of Lytton Strachey until tea-time. Then he comes to life, with its tiresome realities once more, and threshes about among criminological and sociological problems until 7.0, when the dear gin bottle is again brought out.[377]

This humorous vignette of Sprott was not unkindly meant: it was a simple statement of fact from a kindred alcohol-dependant. Ackerley, indeed, had a great deal of respect for Sprott:

You wanted Jack (Sebastian) Sprott's address ... Do invite him along. Though he carries his learning lightly he is one of the wisest of men in all those antiseptic subjects of which I know too little (psychology, philosophy), you might find a chat with him interesting, and K. could tackle him on the subject of the death penalty, he is an expert in criminology.[378]

It was Sprott, in fact, who, along with William Plomer, arranged the small birthday gathering in honour of Ackerley's seventieth. It gave Ackerley a great deal of pleasure:

Darling William I keep thinking of that dinner you and Jack stood me, and the magnificent cheque you sent me, which I had barely time to thank you for. I was so touched by everything. Seldom can a septuagenarian have entered that decade more happy than I, to be feted by my two oldest and dearest friends.[379]

Within seven months of this happy occasion, Ackerley was dead. His death – which occurred in his sleep in the early morning of 4 June 1967 – was quite unexpected. Barely a fortnight earlier, Isherwood, who had met him at the Buckinghams in Coventry, had remarked that he was 'livelier than he had ever seen him before and in apparently excellent health'.[380] Ironically he died a few days after giving up smoking, and at a time when he was negotiating the sale of an obituary article on Forster!:

... when you have recovered from my Memoir, I wonder whether you and Miss LeRoy could sell this for me, here and in America. I had qualms about sending it out – to kill an old friend before he is dead seemed so indelicate – but by holding it up I have lost the place for which I intended it, the *Sunday Times*: they have already secured an obituary article by someone else for their cold storage.[381]

Ackerley had very recently sold his letters from Forster to the University of Texas – without, incidentally, consulting the author! – and at about the same time he had written a begging letter to Forster requesting, in straightforward dignified fashion, he thought, that he be granted a 'solid' settlement of the sort that the Buckinghams had received in 1964. Forster did not reply to the letter; but, 'in the manner of a jovial Father Christmas',[382] he sent Ackerley a cheque for £1000 – a generous gesture, though significantly less than the £10,000 he had bestowed upon the Buckingham family.

By these actions, Ackerley may appear to have revealed a somewhat calculating and mercenary streak in himself; but we might remember the words he wrote to Sonia Brownell Orwell a week before he died:

> I am of course entirely ignorant of the worth of these letters of mine, and am interested not so much in that as in securing for them a sum of money which will enable Nancy and me to drink ourselves carelessly into our graves.[383]

Thus if Ackerley was behaving with uncharacteristic cupidity, he was at least intending to use the money to satisfy a singularly modest ambition. Not so out-of-keeping with the man himself, perhaps?

The 'sixties were sad, difficult years for Charles Lovett and Ted Shread. The house at 74 Dryden Street had been purchased in joint names with so much promise. Indeed, in the 'fifties it had been the scene of many enjoyable parties, some of them attended by people like Morgan Forster, Joe Ackerley and Jack Sprott. I remember visiting on one or two of those occasions and catching the gay, festive mood of my large family of 'uncles'. Gradually, however, the place acquired the look and feel of a boarding-house. Ted, increasingly resentful of the Tuesdays and Thursdays that Charles continued to spend with Jack Sprott, began on those days to seek other friendships. One or two of these men were invited to the house, and because there were spare rooms some overnighting took place. This upset Charles; but he didn't alter his Tuesdays and Thursdays routine – so Ted persisted, and the offering of occasional overnight accommodation gave him an idea. The house was obviously large enough for them to consider taking in lodgers on a formal basis.

First came a publican's wife who wanted a place where she could conduct a clandestine affair with one of the draymen who delivered to the pub. For a while she rented a room which was euphemistically called her 'sitting room'; and the drayman, presumably, carried on delivering! Then came two Chinese male nurses, followed by a woman whose parents owned a well-known furniture business in Nottingham; she wanted somewhere to live with her 'fiancé' until they could get married and find a place of their own.

Shortly after this Ted met George Knight, a barman at Truman's in the city centre. They were mutually attracted, and Ted invited him to take up lodgings in Dryden Street. Charles, sensing the danger, confronted Ted. There was a blazing row, the outcome of which was Ted moving out of the bedroom he shared with Charles and into the room rented by George. For spite, initially, Charles took into his room a young man named Ken Ball whom Ted had encouraged to visit the house.

Ball was a tall, large-boned youth, slow of movement – as if he had outgrown his strength – and even slower of thought and speech; he may have been educationally subnormal. Ackerley refers to him – though not by name – most disparagingly in one of his letters:

> ... but I felt rather vexed, the more so since I had already been bitten, by a dog (canis familiaris), on Saturday when I was staying with Jack in Nottingham. Of this wretched creature, a large, wire-haired terrier, belonging to one of Jack's stupidest working class friends, I had predicted disaster years ago, since it was never let off its lead and lived in a state of perpetual excitement.[384]

The 'wire-haired terrier' was called Rex, and Ackerley might have stopped to reason that there was no call for him to feel unjustly discriminated against: the wretched creature bit anyone and everyone – myself included! – who came within the limit of its tether. It even bit Charles, on the hand that often fed it, and on one of the legs which took it for daily walks while its owner was out at work. Indeed, the owner himself, Ken Ball, had no guaranteed immunity against the dog's indiscriminate aggression.

Rex was but one of three combative animals that, over the years, visitors to Dryden Street and Portland Road had to be on their guard against; and for a period in the early 'sixties the three of them were at work concurrently, opening skin and drawing blood. The other two members of the trio were Charles' black cat, Mau-Mau – aptly named after the Kikuyu terrorists who at that time were bent on driving the whites out of Kenya – and Jack Sprott's cockatoo, more prosaically named Cocky.

The reader has already been introduced to Cocky. This was the caged bird Sprott bought at the time of his friendship with

Harry Dawes; the one Charles thought would let you 'do any-thing with him'; the one Jack said was 'very affectionate, a little noisy, inclined to peck at you'. There is no reason to doubt that these early assessments were made accurately and with genuine enthusiasm. By the time I came to meet Cocky, however, I think it could have been said with some confidence that few, if any, of Jack's guests would have shared such sentiments. By then the old bird had acquired an uncertain temperament, an ear-piercing, heart-stopping shriek, and a penchant for violating human tissue which was accommodated by a cunning ability to lure its victims into a false sense of security. In short, when poor Cocky fell off his perch in 1962, none but his nearest and dearest would have mourned his passing with much sincerity. Typically, though – ever mindful of people's feelings, even if not always shared exactly – Forster sent his condolences:

> I have felt so very sad about Cocky. There is nothing to say, but how many will miss that squawk on entering the house, that showed it was alive. How distressing for Charles, too. I am sure that Ken [Ball] did his best and that no further diagnosis could have prolonged life.[385]

Impressive though Rex and Cocky were in their disregard for the inviolability of human flesh, they couldn't quite match Mau-Mau for sheer maladjustment. They probably spilt more blood, but her behaviour was more bizarre. They enjoyed biting: she enjoyed terrorising. They merely damaged bodies: one quick bite and it was all over. Mau-Mau, on the other hand, specialised in mental torture, creating in the minds of those who were of a nervous disposition – or who were simply not comfortable in the presence of cats – unease, uncertainty, apprehension and fear. There was a further distinction. Excuses were sometimes offered for the anti-social behaviour of Rex and Cocky. After all, Cocky was created for free flight, surely, and here he was cooped up, imprisoned, in a cage. Similarly, Rex was meant for the wild, for free running with the pack, not to be confined to a house or kept on a leash.

By contrast, Mau-Mau had the run of the Dryden Street house and its environs. She was afforded warmth and shelter, and she was well-fed; she was also offered as much affection as she wanted to take. Yet she was a weird, unpredictable, ungrateful creature given to sudden, dramatic changes of mood. One moment she could be lying out on top of the china cabinet, apparently cat-napping, and the next moment she would be flying through the air with a blood-curdling caterwaul to thud into the back of a chair or settee, the claws of all four paws sinking in like grappling irons. Or she would brush up against you in feline fashion, mewing seductively, as if inviting affection – then as you reached out, flattered and beguiled, to stroke her, she would hiss and lash out at you with claws unsheathed, unerringly branding your hand or wrist.

Mau-Mau's tactic with the visitor was first to offer a spectacular demonstration of her wild, unpredictable nature – like the mad flying stunt, or the act of treacherous aggression, with plenty of steel flashing to reveal her potential for violence – and then to crouch motionless, yet fully sprung for action, on the arm of a chair opposite, transfixing the victim with yellow, unblinking eyes. Nervous visitors were mesmerised into a cold sweat by this brand of psychological warfare; and even the strongest, those determined not to be intimidated by a mere cat, were made to feel uneasy under Mau-Mau's calculating gaze.

Yes, Mau-Mau was some cat, and quite the most formidable of this trio of belligerent animals. Once, she almost contrived to get Charles into trouble by her name alone. During the two decades following the war, the bottom end of Dryden Street and the area adjacent gradually became quite a popular housing centre for Afro-Caribbean immigrants. One night Charles went out to call the cat in. 'Mau-Mau', he called, 'Mau-Mau, Mau-Mau.' Then, getting impatient: 'Mau-Mau', he growled, 'Mau-Mau' – and from behind the hedge up popped a huge black man, the whites of his eyes shining menacingly (or was that a Kikuyu knife?), crying, 'Hey, man: who you calling Mau-Mau?'

Charles Lovett's health began to fail towards the end of the 'fifties. When an eightieth birthday party was arranged for Forster in January 1959, it was a much bigger and grander affair – a luncheon, organised by King's College – than the one held ten years earlier. An invitation to his working-class friend may not have been appropriate on this formal, ceremonious occasion – with so many scholars and writers gathered to honour, in the words of the Provost, 'the greatest living Kingsman' – but in any case Lovett would not have felt robust enough to attend. He had started to experience the sort of palpitations which had alarmed his father before him, though his concern had yet to be communicated to Sprott. For the moment, he received a considerate letter from Forster who gave details, not without humour, of what he called the 'big Blowout' at King's:

Dearest Charles, Just a line of love for your Christmas and Birthday attentions. Such a whirl as it has been and I feel rather tired though quite happy. Jack will have told you about his big Blowout. I am afraid that his seating arrangements went rather wrong. I arranged for him to sit next to Sir Michael Seymour, but he didn't, and the Earl of Sandwich, who should have sat opposite him, turned up with a Countess who spread devastation with her constant chatter. I did better, between Sydney Wilkinson and Charles Mauron whom you may remember from far off days when we were in Theatre at Orange.[386]

In the spring of 1963 Lovett had a heart attack. He survived it, but his condition gave rise to serious concern. Characteristically, Forster was quick to offer sympathy and support:

What distressing news about Charles. Give him my love if he is capable of accepting it. Is money, or will it, be required? Let me hear about this.[387]

The news about Charles is certainly disheartening and distressing for you in many ways. Hearts are either tedious or melodramatic, and one must avoid the latter.[388]

My dearest Charles, Jack has been telling us all your news. I wish it had been better, but the worst seems to be past, and anyhow you are lucky to have such friends as Ken to look after you. Be a good boy, don't overtire yourself, do as you are told and I think you will soon be well. Such anyhow is the wish of your loving old Morgan. [N.B. This letter contains an amusing postscript from Joe Ackerley – part of which reads 'and such also is the wish of your loving JOE who hopes to see you soon . . . Well, dear, do as the leeches tell you, for blood pressure has to be brought down if other things are to stand up . . . Much love, dear Charles. Joe][389]

Dearest Charles, I recognised your writing on the envelope at once. It has not got as bad as mine. I am so glad that your news is slightly better. It must have been a great worry to you, as it has been to Jack.

I knew hearts could be hard or soft, but like you I did not know they could change from large to small. I hope yours will turn into a tiny one.

My own health keeps good considering my age, but I am deafer and don't see so well. I was pleased to hear better news of

Jack's health. I have just been talking to a very nice blackamoor
who wants to meet him at the airport in Ghana.

Well, I must end now, for the College Matron is coming to
cut my toe nails. Please give my very kind remembrances to Ken –
how wonderfully he has looked after you – Much love to yourself
from Morgan.[390]

At the beginning of this illness Lovett's bed was brought
downstairs, and thereafter he and Ken Ball lived on the ground
floor in the dining room, leaving Ted Shread and George Knight
to occupy the first-floor rooms; the ground-floor sitting room
was occupied by a paying guest. Recognising instinctively, perhaps, that a capricious dog and a maladjusted cat were somewhat
unsoothing companions for someone convalescing after a heart
attack, Ball bought Lovett a budgerigar in a cage. Later, as another
gift for his elderly friend, he built an aviary for small birds in the
back garden. Lovett developed an interest in these creatures; it
proved to be a therapeutic aid to a tolerable recovery.

Meanwhile, as we have seen, no sooner was he up and about
again than he received news of Sprott's intention to visit Ghana.
Lovett became depressed at the thought of having to manage for
four months without seeing his mentor: rarely had the two men
been separated for such a long period of time. As ever, Forster
was ready to console:

Dearest Charles, You are bound to feel low after Jack's departure,
so I send a line in the hope of cheering you up. It is a great thing
for him going to Ghana and should help him on his career very
much.

He gave me more satisfactory news of your health, and I do
hope it will continue to improve in his absence so that you can
greet him riotously on his return! My own health is good for my
age – no aches and pains, which is something – the main bother is
that I am beginning to use a stick and I lose it between whiles.

I also lose my pen – this one is stolen from a boy and a
very nice one. I hope it will not embitter him against me when he
finds it is gone. My chief news however is about my play, *Where
Angels Fear to Tread*, which, after a rather uncertain start, is now
running in London nicely. A short telecast of it has helped, and
when it ends the BBC will televise the whole of it with their own
actors. I have had great luck with the lady who has dramatised it
– an elderly girl from Texas.

Well I must end now, and try to find my stolen pen – it keeps
conking out and I don't know what to do. Write me a line when
you feel like it. Give my love to Ken, of whose goodness Jack

speaks most warmly, and much love to yourself I needn't say from Morgan.[391]

This was Forster's last letter to my uncle, Charles Lovett. In fact, in his remaining years Forster wrote few letters to anyone. Failing eyesight, increasing absent-mindedness and a hand unsteadied by age and by one or two minor strokes, began to make writing more and more difficult for him. There are no surviving letters to Sprott (whom he had made his executor) after one dated June 1967, in which he wrote on the death of Joe Ackerley – 'naturally a shock'[392] – with typical calmness and resignation.

Forster's own death came early in the morning of 7 June 1970. It was his wish to have a non-religious funeral; nevertheless, Furbank, attending as one of the mourners, was presented with a heaven-sent opportunity to end his admirable biography on a light note:

> ... but as we filed back towards the cars there was a diversion. The undertakers' men were peering inside the bonnet of the leading Rolls, evidently unable to make it start. The chief undertaker approached, pressing his black gloves to his forehead in a theatrical gesture, protesting that never, never in twenty years, had such an unfortunate thing ... And at this Sprott, who had been gloomy, brightened greatly, remarking that Forster's spirit was clearly at work.[393]

The death of a distinguished nonagenarian never takes newspapers and magazines by surprise. Obituaries and appreciations had been 'in the can' for years: the presses were ready to roll. And within a few days of the announcement, the public's curiosity regarding Forster's estate was satisfied through newspaper items like the following:

PROFESSOR NAMED IN NOVELIST'S WILL

A NOTTINGHAM professor is named as executor in novelist E.M. Forster's will, published yesterday. Prof. W.J.H. Sprott (73), Emeritus Professor of Psychology at Nottingham University, receives over £50,000 in trust for the rest of his life under the terms of the will.

After his death the money will go to King's College, Cambridge. Among the effects bequeathed to Prof. Sprott is the manuscript of an unpublished novel, *Maurice*. Written in 1913, the novel tells of a homosexual relationship between two Cambridge undergraduates.

CONTROVERSY

Forster refused to publish it during his lifetime for fear of public controversy, but Prof. Sprott said yesterday that he thinks the novel should be published. It would not detract in any way from Forster's reputation, he said.

Prof. Sprott, of Portland Road, Nottingham, a close friend of the novelist since 1923, will now be discussing publication with his co-executor, Dr Donald Ambrose Parry, Vice-Provost of King's College, Cambridge.

Forster, who died in June, aged 91, left £63,021 net (duty payable £23,843). After legacies of about £7,000 to relatives and friends, the remainder passes in trust to Prof. Sprott.[394]

A few weeks after Forster's death, on 8 September, Lovett himself lay dead following a massive stroke. Ken Ball registered the death the next day, and Sprott took charge of the funeral arrangements. He had his old friend cremated – against Charles's own preference, and despite the fact that a place was reserved for him in the Lovett family grave at Wilford Hill. To the very end, you see – even *after* his death! – Charles Lovett was being organised by Jack Sprott.

Sprott died less than a year later, on 2 September 1971. He died in his bed at the family home, 'Magavelda', in Blakeney, Norfolk, with a fallen book on the floor beside him. A life had ended, it appeared, during an activity which had featured prominently and habitually in its living: namely, in the act of reading.

Sprott had just bought a new car, of which he was proud, using some of the money he had inherited from Forster . . .

Postscript

My story has been one of love and betrayal: of large, unsatis-
factory loves – for none of my characters achieved complete
fulfilment – and small, inconsequential betrayals, trivial because
they harmed no one and were the result, not the cause, of imperfect relationships. It has been a tale of the great and the small,
the famous and the obscure: in short, a tale of unlikely associ-
ations. But we have seen how the lives of the distinguished and
the anonymous can touch, and even be mutually dependent, for
a while. 'Only connect', that is all we have to do.

The chief motive for attempting this study – apart from
my own vanity, that is: never discount vanity in a writer
– was a desire to set the record straight. Charles Lovett, I
contend, deserved to be much more than a footnote in someone
else's biography of Forster. In my attempt to demonstrate this,
I have revealed details of Forster's private life, including some
further evidence of his numerous and frustratingly triangular
emotional entanglements. I have presented the great man – or
allowed him to present himself – warts and wanks, and all.
This, I hope, has not been done irreverently, or pruriently, or
irresponsibly merely to create sensation. The life of each and
every one of us would reveal a difference between the way we
conduct ourselves in private and the way we conduct ourselves
in public; it would reveal discrepancies between our intentions
and our actual behaviour: it would reveal many inner struggles,
inconsistencies and paradoxes. Forster was a distinguished man
of letters, but he was a human being. Stripped of his genius,
he was one of us: a mixture of strengths and frailties. It does
not do Forster – indeed, anyone – a service to deny this. In my
view, too, these revelations, such as they are, in no way detract
from our respect for Forster. Indeed, for some people, they may

help to make him more accessible as a writer; and for all of us, they make him more identifiable as a fellow traveller on life's difficult journey.

There will, of course, be those who would question the legitimacy of penetrating the private life of an artist. W. H. Auden would almost certainly have done so. He branded literary biographers in the mass as 'gossip-writers and voyeurs calling themselves scholars'.[395] Well, I admit to a little weakness for gossip, and there is something of the voyeur in all of us perhaps; but I have no pretensions regarding scholarship. I am not a literary biographer. However, I know what Auden was driving at. He described biographies of writers as:

> . . . always superfluous and usually in bad taste. A writer is a maker, not a man of action. To be sure, some, in a sense all, of his works are transmutations of his personal experiences, but no knowledge of the raw ingredients will explain the peculiar flavour of the verbal dishes he invites the public to taste; his private life is, or should be, of no concern to anybody except himself, his family and his friends.[396]

This represents a minority view of biographies, I would guess, and one which is probably not commonly held by writers themselves. There is now a wider acceptance of the 'all-revealing' form of the genre, though many people, I am sure, would at least agree with Auden that caution must be exercised when considering the degree to which details of an artist's life can shed light upon his work.

Humphrey Carpenter provides us with an example of the more commonly held view. When he was preparing his biography of Benjamin Britten, he contacted many people who knew the composer personally, and he received the following response from Stephen Reiss:

> Especially I would like to know whether your purpose is to give a comfortable or an uncomfortable picture, the true or the fictitious. This sounds terribly threatening, but truly it is not meant to be. I just feel most strongly that B.B. can survive the truth and still come through as one of the most supreme and lovable persons that ever lived, but if the whole truth is not told his image will in fact be impaired and will limp into history.[397]

I am grateful to Messrs Reiss and Carpenter, for this is precisely the way I feel about Forster. His reputation as a writer, and as a caring human being, will not be diminished, I am confident, by the modest contribution I am making to the pool of knowledge about him. 'Yes', you may say, 'the imagery is apt: are you really adding water to the pool, or simply throwing stones, disturbing the surface, causing waves?' Well, I hope that I am adding to the pool – years of work have been in vain otherwise – but I know that you cannot add anything to a liquid without causing some measure of disturbance.

I trust that Forster himself would not have disapproved of my intentions. Evidence from his own pen – a sneaky thing to offer, Morgan, I know! – can be used as some sort of endorsement, perhaps. For example, he once wrote, 'When they write my life they can tell everything'.[398] And remember the comment he made in his review of *My Dog Tulip*, that 'much too much fuss is made over feeling shocked'.

Yes, it is hard to believe that Forster himself would have been shocked by anything I have written. There is a lovely story about a retort he once made to Harry Daley when the two men met after an interval of many years at a dinner in the Savoy hotel. The occasion, which was organised by Joe Ackerley to celebrate his W. H. Smith prize for *We Think the World of You*, is recounted by Furbank in his excellent introduction to Daley's memoirs, *This Small Cloud*:

> The encounter went very amicably. Daley told Forster he was writing his memoirs but Forster was not to worry, for he had become discreet in his old age. Forster replied that he had become indiscreet in his old age, so Harry could write what he pleased.[399]

Interestingly, despite this invitation, Daley stuck to his vow – and, relevant to the argument, a potentially excellent and entertaining memoir was, in the view of many, perhaps the poorer for his discretion.

As regards the Lovett–Forster element of my story, I am aware that the precise nature of the physical relationship between the two men remains unclear. This is hardly surprising when we recall that even in his fiction Forster was never explicit about such matters. Oliver Stallybrass writes:

> For better or worse, however, the actual physical encounters are described briefly and, by the standards of today, with circumspection, not to say circumlocution: 'a muscle thickened up out of

gold' is perhaps the most explicit statement in the book.[400]

But in any case, no gentleman would divulge the secrets of the bedroom – even to a confidant as discreet as Sprott. The sharing of such intimate details would represent a betrayal of the trust which must exist between lovers, and a denial of the sanctity of personal relationships which was such an integral strand of Forster's credo. My interpretation of the erotic element of the affair between the writer and his 'on loan' lover is the closest we are going to get to the truth; it is based on a 'best guess' offered by Ted Shread, who at least had intimate knowledge of the sexual predilections of one member of the partnership. More confident statements, based on much less evidence, are probably made by biographers all the time. Peter Ackroyd, in his fascinating biography of Dickens, is one who is at least honest enough to admit it:

> . . . the real nature of their marriage cannot be recovered . . . but that did not stop me from interpreting it in a very direct way . . . the uncertainty principle is quite impossible to build into biography; of all forms, the biographical one seems to demand certainty and clarity. Once you introduce ambiguities and doubts, the whole enterprise starts to collapse.[401]

Apart from the physical side of the relationship, you may still be left wondering what Forster really thought of Lovett. Yes, we know that he always regarded him with great affection, and that he treated him with modest generosity over the years. There is no doubt, too, that Forster remained a loyal friend to the end: only death, some thirty years after the carnal element of their strange liaison petered out, could terminate their friendship. This may present a touching picture, but it perhaps reveals no more than we would expect of Forster, a man for whom loyalty in friendships was almost a religious tenet. So was there anything more? Was my uncle Charles anything more to Forster than 'a nice piece of coal'[402] that burned brightly and gave a little warmth for a time, leaving behind ashes which the grateful consumer then took care of, respectfully, in characteristic fashion? Perhaps not. And Charles Lovett, a simple, modest man – a Nobody on loan from one Somebody to another – would perhaps have been prepared to settle for that. Not the self-disparaging 'I was Forster's bit of rough', but a prouder, more dignified voice claiming, 'I warmed the heart, shone the face and twinkled the eye of an exceptional human being'.

But there was just a little more to it than that, I am convinced. Forster may not have been looking for gold in his coal-mining days, but he was lucky: he found some. He found some with Bob Buckingham; maybe not a huge nugget, but certainly a small piece. And he found some with Charles Lovett – in this case, not even a solid piece, perhaps, but veins of gold: traces of the precious metal, which melted among the ashes and then solidified, to give Forster something other than sentiment, something of durable value, to keep.

I think it is clear from all the evidence that Lovett, like Buckingham, was elevated to a place among Forster's version of the aristocracy. Forster did not believe in 'Belief', but he had a number of precious beliefs. He believed in 'tolerance', for example, and 'good temper and sympathy', and he placed his trust in the value of personal relationships. Above all, he lived by a simple creed which we find formulated in his essay, 'What I Believe':

> I believe in aristocracy, though – if that is the right word, and if a democrat may use it. Not an aristocracy of power, based upon rank and influence, but an aristocracy of the sensitive, the considerate and the plucky. Its members are to be found in all nations and classes, and all through the ages, and there is a secret understanding between them when they meet. They represent the true human tradition, the one permanent victory of our queer race over cruelty and chaos. Thousands of them perish in obscurity, a few are great names. They are sensitive for others as well as for themselves, they are considerate without being fussy, their pluck is not swankiness but the power to endure, and they can take a joke . . . On they go – an invincible army, yet not a victorious one. The aristocrats, the elect, the chosen, the Best People – all the words that describe them are false, and all attempts to organise them fail . . . their temple, as one of them remarked, is the Holiness of the Heart's Affection, and their kingdom, though they never possess it, is the wide-open world.[403]

Sensitive, considerate and plucky? Yes, I think Charles Lovett met these simple criteria. Further, he could hardly be accused of asceticism – another point in his favour, for Forster preferred that his aristocratic type 'should not be an ascetic one':

> I am against asceticism myself. I am with the old Scotsman who wanted less chastity and more delicacy. I do not feel that my

aristocrats are a real aristocracy if they thwart their bodies, since bodies are the instruments through which we register and enjoy the world . . . Still, I do not insist. This is not a major point. It is clearly possible to be sensitive, considerate and plucky and yet be an ascetic too, and if anyone possesses the first three qualities, I will let him in![404]

I am sure that Forster let Lovett in. I am equally sure that there would have been no life peerage in his Upper House for Shread. However, Shread would certainly deserve to qualify for Forster's aristocracy on one criterion at least: namely, pluck. His indomitable spirit, his power to endure cheerfully in the face of adversity – throughout his life, really, but particularly in the beginning and near the end – are qualities which Forster, had he been able to take a retrospective and more objective view, without Sprott looking over his shoulder, would have found admirable. Sadly, Shread did not live to see the completion of this book. He died of pulmonary carcinoma early in the morning of Monday 26 April 1993, at the City Hospital, Nottingham; he was in his eightieth year.

Sprott himself, of course, was unquestionably one of Forster's aristocrats: not only that, he sat at the master's right hand. True, in his confrontations with Shread he behaved badly – sometimes getting angry, losing control and saying things which he regretted later – and for this reason the reader has been given a somewhat unbalanced view of him. Sprott's reaction to Shread almost always resulted in untypical behaviour – behaviour of which he would not have been proud, however strong the plea of extreme provocation. For to Sprott, Shread was like a red rag to a bull. Indeed, Shread had the capacity – a fearless, cocky type of truculence, not to mention rival love – to rile him, almost instantly, in a way that, from all the evidence, no other man could. Not that Sprott was ever, I think, as adept as Forster at dealing with a badly-behaved adversary. Both men believed that people should know the rules of civilised engagement, but Sprott was the more easily irritated and stirred to action by any ignorance or breach of the code.

Sprott was an interesting, complex character who led a fascinating life. Despite being a lover of Maynard Keynes, a confidant of Lytton Strachey and Dora Carrington, a long-standing, intimate friend – and executor – to Morgan Forster, and a Bloomsbury satellite whose name keeps cropping up in the plethoric literature of that period, almost nothing has been written about my 'uncle' Jack. Until now, that is.

Yet there are gaps in my knowledge of him. I wish I hadn't lost touch with him in the late 'fifties and 'sixties, when I was pursuing my own career. I wish that I had been told more about him when I was younger, and that I could have had the prescience at that time to understand the significance of what little I did know. I wish I had contacted his sister, Velda, earlier, and could have had more than the one interview I had before, sadly, Alzheimer's led her vacantly to her death. I wish I could have reached Ted and Daisy Manning, servants and friends of the Sprott family in Blakeney, earlier than I did, at a time when their memories would have been keener and fresher. Oh, I wish, I wish, I wish!

Sprott was a man of principle and integrity; in the liberal tradition, he was tolerant of other people's ideas and behaviour – and expected the same, in return – but he did not suffer fools gladly. Seen through my eyes – the eyes of a first-generation grammar-school boy, unsure, starting to take the first tentative steps on an academic ladder whose upper rungs were not only out of sight, but beyond imagination – Sprott was a formidable figure. Clearly he was not at ease speaking to a young boy – he may, indeed, have been as nervous of me as I was of him – but he appeared so superior, so aloof. He made me feel nervous. I was half-afraid of him. It wasn't simply his academic status and his exotic accents – though these were intimidating, goodness knows, to a lad from my background – it was his detachment. My mother used to say, 'He's not a warm man, your uncle Jack', and even my uncle Charles conceded that Sprott was not an easy man to reach until you really got to know him. The last time I met him, I was a young teacher in my twenties; and I sensed again that same detachment – as if he was observing, rather than sharing, the moment with you. I think he was one of life's observers, and in that respect he was not unlike Forster. Forster observed life as a writer, Sprott as a social scientist. But Forster was a warmer person. I think Sprott was more content to be on the outside looking in; that way, he needn't become involved. Forster had a greater emotional need to be on the inside, though he probably felt more comfortable looking on from the periphery. Both men had considerable sympathy for the non-joiners in this life. Sprott certainly made his position clear:

> ... no one will deny the ill-effects of a sense of isolation or
> rejection, [or] the exhilaration of cooperative participation ...
> yet many people seem to maintain their equilibrium under the
> ordinary shocks of life with the aid of comparatively few congenial
> friends; not everyone seems to relish group participation. Many
> prefer privacy ... I should like to see the study of small groups
> ... supplemented by a study of healthy non-groupers ... so as
> to discover under what conditions ... it is possible to fashion a
> way of life which is satisfying, but which does not require the
> sustaining encouragement of group membership.[405]

Despite his detachment, Sprott could be charming – to those
he wanted to impress, or to those with whom he felt comfortable
– and his charm was not reserved entirely for men. He had little
time for women in general, but with the few who found favour
with him over the years he proved an entertaining, sometimes
scintillating, companion and a loyal friend. These two or three
favoured women, though vastly different as personalities, had
certain things in common: high intellect, good education, strong-
mindedness, self-reliance, individualism – that is to say, qualities
and attributes that made them free spirits like Sprott himself.
Each of them could enjoy the advantages of Sprott's company
– the gaiety, the wit, the intellectual cut and thrust – without
having to worry about sexual and emotional complications. This
was an important point: for a woman seeking pure friendship, an
epicene partner could be ideal. I think it was Virginia Woolf who
once observed rather bluntly that the society of 'buggers' – as
she would insist on calling homosexuals – had many advantages
if you were a woman; it was simple and honest, and in some
respects it made a woman feel at ease. Certainly this was true in
Dora Carrington's case; she adored Sprott and felt relaxed in his
company. She could, as she put it, write to him 'as one mistress
to another';[406] and she knew him intimately enough to be able to
joke about his androgyny:

> You really are rather a — [picture of a deer] to give me such a
> beautiful present. Truly I have never received anything that gave
> me half-so-much pleasure. What a pity you aren't ... You might
> have added so much pleasure to my life, dear boy. But there; 'it's
> NO good REPINING over lost balls', said the Countess whilst
> playing croquet with the Archbishop of Canterbury.[407]

Like Forster, Carrington felt that she could rely utterly on

Sprott's discretion as a confidant, and there seems little doubt that she treasured her relationship with him. In fact, had Sprott been able to show a sexual interest in Carrington, they might conceivably have been lovers at some point:

> I love you so much, for being so sweet and listening to my tedious confidences but I love you also for better reasons for – but perhaps you will never know. Your loving C. x x x.[408]

As it was, Carrington had to settle for a fine friendship. She was not, of course, unpractised in the art of sublimating the sexual side of her love, having spent years of chaste cohabitation with a man – her beloved Lytton Strachey – whose sexuality was similar to Sprott's.

When Strachey died, Sprott was one of the people to whom a distraught and despairing Carrington turned for help, and he received possibly the last letter she wrote before she killed herself with a shotgun:

> I know these things are bound to happen and are always happening. But if one person really flavours all life for one it is difficult to see how to set about starting a new one . . . You see my weakness is that I only led, or tried to lead, a 'good' life to please Lytton, left to myself I lapse (secretly) into superstition, drink and mooning about. Come, write me on your typewriter a dis-course on 'the object of life'.[409]

So much for Sprott: a rather unemotional, self-sufficient 'people-watcher', who was not disposed to giving much of himself away, even to lovers and close friends. However, once he had committed himself to a firm friendship, he could always be relied upon for complete discretion and loyalty. He was a man of many qualities, but I suspect that he would have been remembered by most people with respect rather than love. Charles Lovett was a notable exception to this view of Sprott. Sprott was always beyond Lovett's permanent reach – in another league, another class, so to speak – but it was Shread's opinion, expressed with sadness, that if called upon Lovett would have died for his beloved employer.

All that remains is for me the tale-teller to thank you the reader for your forbearance. I apologise if the method of telling my tale, and the problems of the biographical process in general, have appeared on occasions to preoccupy me almost as much as the tale itself. But the truth is never simple: it would be dishonest to suggest that it is. It needs exploring; and so do the processes by which we think we can arrive at it. You can't have an interest in one without having an interest in the other: they are interrelated. In your desire to explore the truth, you have to explore the methodology. You cannot rely simply on so-called historical records. Historical records, letters, diaries – even interviews with the subjects themselves – these are not truths: they are versions of the truth. For this reason alone, biographies themselves can never be more than versions of the truth. But this is only one factor. If you then consider Nabokov's reminder that biographical material is 'shaped by the teller, reshaped by the listener, concealed from both by the dead man of the tale',[410] you begin to realise how much scope there is for further distortions of the truth.

Few biographers are prepared to declare these difficulties openly. Peter Ackroyd may be seen as a refreshing exception:

> I have sometimes imposed a pattern where no pattern really exists . . . whenever there might have been a gap or a discontinuity in the narrative, I made a point of hustling together events and images in order to effect a smooth transition. In other words, I cheated.[411]

Such revelations, I appreciate, make life very difficult for the reader. What can he or she believe? They also make life terribly complicated for the honest biographer. What can he or she write that is genuinely believable? What can one hang on to? Small wonder that there are times when one feels like giving up. Thus Ackroyd, in the imaginary conversation he has with his subject, finds himself being consoled by a Charles Dickens who is only too aware of what he calls 'the mystery of my own self':

> You know as little about me as I do. But the important thing, upon which we are agreed, is that you should finish your work. And it is in the very act of completion that some new truth will be revealed.[412]

It seems too much to hope that I might have revealed 'new truths' in my book – to be honest, I am left in awe of the truth: it is so hard to grasp, so inaccessible – but here and there I may have come close, perhaps; or if not, I may have cut a few steps which could assist others in their search for difficult summits.

And what of my methodology? Well, as you know, at times I appeared to be pulled this way and that between novel and biography. I had to settle for the biographical form – who would believe me otherwise? – but I was unwilling to accept that a biographer was simply 'a novelist without imagination'.[413] Thus, I think it was always my intention to write a novel form of biography, rather than a biographical novel or a *roman-à-clef* – or any fictional form – despite the fact that:

> The fascination of novel writing lies in its freedom; the dull parts can be stripped, and the excitements intensified.[414]

The relationship between the novel and the biography interests me enormously: it is closer than many people think. As Phyllis Rose writes:

> ... a life is as much a form of fiction – of guiding narrative structures – as novels and poems, and the task of the literary biographer is to explore this fiction.[415]

In this book I have been attempting, however clumsily, to present an imaginative form of the biographical genre which would do some justice to Virginia Woolf's concept of 'granite' and 'rainbow' – the solid fact and the less tangible individuality – in respect of my four main characters. I have tried to bring Forster, Lovett and Sprott to life – bring them back from the dead, so to speak, to join Shread, who was very much alive at the beginning of the project – using the freedom of the novelist without, I hope, sacrificing the integrity of the biographer. It may not have worked. Some may find it impossible to reconcile the introduction of the Celestial Omnibus with the writing of history.

However, I like to think that Forster himself might not have disapproved too heavily. We know for certain that he approved of fantasy as an element of fiction:

> I liked that idea of fantasy, of muddling up the actual and the impossible until the reader isn't sure which is which.[416]

And it is significant that his own favourite novel, *The Longest Journey*, is a complicated concoction of autobiography and fiction laced with fantasy. However, fantasy in fiction is one thing: fantasy in biography, I recognise, may be quite another. But as long

223

as it remains a separate device, and does not distort 'the facts'. . . ?

Anyway, if I have failed – and with pastiche there is always the risk of falling flat on your back between the stools – I hope that at least you have had an entertaining read, with here and there a bit of fun. For I wanted you to enjoy the ride: my characters did, quite often! I also hope that I have succeeded with what Ackroyd believes to be the main link between a novel and a biography:

> The only real connection between the two as far as I am concerned is the need to make the narrative coherent. To impose a pattern on the world. That is all. You also need similar skills, of course, the most important being to cover up your own inadequacies.[417]

So there you have it. In part, that's what I've been about all this time: covering my own inadequacies, trying to create a coherent narrative – trying to tell a story that holds together. But only in part. There have been other, more important considerations. Like trying to get to know my characters, for example. To be honest, by comparison with this, the narrative has been a secondary preoccupation. Perhaps it shows.

Do you remember what Forster said of the 'story' aspect of novel writing? He likened it to a worm – because its beginning and end are arbitrary – a 'wriggling and interminable . . . naked worm of time', adding:

> That is why I must ask you to join me in repeating in exactly the right tone of voice the words with which this lecture opened. Do not say them vaguely and good-temperedly like a busman: you have not the right. Do not say them briskly and aggressively like a golfer: you know better. Say them a little sadly, and you will be correct. Yes – oh dear yes – the novel tells a story.[418]

Forster felt obliged to concede that the novel tells a story. However, he said this apologetically, and somewhat grudgingly, before moving on to far more important aspects of the novel: namely, *the plot, fantasy, prophecy, pattern and rhythm* – and chiefly, that 'more interesting topic', *people*.

People fascinated Forster; they also frustrated him. He could never get to the reality of them:

> For human intercourse, as soon as we look at it for its own sake and not as a social adjunct, is seen to be haunted by a spectre.

224

Postscript

We cannot understand each other, except in a rough and ready way; we cannot reveal ourselves, even when we want to; what we call intimacy is really only a makeshift; perfect knowledge is an illusion.[419]

Only in the novel, he concluded, could you come to 'know people perfectly'. No wonder he became a fiction writer. No wonder I was tempted.

References

All sources, where appropriate, are dated – except where no date can be attributed to the original, in which case the reference is designated 'undated'. Where there is supporting evidence, approximations are ventured for some undated items.

The following abbreviations are used:

ABD	*Dickens*, Peter Ackroyd
BB	Benjamin Britten
CBB	*Benjamin Britten: A Biography*, Humphrey Carpenter
CCC	Clare College, Cambridge: archives
CLD	*Carrington: Letters and Extracts from her Diaries*, ed. David Garnett
DC	Dora Carrington
DVW	*The Diary of Virginia Woolf*, ed. Anne Olivier Bell
EMF	E. M. Forster
FBF	*E.M. Forster: A Life*, P.N. Furbank
JA	Joe Ackerley
JS	Jack ('Sebastian') Sprott
KCC	King's College, Cambridge: modern archives
LJA	*The Letters of J.R. Ackerley*, ed. N. Braybrooke
LS	Lytton Strachey
LVW	*The Letters of Virginia Woolf*, ed. Nigel Nicolson
MK	Maynard Keynes
RB	Bob Buckingham
SLF	*Selected Letters of E.M. Forster*, eds. Mary Lago and P.N. Furbank
UTA	The University of Texas at Austin: the Harry Ransom Humanities Research Centre
VW	Virginia Woolf

Uncle Jack

1. Extract, letter from DC to Gerald Brenan, dated 18 Dec. 1921: CLD.
2. See vol. 2 (*The Economist as Saviour*) of Robert Skidelski's biography, *John Maynard Keynes*.
3. Extract, letter from LS to JS: KCC.
4. Extract, letter from LS to JS: KCC.
5. Attributed to Henry Sidgwick, a leading nineteenth-century Apostle, as quoted in *A Marriage of True Minds: An Intimate Portrait of Leonard and Virginia Woolf* by George Spater and Ian Parsons.

Patrick

6. Extract, letter from EMF to JS: KCC.
7. Extract, letter from EMF to JS, dated 27 Aug. 1945: KCC.

References

8. Extract, letter from EMF to JS, dated 21 Jan. 1946: KCC.

Uncle Jack
9. Extract, letter no. 231 from EMF to JS: SLF.
10. Extract, letter no. 1371, dated 17 Mar. 1923: LVW.
11. Diary entry for Sat. 17 Mar. 1923: DVW.
12. Extract, letter no. 1422: LVW.
13. Reported in FBF.
14. Extract, letter from DC to Gerald Brenan, dated 18 Dec. 1921: CLD.
15. From VW's Journal, 1905, quoted in Quentin Bell's biography of VW.
16. Diary entry for 12 Sept. 1921: DVW.
17. Extract, letter no. 1524, to Jacques Ravaret, dated 24 Jan. 1924: LVW.
18. Extract, letter no. 1725, to Vanessa Bell, dated 5 Mar. 1927: LVW.
19. Extract, letter from JS to MK: KCC.
20. 'Lady Clare Magazine', Michaelmas Term edition, 1922: CCC.
21. Extract, letter from LS to JS, dated 2 Oct. 1926: KCC.
22. 1925 edition, 'Preferments and Distinctions' section: CCC.
23. Extract, letter from EMF to JS, dated 22 Mar. 1925: KCC.
24. Reported in Skidelsky's biography of Keynes.
25. Extract, letter from EMF to JS, on Reform Club notepaper, dated 25 Jan. 1923: KCC.
26. Extract, letter from EMF to JS, dated 24 Jan. 1925: KCC.
27. Extract, letter no. 1540, dated 18 Feb. 1925: LVW.
28. Extract, letter no. 1544, dated 25 Mar. 1925: LVW.

The Celestial Omnibus
29. In fact, the words are reported in R. F. Harrod's biography, *The Life of John Maynard Keynes*: 'Mr Sprott (Clare College) was still up [1922], debonair, dashing and an acknowledged leader'.
30. The envelope bears the postmark 1 Nov. 1923: KCC.
31. Extract, letter from LS to JS, dated 31 Aug. 1925: KCC.
32. Attributed to James Farmer, a former Cosmo Hon. Sec.
33. Cosmoite, Joseph McCabe, had these words printed on an early syllabus.
34. Attributed to Fred Groocock, an early enthusiast and Hon. Sec. of the Society, printed on a 1903 syllabus.
35. These words, written in 1905, are attributed to James Farmer.

References 32–35 – together with the extracts from the *Nottingham Civic News*, Mar. 1971, which follow them – can be found in File no. L36.8, Nottinghamshire County Council's Local Studies Library, Angel Row, Nottingham.

Uncle Jack
36. Extract, letter JS to EMF; undated, but most probably written in 1928: KCC.
37. Letter no. 255 from EMF to JS, dated 18 Dec. 1926: SLF.
38. Extract, letter EMF to JS, dated 23 June 1927: KCC.
39. Extract, letter EMF to JS: KCC.
40. Extract, letter EMF to JS, dated 7 July 1927: KCC.

Uncle Morgan
41. Extract, letter EMF to JS, dated 30 Aug. 1927: KCC.
42. Extract, letter EMF to JS, dated 29 Oct. 1927: KCC.
43. Extract, letter EMF to JS, dated 8 Nov. 1928: KCC.
44. *Human Groups*, pp. 140–1.

45. See p. 91 (Penguin edition).
46. Forster's 'Terminal Note' on *Maurice*, written Sept. 1960.
47. Extract, letter no. 178, EMF to Florence Barger, dated 8 Oct. 1917: SLF. Selections from these letters for the year 1917 reveal further examples of the extent to which Forster was willing to exchange confidences with Florence Barger. For description of EMF's affair with Mohammed, see FBF, chapter entitled 'Alexandria'.
48. Extract, letter EMF to JA, from Harnham, Weybridge, dated Sat. 20 Sept. 1924: UTA.
49. Extract, letter EMF to JA, from Harnham; undated: UTA.
50. Extract, letter EMF to JA, from Harnham; undated: UTA.
51. Extract, letter EMF to JA, from Harnham; undated: UTA.
52. Extract, letter EMF to JA, dated 17 Oct. 1924: UTA.
53. Extract, letter EMF to JA, dated 16 Jan. 1925: UTA.
54. Extract, letter EMF to JA, dated 19 Jan. 1925: UTA.
55. Extract, letter EMF to JA, from West Hackhurst, Abinger Hammer; undated: UTA.
56. Extract, letter EMF to JA, dated simply 'Friday': UTA.
57. Extract, letter EMF to JA; undated: UTA.
58. Extract, letter EMF to JA; undated: UTA.
59. Extract, letter EMF to JA; undated: UTA.
60. Extract, letter EMF to JA; undated: UTA.
61. Extract, letter EMF to JA; undated, but early June 1925: UTA.
62. Extract, letter EMF to JA, dated 17 June 1925: UTA.
63. Extract, letter EMF to JA, dated 20 July 1925: UTA.
64. Extract, letter EMF to JA, dated 3 Sept. 1925: UTA.
65. Extract, letter EMF to JA; undated, but after Easter 1926: UTA.
66. See FBF, p. 217 (Cardinal paperback edition).
67. According to Peter Parker in his biography, *Ackerley: A Life of J.R. Ackerley*, p. 83 (Cardinal paperback edition).
68. Reported in FBF, p. 157.
69. Ibid., p. 141.
70. Forster's diary; entry under the year 1929: KCC.
71. Extract, letter EMF to JS: KCC.
72. Extract, letter EMF to JS, dated 5 Dec. 1927: KCC.
73. Extract, letter EMF to JS: KCC.
74. Extract, letter EMF to JS, from West Hackhurst, dated 26 Dec. 1927: KCC.
75. EMF's diary entry, 31 Dec. 1927: KCC.
76. Extract, letter EMF to JS: KCC.
77. Extract, letter EMF to JS: KCC.
78. Extract, letter EMF to JS: KCC.
79. Extract, letter EMF to JS: KCC.
80. Extract, letter EMF to JS: KCC.
81. Extract, letter EMF to JS: KCC.
82. Extract, letter EMF to JS: KCC.
83. Extract, letter EMF to JS: KCC.

Patrick

84. FBF, p. 283.

Uncle Charles

85. Extract, letter EMF to JS, dated 10 Apr. 1929: KCC.
86. Extract, letter EMF to JS, dated 15 Jan. 1929: KCC.

References

87. Extract, letter JA to EMF, from Putney, dated 23 Dec. 1963: KCC.
88. Ibid.

Patrick
89. Extract, letter EMF to André Deutsch, publishers, dated 12 Nov. 1956: KCC.

Uncle Charles
90. Extract, letter EMF to JS, from Hotel des Alpes, Switzerland, dated 6 June 1928: KCC.
91. Extract, letter EMF to JS, dated 13 Aug. 1928: KCC.
92. Extract, letter EMF to JS, dated 23 Sept. 1928: KCC.
93. Extract, letter EMF to JS, dated 28 Nov. 1928: KCC.
94. Extract, letter EMF to JS, dated 15 Jan. 1929: KCC.
95. Extract, letter EMF to JS, dated Mar. 1929: KCC.
96. Extract, letter EMF to JS, dated 26 Mar. 1929: KCC.
97. Extract, letter EMF to JS, dated 2 Apr. 1929: KCC.
98. Extract, letter EMF to JS, dated 8 May 1929: KCC.
99. Extract, letter JS to EMF, dated 14 May 1929: KCC.
100. Extract, letter EMF to JS, dated 28 May 1929: KCC.
101. Extract, letter EMF to JS, dated 11 Oct. 1929: KCC.
102. Extract, letter EMF to JS, dated 14 Oct. 1929: KCC.
103. Extract, letter EMF to JS, dated 1 Nov. 1929: KCC.
104. Extract, letter EMF to JS, dated Dec. 1929: KCC.
105. Extract, letter EMF to JS, dated 28 Dec. 1929: KCC.
106. Extract, letter EMF to JS, dated 13 Jan. 1930: KCC.
107. Extract, letter EMF to JS, dated 3 Feb. 1930: KCC.
108. Extract, letter EMF to JS, dated 10 Feb. 1930: KCC.
109. Extract, letter EMF to JS, dated 5 May 1930: KCC.
110. Extract, letter EMF to JS, dated 12 May 1930: KCC.
111. *Aspects of E.M. Forster*, ed. O. Stallybrass, p. 75. Reproduced by permission of Hodder & Stoughton Ltd.
112. *This Small Cloud: A Personal Memoir.*
113. Extract, letter JS to EMF; undated, but written some time in 1928: KCC.
114. Extract, letter JS to EMF, from 19a Clumber Street, dated simply 'Friday': KCC.
115. Extract, letter JS to EMF; undated, but 1928: KCC.
116. Extract, letter JS to EMF; undated, but early Oct. 1932: KCC.
117. See letter to Sprott, dated Sun. 6.30, early Mar. 1929: CLD.
118. See letter to Sprott, dated Sun. Jan. 1932: 'Darling Sebastian, I wanted to give you these ties and the belt to keep.': CLD.
119. Extract, letter EMF to JS, dated 19 June 1930: KCC.
120. Extract, letter EMF to JS, dated 15 Mar. 1931: KCC.
121. Extract, letter EMF to JS, dated 20 Apr. 1931: KCC.
122. Extract, letter EMF to JS, dated 1 Jan. 1932: KCC.
123. Extract, letter EMF to JS, dated 24 Jan. 1938: KCC.
124. Extract, letter EMF to JS, dated 24 Mar. 1938: KCC.

Patrick
125. Forster's biography of Goldsworthy Lowes Dickinson: the epilogue.
126. Ibid, main text.
127. Ibid.
128. Extract, letter EMF to JS, dated 22 Apr. 1937: KCC.

A Kind of Private Magic

Uncle Charles
129. Extract, letter JS to EMF, dated 21 Aug. 1929: KCC.
130. Extract, letter JS to EMF, dated 20 Jan. 1930: KCC.
131. EMF's diary for 1910: reported in FBF, p. 183.
132. EMF's diary entry for 1927. See note 75 above.
133. Extract, letter EMF to JS, dated 21 Mar. 1930: KCC.
134. Extract, letter DC to JS, dated 14 Mar. 1928: CLD.
135. Extract, letter EMF to JS, dated 3 Jan. 1930: KCC.
136. Extract, letter JS to EMF, from 19a Clumber Street, dated 17 Jan. 1932: KCC.
137. Extract, letter EMF to JS, dated 28 May 1929: KCC.

The Celestial Omnibus
138. Reproduced by kind permission of Nick Furbank.

Patrick
139. From 'Conservation in Notts.: Spring 1983', File no. L37.3 ('Ragged School'): Nottinghamshire C.C. Local Studies Library.
140. Ibid.

Uncle Morgan
141. Reported in Nicola Beauman's *Morgan: A Biography of E.M. Forster*, p. 14. Reproduced by permission of Hodder & Stoughton Ltd.
142. See FBF: p. 10.
143. *Marianne Thornton, p. 224.*

Patrick
144. *Howards End*, p. 188 (Penguin edition).
145. The American, William Roerick. See Roerick's essay, 'Forster in America', in *Aspects of E.M. Forster*, ed. O. Stallybrass, p. 65. Reproduced by permission of Hodder & Stoughton Ltd.
146. Marianne Thornton's nickname for the infant Forster.

Uncle Ted
147. Taken from letter no. 290, EMF to JS, dated 4 Oct. 1932: SLF.
148. Martin Amis in his review of William Burroughs' novel, *Queer*.
149. Extract, letter JS to EMF, dated 8 May 1931: KCC.
150. Extract, letter EMF to JS, dated 5 Oct. 1931: KCC.
151. Extract, letter EMF to JS, dated 22 July 1932: KCC.
152. Extract, letter EMF to JS, dated 20 Aug. 1932: KCC.
153. Extract, letter EMF to JS, dated 15 May 1933: KCC.
154. Extract, letter EMF to JS, dated 11 Aug. 1941: KCC.
155. Extract, letter EMF to JS, dated 5 Apr. 1943: KCC.
156. Extract, letter EMF to JS, dated 20 Apr. 1943: KCC.
157. Extract, EMF's diary entry, dated 21 Apr. 1943: KCC.
158. Extract, letter EMF to JS, dated 1 June 1946: KCC.
159. Extract, letter EMF to JS; undated: KCC.
160. Extract, letter EMF to JA, dated 9 Nov. 1951: UTA.
161. Extract, letter EMF to Charles Lovett, dated 12 Jan. 1959: KCC.
162. Extract, letter JS to EMF; undated, but some time in 1931 because the letter includes a scornful criticism of VW's newly-published novel *The Waves*: KCC.
163. Extract, letter EMF to JS, dated 7 Oct. 1932: KCC.
164. Extract, letter EMF to JS, dated 13 Feb. 1933: KCC.

References

165. Extract, letter EMF to JS, dated 22 Feb. 1943: KCC.
166. Extract, letter EMF to JS, dated 20 Mar. 1943: KCC.
167. Extract, letter EMF to JS, dated 23 June 1945: KCC.
168. Extract, letter EMF to JS, dated 28 Oct. 1960: KCC.

Uncle Ted
169. Extract, letter EMF to JS, dated 9 July 1935: KCC. The alleged reciter was Reg Palmer.
170. Extract, letter James Strachey to his wife, Alix, dated 26 Sept. 1924: *Letters of James and Alix Strachey*, eds. Miesel and Kendrick.
171. Ibid., extract of letter dated 17 Feb. 1925.
172. Written by Ted Shread, at the author's request, on 18 Aug. 1992.

Patrick
173. VW's essay on 'Sterne' (*TLS* 1909).
174. From his book *A History of the World in 10½ Chapters*.
175. *Aspects of the Novel*, p. 54 (Pelican edition).
176. In 'The New Biography', from 'The Art of Biography', in *Granite and Rainbow: Essays by Virginia Woolf*, ed. Leonard Woolf.
177. Ibid.

Uncle Ted
178. Extract, letter EMF to JS, from 33 Marine Parade, Dover; dated simply 'Friday': KCC.

The Celestial Omnibus
179. See note 134 above.
180. *My Sister and Myself: The Diaries of J.R. Ackerley*, entry for 23 July 1949.
181. Extract, letter JS to EMF, from 29a Clumber Street; undated: KCC.

Patrick
182. From foreword to Ackerley's autobiographical piece, *My Father and Myself*.
183. In *Remembrance of Things Past*, p. 47 (English trans.).
184. From an article entitled 'Recollections', written by Forster for *New Statesman and Nation*.
185. Extract, letter no. 9, written from the BBC, Savoy Hill, WC2, on 3 Oct. 1929: LJA.
186. Extract, letter EMF to JS, dated 12 May 1930: KCC.
187. Extract, letter EMF to JS, dated 15 Mar. 1931: KCC.
188. Extract, letter no. 284, EMF to JS, dated 16 July 1931: SLF.
189. Extract, letter EMF to Charles Lovett, dated 5 Mar. 1929: KCC. This is the only pre-war letter from Forster to Lovett which has survived.
190. Extract, letter EMF to JS, dated Mar. 1929: KCC.
191. Extract, letter EMF to JA, dated 31 Mar. 1929: UTA. In this letter, Forster refers to the various people he has been having 'trouble' with, particularly Charles Day.
192. Extract, letter EMF to JA, dated 15 May 1929: UTA.
193. Extract, letter EMF to JA, dated 1 Oct. 1929: UTA.
194. Extract, letter EMF to JA, dated 6 Jan. 1930: UTA.
195. Extract, letter EMF to JA, dated 9 Jan. 1930: UTA.
196. Extract, letter EMF to JA, dated 25 Jan. 1930: UTA. The 'flowers' are, of course, a reference to his many relationships.
197. Extract, letter EMF to JA, dated 14 Feb. 1930: UTA.

198. Extract, EMF's diary, dated 11 Jan. 1931: KCC.
199. Extract, letter EMF to JA, dated 26 Feb. 1931: UTA.
200. Extract, letter EMF to JA, dated 17 Mar. 1931: UTA.
201. Extract, letter EMF to JA, dated 28 Mar. 1931: UTA.
202. Extract, letter EMF to JS, dated 11 Apr. 1931: KCC.
203. Extract, letter EMF to JS, dated 27 June 1931: KCC.
204. Extract, letter EMF to JS, dated 18 Nov. 1931: KCC.
205. Extract, letter EMF to JS, dated 30 Nov. 1931: KCC.
206. Extract, letter EMF to JS, dated 1 Jan. 1932: KCC.
207. Reported to the author during conversation with Ted Shread.
208. Extract, letter no. 284, EMF to JS, dated 16 July 1931 (quoted from earlier, see note 188): SLF.
209. Extract, letter EMF to Forrest Reid, dated 17 Nov. 1931: reported in FBF, p. 169.
210. FBF, p. 169
211. Extract, letter EMF to RB, dated 15 Aug. 1932: KCC.
212. Extract, letter no. 290, EMF to JS, dated 4 Oct. 1932: SLF.
213. Extract, letter EMF to JS, dated 10 Feb. 1933: KCC.
214. Extract, letter EMF to JS, dated 24 Apr. 1933: KCC.
215. Extract, letter EMF to JS, dated 12 June 1933: KCC.
216. Extract, letter EMF to JS, dated Nov. 1933: KCC.
217. Extract, letter EMF to JS, dated 1 Dec. 1933: KCC.
218. Extract, letter EMF to JS, dated 10 Mar. 1934: KCC.
219. Extract, letter EMF to JS, dated 25 May 1934: KCC.
220. Extract, letter EMF to JS, dated 2 June 1934: KCC.
221. Extract, letter EMF to JS, dated 5 June 1934: KCC.
222. Extract, letter EMF to JS, dated 31 Oct. 1934: KCC.
223. Extract, letter EMF to JS, dated 25 Dec. 1934: KCC.
224. Extract, EMF's diary entry, dated 31 Dec. 1934: KCC. It was customary for Forster to make an entry on New Year's Eve, which was also the eve of his birthday.
225. KCC.
226. FBF, p. 186.
227. Phrase used in letter from Forster to Christopher Isherwood, 12 Oct. 1932: see Isherwood's *Christopher and His Kind*, p. 88.
228. End of year entry in EMF's Commonplace Book: quoted in FBF, p. 169.
229. FBF, p. 184.
230. Extract, letter EMF to JS, dated 24 Apr. 1933: KCC.

The Celestial Omnibus
231. Taken from a letter from Benjamin Britten to Forster: quoted in CBB, narrative for 1963.
232. Extract, letter BB to Peter Pears: quoted in CBB.
233. Quoted in *The Loving Friends* by David Gadd, p. 86.
234. Forster once wrote in his diary (1935), 'I want to love a strong young man of the lower classes and be loved by him and even hurt by him. That is my ticket': KCC.
235. Described in CBB. 'Nipper' was, according to Carpenter, a boy named Robin Long.

Patrick
236. Extract, letter EMF to JS, dated 2 June 1933: KCC.
237. Extract, letter EMF to JS, dated 25 June 1933: KCC.

238. Extract, letter no. 295, EMF to Christopher Isherwood, dated 16 July 1933: SLF.
239. Reported in FBF, p. 185.
240. Extract, letter no. 294, EMF to RB, dated Sun. [early June] 1933: SLF.
241. Ibid.
242. Extract, letter JS to EMF, dated 17 Aug. 1933: KCC.
243. Extract, letter EMF to May Buckingham, dated 7 Apr. 1935: KCC.
244. Extract, letter EMF to May Buckingham, dated Apr. 1935: KCC.
245. The same 1949 BBC broadcast, in which Forster was reading from his essay 'In My Library', taken from *Two Cheers for Democracy*, pp. 309–12.
246. Extract, letter EMF to RB, dated 3 July 1935: KCC.
247. Extract, letter EMF to May Buckingham, dated 10 Aug. 1935: KCC.
248. Extract, letter EMF to JS, dated 2 July 1935: KCC.
249. See FBF, p. 206.
250. *Morgan: A Biography of E.M. Forster*, p. 350.
251. Ibid., p. 362. (References 250 and 251 reproduced by permission of Hodder & Stoughton Ltd.)
252. Quoted earlier (see note 75), the phrase Forster used in his diary entry for 31 Dec. 1927, referring to his love for Charles Lovett.
253. Extract, letter EMF to JA, dated 4 June 1935: UTA.
254. Extract, letter EMF to JS, dated 1 Nov. 1935: KCC.
255. Extract, letter EMF to JS, dated 27 Nov. 1935: KCC.
256. Extract, letter no. 311, EMF to RB, dated 17 Dec. 1935: SLF.
257. Extract, letter no. 312, EMF to Forrest Reid, dated 16 Jan. 1936: SLF.
258. Extract, letter EMF to RB, dated 11 Feb. 1936: KCC.
259. Extract, letter EMF to RB, dated 19 Feb. 1936: KCC.
260. Extract, letter EMF to RB, dated 24 Apr. 1936: KCC.
261. Described in FBF, p. 211.
262. Extract, letter EMF to RB, dated 9 Mar. 1937: KCC.
263. Extract, letter EMF to JA, dated 5 Jan. 1937: UTA.
264. Extract, letter EMF to JS, dated 6 June 1937: KCC.
265. Extract, letter EMF to RB, dated 15 Aug. 1937: KCC.
266. FBF, p. 212.
267. Extract, letter EMF to JA, dated 31 May 1938: UTA.
268. Extract, letter EMF to JA, dated 19 June 1938: UTA.
269. Extract, letter EMF to JS, dated 6 July 1938: KCC.
270. Extract, letter EMF to JA, dated simply 'Wednesday': UTA.
271. Extract, letter EMF to JA; undated, probably June 1938: UTA.
272. Reported in FBF, p. 226.
273. Extract, letter no. 330, to Christopher Isherwood, dated 28 Aug. 1938: SLF.
274. Extract, letter no. 336, EMF to RB, dated 19 July 1939: SLF.
275. Extract, EMF's diary entry, dated 1 Sept. 1939: KCC.
276. Extract, letter EMF to JA, dated 8 Sept. 1939: UTA.

The Celestial Omnibus

277. Genesis, ch. 38.
278. Referred to earlier (note 234): diary entry for 1935: KCC.
279. In Ackerley's *My Father and Myself*, p. 157. He worked on *Judcote* in 1924.
280. *Christopher and His Kind*.
281. Referred to in Parker's biography of Ackerley, p. 120.
282. *My Father and Myself*, p. 71.
283. Ibid., pp. 109–10.
284. From *Oscar Wilde: Three Times Tried* by Christopher Millard (Wilde's first biographer, writing under the pseudonym Stuart Mason), p. 258.

285. Ibid.
286. *Plato: Phaedrus and Letters VII and VIII*, trans. Walter Hamilton, pp. 61–2.
287. Letter from Forster to Ackerley, dated 18 Aug. 1939: referred to in Parker's biography of Ackerley, p. 118.

Patrick

288. Extract, letter EMF to JS, dated 9 Oct. 1939: KCC.
289. Extract, letter EMF to JS, from 9 Arlington Park Mansions, Chiswick, dated 13 Nov. 1939: KCC.
290. Extract, letter EMF to JA, undated, but written shortly after the air raids on London began: UTA.
291. Extract, letter no. 342, EMF to RB, dated 28 Feb. 1940: SLF.
292. Extract, letter no. 343, EMF to RB, dated 29 May 1940: SLF.
293. Extract, EMF's diary entry, dated 4 Sept. 1940: KCC.
294. Extract, EMF's diary entry, dated 8 Sept. 1940: KCC.
295. Extract, letter no. 351, EMF to Cecil Day-Lewis, dated 14 Feb. 1941: SLF.
296. Extract, letter EMF to JS, dated 4 Dec. 1940: KCC.
297. Extract, letter EMF to JA; dated simply 'Sunday', but 1941: UTA.
298. Extract, letter EMF to JS, dated 31 July 1941: KCC. (a) Sprott used to try his hand at knitting. (b) The 'vexatious' situation referred to in this letter was a break-in at Sprott's Nottingham house, 116 Portland Road.
299. Extract, letter no. 357, EMF to JS, dated 20 Sept. 1941: SLF. There is a further comment on the break-in referred to in note 298 above.
300. Extract, letter EMF to JS, dated 20 Dec. 1941: KCC.
301. Extract, letter EMF to JS, dated 3 Aug. 1932: KCC.
302. Extract, letter EMF to JS, dated 17 Dec. 1942: KCC.
303. Extract, letter EMF to JS; undated, but obviously approaching Christmas 1942: KCC.
304. Extract, letter EMF to JS, dated Christmas Day 1942: KCC. Forster is referring to the slippers he received from Sprott as a Christmas present.
305. Extract, letter no. 360, EMF to RB, dated 18 Jan. 1942: SLF.
306. Extract, letter no. 363, EMF to RB, dated Sat. 20 Feb. 1943: SLF.
307. Letter, EMF to JS, dated 20 Mar. 1943: KCC.
308. Extract, letter EMF to JS, dated 5 Apr. 1943: KCC.
309. KCC.
310. Extract, letter EMF to JS, dated 20 Apr. 1943: KCC. The impassioned 'Oh, how *can* Charles' was more than a comment on the occasion; it doubtless expressed Forster's amazement that Charles could pair off with such a man.
311. Recounted in *Christopher and His Kind*. Towards the end of 1937, just before Isherwood's intended departure for the Spanish Civil War with Auden, friends advised him to make a will. EMF was one of the witnesses who signed it – after which he was then asked the question, 'Why don't you go to Spain, Morgan?'
312. Reported in FBF, p. 248.
313. The 'girl' Nicola Beauman names in her biography of Forster. See note 251 above.
314. Extract, EMF's diary entry, dated 2 May 1943: KCC.
315. Extract, EMF's diary entry, dated 19 May 1943: KCC.
316. Extract, letter EMF to JS, dated 19 May 1943: KCC. The 'latest news' being Buckingham's 'escape' from the RAF.
317. Extract, letter EMF to JA; undated, but written in 1944: UTA.
318. Extract, letter EMF to JS, dated 10 Mar. 1945: KCC.
319. Extract, letter EMF to JA, dated 13 Mar. 1945: quoted in FBF, pp. 255–6.

320. Extract, letter no. 369, EMF to RB, dated 'Tuesday', but postmarked 13 Mar. 1945: SLF.
321. FBF, p. 256.
322. Extract, letter EMF to JS, dated 9 June 1945: KCC. 46 Welbeck Street (now demolished) was the house Charles and Ted shared throughout the 1940s.
323. Extract, letter no. 375, EMF to RB, from India, dated 24 Oct. 1945: SLF.
324. Extract, EMF's diary entry, dated 13 Aug. 1945 – written after attending Walton Regatta with RB: quoted in FBF, p. 257.
325. Extract, letter EMF to JS, dated 25 June 1947: KCC.
326. Extract, letter EMF to RB, dated 28 Jan. 1946: KCC.
327. Extract, letter no. 378, EMF to John Hampson Simpson, dated 4 Oct. 1946: SLF.
328. The original letter is in the author's possession.
329. Extract, letter EMF to JA; undated, but late 1948: UTA.
330. Extract, letter EMF to JA, dated 2 Dec. 1949: UTA.
331. Only four letters from Forster to Lovett survived the post-war period.
332. Written, by Christopher Isherwood when Forster was fifty-three years old: recounted in *Christopher and His Kind*, p. 85.
333. Extract, letter no. 373, EMF to RB, dated 27 July 1945: SLF.
334. Extract, letter no. 401, EMF to RB, dated 9 Feb. 1953: SLF.
335. Extract, letter no. 441, EMF to RB; autumn 1966: SLF.

The Celestial Omnibus

336. Reported in FBF.
337. Expressed by J.T. Sheppard in the famous paper he read to a meeting of the Apostles (attended by Forster) in the autumn of 1903, reported in FBF, vol. 1, p. 105.
338. In *My Sister and Myself: The Diaries of J. R. Ackerley*, entry for 11 Dec. 1948.
339. Ibid., entry for 11 Dec. 1948.
340. Ibid., entry for 1 Nov. 1948.
341. Ibid., entry for 11 Dec. 1948.
342. Extract, EMF's diary entry, dated 24 Mar. 1925: KCC.
343. Quoted in Parker's biography of Ackerley, p. 133.
344. Extract, letter EMF to JS, dated Christmas Day 1939, on the subject of Lovett changing his war work: KCC.
345. Extract, EMF's diary entry: the entry for 14 Oct. 1923 reads: 'I don't quite like Ackerley, though he has intelligence and charm. I suspect him of cruelty, but perhaps this is merely that I suspect all young men. I have no friend under thirty now. Also, I remember his his ill-bred ancestry': KCC.
346. Joe Ackerley's father, Roger Ackerley, was a director of Elder & Fyffes, the banana importers.
347. See FBF, p. 117.
348. From the essay 'In My Library' in *Two Cheers for Democracy*, p. 312.
349. Extract, letter EMF to Goldsworthy Lowes Dickinson, dated 25 June 1917 – though this is actually a continuation of letter no. 165 begun on 5 May 1917: SLF.
350. To be found in *Lions and Shadows*, the first volume of Isherwood's autobiography, p. 111.
351. From *Christopher and His Kind*, the second volume of Isherwood's autobiography.
352. Daft was Mrs Lovett's maiden name.

Patrick

353. Extract, letter EMF to JA, dated 29 Jan. 1924: UTA.
354. Extract, letter EMF to JA, dated 12 Mar. 1924: UTA.
355. Extract, letter EMF to JA, dated 13 Nov. 1933: UTA.
356. Extract, letter EMF to JA, dated 28 Sept. 1956: UTA.
357. KCC.
358. Extract, letter EMF to JA, dated 12 Dec. 1926: UTA.
359. The term he used in a letter to Sprott in 1949, reported in FBF, p. 280.
360. One of two newspaper clippings (source unidentified) given to the author by Ted and Daisy Manning.
361. Extract, letter EMF to JA, dated 12 Nov. 1956: UTA. Forster was describing a story he was attempting to write.
362. Extract, letter EMF to JA, dated June 1958: UTA.
363. Extract, letter no. 194, JA to EMF, written from Japan, dated 21 Sept. 1960: LJA.
364. Extract, letter EMF to JA, dated Sat. 29 [Sept.] 1960: UTA.
365. Extract, letter JA to EMF, dated 23 Dec. 1963: KCC. 'Ken' is Ken Ball. 'Velda' is Sprott's sister.
366. Extract, letter no. 250, JA to Paul Cadmus, dated 3 Jan. 1964: LJA.
367. Extract, letter JA to EMF, dated 31 Dec. 1963: KCC. 'Dorothy' was the author's mother, Dorothy Portington (after her divorce from Tom Belshaw, she remarried), and her daughter is the author's younger sister, Jill.
368. Extract, letter EMF to JA, dated 15 Dec. 1964: UTA.
369. Extract, letter EMF to JA, dated 25 Mar. 1965: UTA.
370. Extract, letter EMF to JA, dated 3 Apr. 1965: UTA.
371. Extract, letter no. 331, JA to EMF, dated 1 Mar. 1967: LJA.
372. Extract, letter no. 224, JA to William Plomer, dated 28 June 1962: LJA.
373. Extract, letter no. 262, JA to Francis King, dated 19 Oct. 1964: LJA.
374. Extract, letter no. 267, JA to Sonia Brownell Orwell, dated 13 Jan. 1965: LJA.
375. Extract, letter no. 297, JA to Paul Cadmus, dated 1 Jan. 1966: LJA.
376. *My Sister and Myself: The Diaries of J.R. Ackerley*: entry for 2 Apr. 1949. 'Bunny' was JA's aunt. 'Ann', her friend, was formerly Ackerley's mother's servant.
377. Extract, letter no. 295, JA to Geoffrey Gorer, dated 12 Dec. 1965: LJA.
378. Extract, letter no. 273, JA to Lady Clark, dated 29 Apr. 1965: LJA.
379. Extract, letter no. 319, JA to William Plomer, dated 6 Nov. 1966: LJA.
380. Reported by Neville Braybrooke in his introduction to *The Letters of J.R. Ackerley*, p. xxxi.
381. Extract, letter no. 334, JA to David Higham, dated 19 Apr. 1967: LJA.
382. Neville Braybrooke's introduction to *The Letters of J.R. Ackerley*.
383. Extract, letter no. 336, JA to Sonia Brownell Orwell, dated 27 May 1967: LJA. 'Nancy' was Ackerley's sister.
384. Extract, letter no. 294, JA to William Plomer, dated 2 Dec. 1965: LJA. (Ackerley felt 'vexed' because he had been bitten by a recent remark of Forster's.)
385. Extract, letter EMF to JS; the letter is dated simply 'Tuesday': KCC.
386. Extract, letter EMF to Charles Lovett, dated 12 Jan. 1959: KCC.
387. Extract, letter EMF to JS, dated simply 'Wednesday', but May 1963: KCC.
388. Extract, letter EMF to JS; undated, but May 1963: KCC.
389. Extract, EMF to Charles Lovett, dated 22 May 1963 – with postscript from JA: KCC.
390. Letter, EMF to Charles Lovett, dated 9 Aug. 1963: KCC.
391. Letter, EMF to Charles Lovett, dated 3 Dec. 1963: KCC.
392. Taken from letter, EMF to JS: KCC.

References

393. FBF, p. 325.
394. One of two newspaper clippings (source unidentified) given to the author by Ted and Daisy Manning.

Postscript

395. Reported in Humphrey Carpenter's, *W.H. Auden: A Biography*.
396. See the preface to Carpenter's biography of Auden.
397. Written on 5 Feb. 1991: quoted in CBB, introduction.
398. In a letter to T.E. Lawrence.
399. The occasion is also observed in FBF, p. 333.
400. In his introduction to Forster's *The Life to Come and Other Stories* (Penguin edition).
401. ABD, section starting on p. 892.
402. See note 287 above.
403. Written in 1939 and included in Forster's *Two Cheers for Democracy*, pp. 77–85.
404. Ibid., p. 83.
405. *Science and Social Action*, p. 84.
406. Reported in Mary Ann Caws, *Women of Bloomsbury*.
407. Extract, letter DC to JS, dated Sun. 6.30 [early Mar.] 1929: CLD.
408. Extract, letter DC to JS, dated Sun. 30 July 1930: CLD.
409. Extract, letter DC to JS, dated Mar. 1932: CLD.
410. Quoted in the prologue of ABD.
411. ABD, section starting on p. 892.
412. ABD, section starting on p. 753.
413. Ibid.
414. Virginia Woolf, in her essay on 'Sterne' (*TLS* 1909).
415. Preface to her *Woman of Letters: A Life of Virginia Woolf*.
416. *Two Cheers for Democracy* (which is dedicated to Jack Sprott), writing of *Erewhon* in his essay 'A Book that Influenced Me', p. 227.
417. ABD, in section VI.
418. *Aspects of the Novel*, chapter on 'The Story', p. 49 (Pelican edition).
419. Ibid., chapter on 'People', p. 70.

Bibliography

Ackerley, J.R., *My Father and Myself*, Bodley Head, 1968.
—— *My Sister and Myself: The Diaries of J.R. Ackerley*: see King, ed.
—— *We Think the World of You*, Bodley Head, 1960.
—— *My Dog Tulip: Life with an Alsatian*, Secker & Warburg, 1956.
—— *Hindoo Holiday: An Indian Journal*, Chatto & Windus, 1932.
—— *Prisoners of War: a play*, Chatto & Windus, 1925.
—— *The Letters of J.R. Ackerley*: see Braybrooke, ed.
Ackroyd, Peter, *Dickens*, Sinclair-Stevenson, 1990.
Alexander, Peter F., *William Plomer: A Biography*, Oxford, 1989.
Barnes, Julian, *A History of the World in 10½ Chapters*, Cape, 1989.
Batchelor, John, *The Edwardian Novelists*, Duckworth, 1982.
Beauman, Nicola, *Morgan: A Biography of E.M. Forster*, Hodder, 1993.
Bedient, Calvin, *Architects of the Self*, Univ. of California Press, 1972.
Bell, Anne Olivier, ed., *The Diary of Virginia Woolf*, Hogarth Press, 1977.
Bell, Quentin, *Bloomsbury*, Weidenfeld & Nicolson, 1968.
—— *Virginia Woolf: A Biography*, Hogarth Press, 1972.
Beer, J.B., *The Achievement of E.M. Forster*, Chatto & Windus, 1962.
Bowlby, Rachel, Introduction to Virginia Woolf's *Orlando*, OUP World Classics edition, 1992.
Bradbury, Malcolm, 'E.M. Forster', *The Independent* magazine, 1 Dec. 1990.
Braybrooke, Neville, ed., *The Letters of J.R. Ackerley*, Duckworth, 1985.
Carpenter, Humphrey, *W.H. Auden: A Biography*, Allen & Unwin, 1981.
—— *Benjamin Britten: A Biography*, Faber & Faber, 1992.
Carrington, Dora, *Letters and Extracts from her Diaries*: see Garnett, ed.
Caws, Mary Ann, *Women of Bloomsbury: Virginia, Vanessa and Carrington*, Routledge, 1990.
Colmer, John, *E.M. Forster: The Personal Voice*, Routledge, 1975.
Crews, F.C., *E.M. Forster: The Perils of Humanism*, OUP, 1962.
Daley, Harry, *This Small Cloud: A Personal Memoir* (with foreword by P.N. Furbank), Weidenfeld & Nicolson, 1986.
Darroch, Sandra Jobson, *Ottoline: The Life of Lady Ottoline Morrell*, Chatto & Windus, 1976.
David, Hugh, *Stephen Spender: A Portrait With Background*, Heinemann, 1992.
Edel, Leon, *Bloomsbury: A House of Lions*, Hogarth Press, 1979.
Forster, E.M. NOVELS: *Where Angels Fear to Tread*, Arnold, 1905.
    The Longest Journey, Arnold, 1907.
    A Room with a View, Arnold, 1908.
    Howards End, Arnold, 1910.
    A Passage to India, Arnold, 1924.
    Maurice, Arnold, 1971 (posthumous).
  STORIES: *Collected Short Stories*, Sidgwick & Jackson, 1947.
    The Life to Come and Other Stories, Arnold, 1972.
  BIOGRAPHY: *Goldsworthy Lowes Dickinson*, Arnold, 1934.

Bibliography

Marianne Thornton: A Domestic Biography, Arnold, 1956.

OTHER: *Pharos and Pharillon*, Hogarth, 1923.
Aspects of the Novel, Arnold, 1927.
The Hill of Devi, Arnold, 1953.
Abinger Harvest, Arnold, 1936.
Two Cheers for Democracy, Arnold, 1951.
Selected Letters: see Lago and Furbank, eds.

Furbank, P.N., *E.M. Forster: A Life*, 2 vols., Secker & Warburg, 1977 and 1978.

Gadd, David, *The Loving Friends*, Hogarth Press, 1974.

Gardner, Philip, ed., *E.M. Forster: The Critical Heritage*, Routledge, 1973.

Garnett, David, ed., *Carrington: Letters and Extracts from her Diaries*, Cape, 1970.

—— ed., *The Letters of T.E. Lawrence*, original pub. 1938; Spring Books, 1964.

—— *Great Friends*, Macmillan, 1979.

Glendinning, Victoria, *Vita: The Life of V. Sackville-West*, Weidenfeld & Nicolson, 1983.

Hanley, James, *Boy*, Borriswood, 1931 and 1934; Deutsch, 1990.

Harrod, R.F., *The Life of John Maynard Keynes*, Macmillan, 1951.

Hayes, Denis, *Challenge of Conscience: The Story of the Conscientious Objectors of 1939–1949*, Allen & Unwin, 1949.

Herz, J.S., and Martin, R.K., eds., *E.M. Forster: Centenary Revaluations*, Macmillan, 1982.

Holroyd, Michael, *Lytton Strachey: The Years of Achievement*, Heinemann, 1968.

Hyde, H. Montgomery, *The Other Love*, Heinemann, 1970.

—— *The Trials of Oscar Wilde*, Penguin, 1962; Dover, 1973.

Isherwood, Christopher, *Lions and Shadows: An Education in the Twenties*, Hogarth Press, 1938.

—— *Christopher and His Kind, 1929–39*, Methuen, 1977.

Johnstone, J.K., *The Bloomsbury Group*, Secker & Warburg, 1954.

King, Francis, ed., *My Sister and Myself: The Diaries of J.R. Ackerley*, Hutchinson, 1982.

Lago, Mary, and Furbank, P.N., eds., *Selected Letters of E.M. Forster*, vol. 1, *1879–1920*, Collins, 1983; vol. 2, *1921–1970*, Collins, 1985.

Mason, Stuart, *Oscar Wilde: Three Times Tried*, privately printed Paris, 1912.

McNeillie, Andrew, ed., *The Essays of Virginia Woolf*, vol. 3, *1919–1924*, Hogarth Press, 1988.

Meyers, Jeffrey, *Homosexuality and Literature: 1890–1930*, Athlone, 1977.

Miesel, Perry, and Kendrick, Walter, eds., *The Letters of James and Alix Strachey: 1924–5*, Chatto & Windus, 1986.

Moody, A.D., *Virginia Woolf*, Oliver & Boyd, 1963.

Moore, G.E., *Principia Ethica*, CUP, 1903; OUP, 1963.

Nicolson, Harold, *Some People*, Constable, 1927; OUP, 1983.

Nicolson, Nigel, ed., *The Flight of the Mind: The Letters of Virginia Woolf*, vol. 1, *1888–1912*, Hogarth Press, 1975.

—— ed., *The Question of Things Happening: The Letters of Virginia Woolf*, vol. 2, *1912–1922*, Hogarth Press, 1976.

—— ed., *A Change of Perspective: The Letters of Virginia Woolf*, vol. 3, *1923–1928*, Hogarth Press, 1977.

—— *Portrait of a Marriage*, Weidenfeld & Nicolson, 1973.

Parker, Peter, *Ackerley: A Life of J.R. Ackerley*, Constable, 1989.

Partridge, Frances, *Love in Bloomsbury: Memories*, Little Brown, 1981.

Petre, Diana, *The Secret Orchard of Roger Ackerley*, Hamish Hamilton, 1975.

Plato, *The Symposium*, trans. Walter Hamilton, Penguin Classics, 1951.

—— *Phaedrus and Letters VII and VIII*, trans. Walter Hamilton, Penguin Classics, 1973.

Plomer, William, *At Home: Memoirs*, Cape, 1958.

Plummer, Kenneth, ed., *The Making of the Modern Homosexual*, Hutchinson, 1981.

Porter, Kevin, and Weeks, Jeffrey, *Between the Acts: Lives of Homosexual Men 1885–1967*, Routledge, 1990.

Proust, Marcel, *Remembrance of Things Past (À la Recherche du Temps Perdu)*, part 1, *Du Côté de Chez Swann*, 1913; English translation, Chatto & Windus, 1981.

Rose, Phyllis, *Woman of Letters: A Life of Virginia Woolf*, Routledge, 1978.

Shone, Richard, *Bloomsbury Portraits*, Phaidon and Dutton, 1976.

Skidelski, Robert, *John Maynard Keynes*, 2 vols., Macmillan, 1983 and 1992.

Spater, George, and Parsons, Ian, *A Marriage of True Minds: An Intimate Portrait of Leonard and Virginia Woolf*, Cape and Hogarth Press, 1977.

Spring, Ernest, *Conchie: The Wartime Experiences of a Conscientious Objector*, Leo Cooper, 1975.

Sprott, W.J.H., *Sociology*, Hutchinson, 1949.

—— *Social Psychology*, Hutchinson, 1952.

—— *Science and Social Action*, Josiah Mason Lectures to Birmingham Univ., Watts & Co., 1954.

—— *Human Groups*, Penguin, 1958.

Stallybrass, Oliver, ed., *Aspects of E.M. Forster*, Arnold, 1969.

Stone, Wilfred, *The Cave and the Mountain*, Stanford Univ. Press, 1966.

Storr, Anthony, *Sexual Deviation*, Penguin, 1964.

Strachey, Lytton, *Eminent Victorians*, Chatto & Windus, 1918.

—— *Queen Victoria*, Chatto & Windus, 1921.

Tomalin, Claire, *The Invisible Woman: The Story of Nelly Ternan and Charles Dickens*, Viking, 1990.

Woolf, Leonard, ed. *Granite and Rainbow: Essays by Virginia Woolf*, Hogarth Press, 1958.

Woolf, Virginia, *Orlando*, Duckworth, 1928.

—— *Letters*: see Nicolson, ed.

—— *Diary*: see Bell, ed.

—— *Essays*: see Woolf, ed.